RESISTING DISCRIMINATION: WOMEN FROM ASIA, AFRICA, AND THE CARIBBEAN AND THE WOMEN'S MOVEMENT IN CANADA

In her introduction to *Resisting Discrimination*, Vijay Agnew quotes Keibo Oiwa: 'We rarely encounter accounts of what the persecuted themselves felt, thought, wished to do, and actually did or failed to do; what meanings they attached to their thoughts and actions.' As Agnew observes, there is little Canadian feminist literature, from a minority perspective, on racism in feminist practice. *Resisting Discrimination* is a ground-breaking book. Focusing on the experiences of women from Asia, Africa, and the Caribbean, the volume explores the realities of race, class, and gender discrimination in twentieth-century Canada.

Agnew uses an integrated approach, adopting methodologies from political science, history, sociology, and women's studies to investigate the history and politics of Asian and black women throughout this century and the exclusion of these women from theory and practice of mainstream feminism. She also looks at the relationship between the state and community-based organizations of immigrant women, and the struggles of these women to provide social services to non–English-speaking working-class women through their community-based organizations.

Agnew's views are critical of white feminist theories and practices. Her goal is to sensitize the reader to another perspective and to empower minority women by making them the subject of their own recent history and politics. She seeks to open up the possibility of fuller cooperation among feminists across lines of race and class, and to suggest new lines of development for feminist theories and methodologies.

VIJAY AGNEW is an associate professor in the Division of Social Sciences, York University. She is author of *Elite Women in Indian Politics*.

D1444501

VIJAY AGNEW

Resisting Discrimination: Women from Asia, Africa, and the Caribbean and the Women's Movement in Canada

UNIVERSITY OF TORONTO PRESS
Toronto Buffalo London

© University of Toronto Press Incorporated 1996
Toronto Buffalo London
Printed in Canada

ISBN 0-8020-0674-4 (cloth)
ISBN 0-8020-7627-0 (paper)

Printed on acid-free paper

Canadian Cataloguing in Publication Data

Agnew, Vijay, 1946–
    Resisting discrimination : women from Asia,
    Africa, and the Caribbean and the women's movement
    in Canada

    Includes index.
    ISBN 0-8020-0674-4 (bound)   ISBN 0-8020-7627-0 (pbk.)

    1. Women immigrants – Canada – Social conditions.
    2. Minority women – Canada – Social conditions.
    3. Working class women – Canada – Social conditions.
    4. Sex discrimination against women – Canada.
    5. Race discrimination – Canada.   6. Feminism –
    Canada.   I. Title.

    HQ1453.A45 1996   305.48'8'00971   C95-932057-1

University of Toronto Press acknowledges the financial assistance to its
publishing program of the Canada Council and the Ontario Arts Council.

This book has been published with the help of a grant from the Social Science
Federation of Canada, using funds provided by the Social Sciences and
Humanities Research Council of Canada.

For my daughter Nicole
and
for the daughters of all my immigrant friends

Contents

viii   Contents

9
Immigrant Women and Wife Abuse 194

10
Conclusion 224

Acknowledgments

It is customary for authors to acknowledge their debts to individuals who contributed to the writing of their book, but there were a number of unpleasant incidents in my life that made me want to understand race, class, and gender discrimination better, and their contribution must be noted too. These unhappy experiences led to many conversations with women from Asia, Africa, and the Caribbean who had shared similar experiences; we attempted to come to terms with them and to exorcise their ghosts from our minds. These discussions provided insight into the ways in which racism, classism, and sexism shadow the lives of women from Asia, Africa, and the Caribbean in Canada, and I owe a tremendous debt of gratitude to the women who shared their thoughts with me. Their stoic courage and humour encouraged me to write this book.

I would like to thank the administration of York University, particularly the Office of Research Administration, for awarding me several grants that enabled me to develop my research plans. A three-year research grant from the Social Sciences and Humanities Research Council enabled me to complete the major part of the research that is presented in this book.

In the three years that it took me to research and write this book, I presented many papers at conferences. I would like to thank the conference participants – white feminists and feminists from Asia, Africa, and the Caribbean – for their insights. The questions that they raised frequently led me to reformulate and clarify my ideas. I am specially grateful to Professors Monica Boyd, Helen Ralston, Vanaja Dhurvarajan, Josephine Naidoo, and Jean Burnet for their encouragement and support. Colleagues and staff at York, particularly in the Division of Social Science, were invariably helpful and supportive, and I would like to thank them all.

I am particularly indebted to the anonymous reviewers who read the complete manuscript for their close scrutiny of the research presented in this book. I would also like to thank the many anonymous reviewers for reading the articles that I submitted to journals or who evaluated my research proposals. I am grateful to John Shafer, of the Centre for Academic Writing at York University, for his criticism of earlier drafts and to Virgil Duff at the University of Toronto Press, Linda Biesenthal, and Riça Night for their help in preparing the manuscript for publication.

I thank my husband, Tom, who has always supported me with his love and who has never complained when I remained absorbed in my work for weeks on end, and I am grateful to my sister-in-law Debbie for always making me feel a loved member of the family. When my daughter, Nicole, was twelve years old, she pointed out that several of her white friends' fathers had academic positions higher than mine. She decided that with her encouragement and support I could write a book and get promoted. Although in the intervening years she gained more insight into my situation, her support for my work has never wavered, and she spent one summer retyping drafts of most of the chapters and checking references. This book is dedicated, with love, to Nicole and to my nieces Aarti and Anjali and my nephews Arjun and Gautam, with the hope that life will be a bit easier for them than it has been for their mothers.

VIJAY AGNEW

RESISTING DISCRIMINATION:
WOMEN FROM ASIA, AFRICA, AND THE
CARIBBEAN AND THE WOMEN'S MOVEMENT
IN CANADA

1

Introduction

During the 1980s it became customary for white, middle-class feminists to acknowledge that, in their struggle against gender oppression, they had all but ignored the ways in which race and class prejudices intersect with gender bias to oppress women of colour and working-class women, and also to admit that their own feminist theory and practice exhibited race and class biases. They affirmed that gender, race, and class are interconnected and that many women experience a combination of oppressions that the narrow fight against gender discrimination cannot overcome. However, in the early 1990s feminists from Asia, Africa, and the Caribbean complained that the mantra of 'race, class, and gender' was repeated so routinely that all its force as a critique of mainstream feminism had been lost. Repetition of the phrase gave the impression that the problem of bias in mainstream feminism had been resolved, but feminists from Asia, Africa, and the Caribbean contend that attempts to deal with the problems stopped at the point of acknowledging the biases.[1]

This issue evokes a great deal of emotion and anger on both sides. White feminists feel that their attempts to incorporate the experiences of others have been discounted, and women from Asia, Africa, and the Caribbean express strong reservations about feminist theories and practices dominated by the experiences of white, middle-class women. Little work has been done by mainstream feminists on race and class biases against women, and little has been learned about the ways in which race, class, and gender intersect in the lives of women who have immigrated to Canada from Asia, Africa, or the Caribbean. And little is known about how these women have struggled against their oppressions or about the organizations they have formed to advance their struggles. This book aims to analyse some of the ways in which race, class, and gender biases have excluded them from the larger society and marginalized them in the feminist movement, and some of the ways in which they have fought back.

Keibo Oiwa writes in her introduction to a history of Japanese Canadians in Canada: 'We rarely encounter accounts of what the persecuted themselves felt, thought, wished to do, and actually did or failed to do; what meanings they attached to their thoughts and actions' (1991, 15). The existing literature on women from Asia, Africa, and the Caribbean is informed by personal experiences of oppression and exploitation on the basis of ethnicity, race, and gender, but it still reflects the power relations of society, and our understanding of these experiences is mediated by the discourses of the dominant groups. My discussion 'centres' women who came to Canada from Asia, Africa, and the Caribbean and focuses on their recent history and politics in Canada.[2] It analyses how race, class, and gender biases have oppressed women from Asia, Africa, and the Caribbean in Canada between 1900 and the 1990s and how they have struggled against these biases through their community-based organizations. It examines the dissatisfaction of women from Asia, Africa, and the Caribbean with mainstream women's organizations and the conflicts between women across lines of race and class.

Determining what is to count as knowledge belongs to those who have power, and in the past they have most frequently been white, university-educated males (Code 1991). Mainstream (white, middle-class) feminists have critiqued the power dynamics that exist within male-dominated epistemology, but other oppressed groups, like women from Asia, Africa, and the Caribbean, have exposed similar hierarchies of power within feminist theories and practices (hooks 1984, 1988). bell hooks observes that those 'whose work is oppositional' or who write 'against the grain' may find their work subjected to 'forms of dismissal and devaluation' (1991, 10). Patricia Williams writes about the difficulties of blacks taking on a 'subject position' that has both authenticity and authority (1991, 256). All this makes documenting the history and politics of women from Asia, Africa, and the Caribbean problematic. Who is to decide what is significant – and true? Readers of this book may be open to different perspectives, but difficulties may emerge nevertheless.

I have documented my arguments carefully, but my different location from some of my feminist readers may lead them to see me, a South Asian, as an 'outsider' who lacks their perspective on Canadian history, on women's movements with which they are familiar, or on the forms of feminism to which they subscribe. My intention is not to create feelings of guilt in white feminists, however, but to document, from their own perspective, the recent history and politics of women from Asia, Africa, and the Caribbean, particularly within the women's movement. This perspective places me in an oppositional mode that is critical of white feminist theories and practices. But as Charlotte Bunch advises, we do not need to agree on everything; 'we do need to be able to challenge each other from the assumption that change is possible' (1990, 55). Consciousness of the views of others is a necessary step in building antiracist feminist theories and practices.

My goal in making women from Asia, Africa, and the Caribbean the subjects of their own recent history and politics is to empower them. In doing so, I expose the divisions and disputes between feminists, and some might argue that this approach undermines the women's movement by further fragmenting its already precarious political unity and providing evidence to an androcentric society of shortcomings in feminist theories and practices. But I believe that the book opens up the possibility of fuller cooperation among feminists across lines of race and class and suggests fresh insights into the further development of feminist theories and methodologies.

FEMINIST METHODOLOGY

A feminist book on women from Asia, Africa, and the Caribbean must begin by identifying the voice of the author and her location. Feminist theorists have condemned what they term 'the view from nowhere' or 'the god's eye view,' arguing that all analyses stem from specific identities and locations (Di Stefano 1990; Harding 1990). Who one is and what one's relationship is to the subject under investigation are issues that determine both one's questions and, to some extent, one's answers about the subject. Androcentric knowledge of white, university-educated, middle-class males has ignored the experience of women while claiming to establish universal truths. Feminists have protested exclusion and marginalization by the power dynamics that underlie 'knowledge making' or epistemology (Harding 1987; Martin 1988; Sawicki 1986; Cancian 1992), but the perspective of white, middle-class, university-educated women dominates feminist theories and practices in Canada, as elsewhere.

I am a woman who was born and raised in India, immigrated to Canada, and received a PhD in history at the University of Toronto. For the last twenty years I have taught social science at York University. My physical appearance is that of a South Asian woman – a Canadian label for a member of what is in fact a very diverse group. In Western societies the colour of one's skin has almost always been used to rationalize and assign inferior and disadvantageous positions to black and Asian women. But 'black,' 'Asian,' or 'South Asian' are not fixed and rigid identities. Gender and race are sociopolitical constructs, and different sets of values and norms have been associated with skin colour and sex at different periods of history and in different contexts. Postmodern feminist analysis of the shifting nature of 'identity' and 'location' shows that attempting to locate my voice runs the risk of making an essentialist or stereotypical assessment of my identity (Alcoff 1988). Indeed as I did the research for this book, I found that the significance attached to my racial identity as a South Asian woman differed in different contexts.

In academic environments I was often grouped with non-white women in a category variously referred to as 'visible-minority women,' 'women of colour,' 'racial-minority women,' or 'black women.' White feminists often invite Chinese, or black, or South Asian women to 'their' meetings and rallies, partly to legitimize their claim to be representative of 'all' women. In this context I was located on the margin and defined as the 'other.' But within community-based groups of immigrant women or visible-minority women, I was positioned as a member of a privileged group. I had a secure, full-time job, while many of the women I interviewed were on short-term contracts with no job security. And there were differences in how I was regarded within these groups as well. While South Asian women treated me as one of their own, black women were sometimes more reserved in their interactions with me and considered me an outsider. In India I was identified not by my race but by my status as a resident of Canada or as a Western academic collecting data for research. Unlike most feminists in India, I had access to libraries, I could buy books and xerox documents, and I had the resources for travelling and doing research.

These shifting locations, sometimes placing me with other oppressed women and sometimes identifying me as a privileged individual, provided me with some epistemic advantages. I learned to listen to the anger and frustration of my respondents without imposing my academic or research needs upon them, or asking them to validate my own feelings and experiences. I used language familiar to them and with which they felt comfortable, rather than asking them to adopt feminist language or to fit their experiences into academic feminist categories.

Many of my respondents would have felt uncomfortable had I asked them directly whether they were feminists – let alone whether they were liberal, socialist, or radical feminists. Some respondents used these categories themselves, but most simply discussed their work. Recognizing the shifting nature of identity does not, however, remove the necessity of locating myself with respect to the political and social issues I address in my research (Bordo 1990; Mohanty 1991). In this book, then, I speak as a South Asian woman immigrant in Canada who shares similar experiences of racial and gender oppression with women from other parts of Asia, from Africa, and from the Caribbean.

In this book I often contrast 'white women' with women from Asia, Africa, and the Caribbean. By the term 'white women' I mean to identify women of northern European (primarily British) descent. Women of southern or eastern European descent have been racialized as non-white in societies, like Canada's, that are dominated by people of northern European descent.

The category of 'white feminist,' however, may include women of eastern or southern European descent, and it has the added fault of failing to distinguish between middle-class and working-class white feminists. For this reason I try to give detailed characterizations of the varieties of 'white feminism' (e.g., 'mainstream,' 'socialist'). The term has also been criticized for its derogatory connotations. Catharine MacKinnon argues that the category of 'white feminists' locates women as privileged, self-indulgent, pampered whiners who, from a 'simple lack of anything meaningful to do,' think they need to be 'liberated.' Such stereotyping denies the oppression of white feminists by male domination, rape, battering, poverty, and discrimination (MacKinnon 1991, 19). But, as I argue in chapter 2, some categorization is necessary if we are to analyse the experience of racism, classism, and gender discrimination of women from Asia, Africa, and the Caribbean, and to understand their strategies for overcoming their oppression.

The research topics of feminism, racism, and the work of community-based women's groups emerged through my interactions with women from Asia, Africa, and the Caribbean. We could, as part of a larger community of women from Asia, Africa, and the Caribbean living in Canada, Britain, and the United States, unmask the ethnocentric biases of many white feminist theories and critique their claims to represent 'all' women. But to move forward, in either developing an antiracist feminist theory or participating in creating knowledge that speaks to the experiences of racially identified women, we need to substantiate and document our own experiences.[3] This work is hindered by our class and race position and by our near absence from academic life, but women with diverse identities and politics cooperated and shared their experiences with me. Many gave advice on what myths and stereotypes I should dispel, such as those that treated them as poor and uneducated or as victims of their race and gender. My book forms part of a collective process of constructing knowledge about women from Asia, Africa, and the Caribbean in Canada; it documents their oppressions and can also serve as a basis for political action.

The literature on this subject (discussed in detail in chapter 5) articulates the concerns of women from Asia, Africa, and the Caribbean and gives direction to the book. However, the literature does not present a unitary perspective but reflects the divisions among women based on their class, country of origin, and ideology. While academic feminists from Asia, Africa, and the Caribbean debate theoretical issues with white feminists, writers from community-based groups analyse the everyday experiences of ethnically and racially identified women.

My research was motivated by a desire to bring about social change. It attempts to describe and explain the everyday experiences of women (e.g., how they understand the racial stereotypes that oppress them and the dilemmas and struggles of being immigrant women). But I do not merely reflect and reproduce those views. I attempt to distil and organize the experiences of these women, to locate patterns and identify commonalities, and to show how the structures of race, class, and gender domination give particular shapes to their experiences.

Dorothy Smith observes that a feminist sociologist must begin from the everyday experience of women and analyse how the everyday world of women is structured and embedded in the power relations of society. In explaining the 'standpoint of women in the everyday world' she writes: 'In the research context this means that so far as their everyday worlds are concerned, we rely entirely on what women tell us, what people tell us, about what they do and what happens. But we cannot rely upon them for an understanding of the relations that shape and determine the everyday. Here then is our business as social scientists, for the investigation of these relations and the exploration of the ways they are present in the everyday are and must be a specialized enterprise, a work, the work of a social scientist' (1987, 110).

My book sometimes describes the conflicts and struggles between women, particularly between white feminists and feminists from Asia, Africa, and the Caribbean. White feminists frequently express in their public statements or in their writings a desire to be antiracist and to 'include' all women. Conflicts emerge because there is a discrepancy between what they say or do and the ways in which their words or actions are understood and experienced by women from Asia, Africa, and the Caribbean. In their desire to 'include others' white feminists may nevertheless offend. One South Asian woman from Pakistan writes: 'At a recent Commonwealth Women's Conference in Toronto, one of our Canadian sisters was quite eager to show a video on bride burning in India. I asked her if she also intended to show one on incest in Canada. She was quite bewildered by my question' (Javed 1992, 3–4).

When some aspects of racial domination in the larger society are reproduced in feminist practice, they create conflicts and bitterness and result in charges and countercharges which distract feminists from their common struggles. Feminists from Asia, Africa, and the Caribbean believe that they must organize themselves in autonomous organizations to resist oppression and domination and that gender politics dominated by white women do not necessarily provide a 'home' for them. But this disjuncture allows us to see how race positions women in different locations and structures the conflicts between them.

Women from Asia, Africa, and the Caribbean are active, participating subjects of this book. Their voices are heard throughout the text. Sometimes they speak for their own ethnic or racial group and at other times for larger more diverse groups. A unity thus emerges based on the women's location – marginality in white feminist theory and practice – but there are also fissures of ideology and politics between racially identified women.

The book employs a feminist methodology that preserves women in their role as 'knowers and actors' (Smith 1987, 105). This methodology requires a collaborative and interactive relationship between the researcher and her subjects – a relationship that is open, equal, and non-exploitative (Pennell 1992; Whyte, Greenwood, and Lazes 1991; Geiger 1990; Jayaratne and Stewart 1991; Acker, Barry, and Esseveld 1991). It rejects conventional interview techniques, which maintain a distance between researchers and subjects and relegate subjects to a 'narrow and objectified function as data.' Instead, feminist research uses the interview to validate 'women's subjective experiences as women and as people' (Oakley 1981, 30; also Acker, Barry, and Esseveld 1991). By being a responsive listener, the researcher provides an opportunity for the subject to gain a voice.

Feminist research also requires resisting some traditional male perspectives and categories. As Lyn Brown and Carol Gilligan explain, 'in listening to ... women's voices, we listen for and against conventions of relationship within a society and culture that are rooted psychologically in the experience of men' (1992, 29). Sometimes female anthropologists, by scrupulously adhering to the local dress and behaviour codes, gained entry to the world of women of another culture. The resulting trust provided access to experiences and perspectives not available to outsiders (Pettigrew 1981). But some Third World feminists complain that gender similarity between researcher and subjects can still reproduce stereotypical analysis derived from categories of androcentric knowledge. For example, women who observe purdah in Islamic countries have been portrayed by Western feminists as victims of their religion and culture (Lazreg 1990; Mohanty 1989; Harding 1986, 163–96; Collins 1991).

A shared gender and racial identity between my respondents and me, and similarities in our experiences as 'non-whites' in Canadian society, created a safe place for them to articulate their perceptions and experiences. They were being heard. I could pick up subtle nuances of body language and facial expressions and let the interview develop in directions indicated by my respondents. Often what began as a formal interview was transformed by a shared moment or a smile into a dialogue in which we sought to validate each other's experiences and together engaged in discovering and understanding the nature of women's everyday experiences.

An example of the shared understanding that often emerged in my interviews occurred when I talked with the one South Asian woman who was dressed in South Asian clothes. I complimented her on her appearance, and she immediately gave me a vivid description of how white Canadians usually reacted to her dress. They took it to indicate that she was mild-mannered and reticent, and they were consequently surprised when they heard her make militant denunciations of racism in Canadian society. One white woman asked her to come to a meeting in her 'costume.' She responded by saying she hoped the other woman would come in her costume too. The irony was lost on the white woman (Interview, 7 Sept. 1992).

My respondents did not see themselves as passive subjects of my research but confidently assumed the role of knowers and experts. They enjoyed meeting with me and guiding me, but they did not always share my view that a better understanding of the forces oppressing us could help us politically to organize, lobby, and advocate on our own behalf. Community-based women's groups cast me in the role of an academic feminist, and in contrast members of these groups described themselves as activists and 'frontline workers.' Many women from the Caribbean or Africa considered the research as my project only, despite my efforts to get them to engage more fully in it.

Feminist research has the potential of transforming the consciousness of both researcher and subjects (Smith 1987, 151–80; Whyte, Greenwood, and Lazes 1991; Collins 1991). In the course of my research I came to know communities of women from Asia, Africa, and the Caribbean, and this experience energized and empowered me. Despite their many differences, women in these groups have come together to work, laugh, support, and encourage each other. Meeting and sharing experiences with others who can understand and support their feelings encourages these women to engage in antiracist and antisexist activities.

But the research also made me conscious of the extent to which my respondents and I had absorbed Canadian society's negative evaluations of our gender and racial identity. This awareness made some of us defensive and others defiant. Although race and gender biases have wasted some of our energies, they have not immobilized us or consumed us with bitterness. The consciousness of the integrated nature of race, class, and gender oppression has informed our struggles. Although the initial coming together of women from Asia, Africa, and the Caribbean may have been a reaction to the gender, class, and race biases of society, these communities have become useful platforms from which women from Asia, Africa, and the Caribbean can respond to painful and oppressive circumstances in ways that empower them. By understanding the commonalities in our experiences, we can shed the burdens of self-blame or self-hate that are so often a consequence of racism and classism, and begin to realize our collective strength, create solidarity, and move to political action.

DEFINING FEMINISM

There is no consensus among scholars about what feminism is or what constitutes feminist activity. They seem to agree only that it is difficult to give a precise meaning to the term. The word 'feminism' has been used historically to refer to the general doctrine of sexual equality and to the organized activity of women engaged in changing their social, political, or economic situation, but the nature of their acts, their motivations, and their objectives have varied in different cultures and historical periods. Defining feminism becomes particularly problematic at a time when deconstructionists have questioned the very concept of who is a woman and when postmodern feminists have critiqued the notion of a unitary, constant, and unchanging 'female subject.'

Most scholars have adopted wide definitions of feminism. Alison Jaggar writes that 'feminism' is commonly used 'to refer to all those who seek, no matter on what grounds, to end women's subordination.' She justifies the use of such an inclusive definition by arguing that her interest is not to discover a 'Platonic ideal form of feminism' but to contribute to formulating a conception of feminism that will 'help women to achieve the fullest possible liberation' (1983, 5). Similarly, Rosalind Delmar opts for a wide definition. She observes that 'feminism is usually defined as an active desire to change women's position in society. Linked to this is the view that feminism is par excellence a social movement for change in women's position' (1986, 13).

Racialized women have sought to define feminism by focusing on how different systems of domination work simultaneously to oppress them. Black feminist bell hooks writes that, to end sexist oppression, it is necessary to attack more than gender bias. Feminism for her is 'a struggle to eradicate the ideology of domination that permeates Western culture on various levels as well as a commitment to reorganizing society so that the self-development of people can take precedence over imperialism, economic expansion, and material desires. Defined in this way, it is unlikely that women would join the feminist movement simply because we are biologically the same. A commitment to feminism so defined would demand that each individual participant acquire a critical political consciousness based on ideas and beliefs' (1984, 24).

Maria Mies observes that in Third World countries the word 'feminism' is often used with the pejorative adjective 'Western,' or sometimes 'bourgeois,' suggesting that feminism belongs in the same category as colonialism or capitalist class rule (1986, 6). Despite some resistance among Third World women to labelling themselves or their activities as feminist, she identifies as feminist women's attempts to form grassroots organizations to struggle against their oppression and exploitation (6–23).

Although feminists agree that 'women are oppressed and exploited by virtue of being women,' they do not agree on the roots or causes of women's oppression. Theories of women's oppression have also evolved over a period of time, often reflecting changes in women's experiences. In the past, feminist theorists attempted to locate the cause of women's oppression in a single factor. Linda Nicholson writes: 'Such attempts have ranged from Shulamith Firestone's very early appeal to biological differences between women and men, to the postulation by many influential feminist anthropologists in the 1970s of a cross-cultural domestic/public separation, to later appeals in the late 1970s and early 1980s to women's labour, to women's sexuality, and to women's primary responsibility for child bearing' (1990, 5–6). Feminist theorists have more recently moved away from locating a single factor to acknowledging the multiple sites of women's oppression and their interconnected and integrated nature.

When writing this book I was aware of the constant tension between the need to take a wide view of feminism and at the same time to be specific, or 'local,' and avoid the pitfalls of overgeneralizations. This tension is discussed in greater detail with reference to terminology in chapter 2. In other chapters I discuss theoretical issues and then go on to analyse specific examples of feminist practices in various periods and provinces of Canada. Feminist organizations and the practices of different ethnic and racial groups are discussed in case studies of their advocacy and in analyses of the cultural dimensions of some of the services provided by them.

My discussion of women from Asia, Africa, and the Caribbean in Canada spans about ninety years – from the early 1900s to the 1990s – and shows how feminism changed over this time. Feminist theory from the early 1900s to the Second World War was predominantly, although not exclusively, about women's struggles to gain equal rights and opportunities. My discussion here focuses on the ethnocentrism of that feminism and its exclusion of women from Asia, Africa, and the Caribbean – for example, Chinese, Japanese, and South Asian women in British Columbia. In chapter 3 I expand my discussion to later feminist theories and the extent to which they too excluded or marginalized race in their formulations of what oppresses women. In chapter 4 I focus on examples of feminist practices that stem from different ideological positions and describe the difficulties of living up to feminist ideals.

LIBERAL AND SOCIALIST-FEMINIST PRACTICES

Feminist theoreticians differ in their views of the role of the state in the lives of women. Liberal feminists believe that the state can guarantee women equal rights, ensure equality of opportunity, and help to eliminate discrimination. They do not view the oppression of women as a structural feature of the capitalist economic system. Socialist feminists take the view that the state is an instrument of the capitalist ruling class which is implicated in women's oppression and exploitation. Women need to come together to struggle against and to overthrow the class, race, and gender domination epitomized and maintained by the state.

Historically, liberal feminists have struggled to win formal legal equality, equal educational opportunities, and freedom from gender discrimination (Cramer 1992; Strong-Boag 1986). In the period following the Second World War, liberal feminists began to recognize the limited value of formal legal equality within a structure of sexual, economic, and racial inequality. They acknowledged that equal opportunity, in the abstract sense that all individuals 'can rise according to the amount of initiative, intelligence, and energy they have,' does not adequately address the multiple sources of women's inequality (Eisenstein 1981, 231; see also Jaggar 1983; Pateman 1987). Liberal feminists therefore have moved to advocating affirmative action programs, such as pay equity and employment equity. They have developed analyses of other issues, such as those relating to wife abuse, that implicitly recognize the interconnections between women's public and private lives, and they have acknowledged the integrated nature of gender, class, and racial discrimination.

Socialist feminists like Zillah Eisenstein have argued that there is an inherent contradiction between 'liberalism (as patriarchal and individualist in structure and ideology) and feminism (sexual egalitarian and collectivist),' but this incompatibility has the potential of radicalizing liberal feminism (1981, 3). Socialist feminists believe that private life is structured by the power relations of society (the personal is political), and they advocate collective forms of organizations that disavow the hierarchies of society and the authority of the capitalist, patriarchal state (Adamson, Briskin, and McPhail 1988; Randall 1988, 1989). Alison Jaggar predicts that as women continue to struggle for state-instituted reforms they will come to realize that the capitalist, patriarchal state is 'unable to guarantee genuine equality for women; consequently, liberal feminists will come to a more radical understanding of the function of the state and to a radical critique of the system that sustains it' (1983, 201–2).

Linda Briskin contrasts the two opposing poles of disengagement, as advocated by socialist feminists, and mainstreaming, as pursued by liberal feminists. She explains: 'Disengagement, which operates from a critique of the system and a standpoint outside of it, and a desire, therefore, to create alternative structures and ideologies, can provide a vision of social transformation. Mainstreaming operates from a desire to reach out to the majority of the population with popular and practical feminist solutions to particular issues, and therefore references major social institutions, such as the family, the workplace, the educational system and the state' (1991, 30).

The socialist-feminist desire for disengagement has most frequently led to the establishment of 'alternative' organizations, but these have been compromised by the difficulty of 'establishing any social/political/ economic space outside of patriarchal capitalism.' Briskin argues that feminist practices that maintain a rigid separation from the state run the risk of marginalization and invisibility. Mainstreaming, which proposes practical solutions to concrete problems encountered by women in the family or the workplace, has led to engagement with the government and the state, but 'engagement with mainstream institutions leads to co-optation and institutionalization' and risks losing sight 'of the larger goals of radical social transformation' (1991, 34).

Jill Vickers believes that most of the contemporary Canadian women's movement leans towards working with the state: 'Despite an important counter-current, the dominant mode of political discourse involves a ... positive view of the state as a utility of value for women. This has focused women's movements on building co-operative political structures to interact with states and on retaining a tension between autonomy and integration. The movements' service orientation and willingness to depend on the state for financial support also moderates their stance' (1992, 59–60).

Although socialist feminism and liberal feminism have different theories about the cause of women's oppression, their pragmatic political strategies narrow the gap between them in their practice. Some feminist demands, particularly those from before the Second World War, have become an established part of the state's agenda (equal political rights and equality of opportunity, for example). In the post-1970s period the state has shown some willingness to address the concerns of women by establishing the Royal Commission on the Status of Women (1970), introducing women's directorates in its bureaucracy, and initiating new legislation. Consequently, socialist feminists feel 'entangled' in the agenda of the state. Sue Findlay observes:

The 1980s has seen the state 'take up' many of our [socialist-feminist] issues – affirmative action, racism and the particular issues of visible minority women, wife abuse, child sexual abuse, rape, reform of the Indian Act, day care, equal pay for work of equal value, and even abortion. In so doing, the state has offered us an opening to exercise our influence. In fact, the way in which the state has taken up our issues has in many cases presented us with the opportunity to participate in the development of state policy, just what we have always wanted. And even if this hasn't been our wildest dream, dare we decline on principle? If we don't participate, who *will* speak for women? (1988, 7)

Socialist feminists have questioned their participation in policy debates initiated by the state or in the implementation of policies. They have complained that the state has reformulated and redefined feminist issues in ways that obscure feminist critiques of gender relations (Barnsley 1985; Randall 1988; Walker 1990). Consciousness of the constraints imposed by state funding is counterbalanced by the recognition that most women's organizations would not be able to survive without these resources. Feminist organizations are dependent on state funding for many activities, including lobbying on behalf of particular groups of women, such as domestic workers and native women. During the referendum on the Charlottetown constitutional accord, the National Action Committee on the Status of Women publicly endorsed a vote against the government. Judy Rebick, its president, noted that this stand might have jeopardized the organization's $3-million grant from the government. The National Action Committee could take this stand because it had also successfully raised funds privately. But Rebick knew of hundreds of organizations that felt compelled to go along with the government rather than risk their funding.[4] While some feminists despair that there is 'no cohesive strategy for dealing with the state in contemporary society' (Randall 1988, 15), others are preoccupied with dealing with immediate political issues. Their 'hopes for the transformation of society in the near future have faded' (Findlay 1988, 8).

Feminist theory was not of immediate concern to the subjects of my research, although some identified themselves as either liberal feminists or socialist feminists. Some saw contradictions between feminism and the hierarchical structure of some of their community-based organizations. But theoretical differences were not perceived as reasons for dispute or disagreement. This view is particularly true of representatives of umbrella organizations, whose member agencies subscribe to different ideological beliefs. For example, the National Action Committee has over 500 member organizations; there are conflicts between member agencies and the executive, but they mostly concern priorities and agendas, pragmatic politics rather than ideological beliefs (Vickers 1992).

Feminists committed to different ideological positions cooperate with one another in pursuit of the immediate goals of securing funding to provide services for women and obtaining equal access to social services for women from their ethnic and racial groups. Community-based groups aim to ensure that women's cultural values and norms are respected in the delivery of services to them, such as in counselling victims of wife abuse and in gaining equal language-training opportunities for women by demanding that they receive training allowances similar to those available to men and that provisions for child care be made at the places of instruction.

Community-based groups do not view themselves as independent of the state, but believe that some redistribution of power and resources can be achieved by cooperating with the state. For them, as for white, middle-class feminists, the state is 'the main recourse of women.' They perceive it as a provider of useful services rather than as a reinforcer of patriarchal norms (Vickers 1992, 45).

Middle-class women from Asia, Africa, and the Caribbean have been engaged with white, middle-class women in conceptualizing and theorizing about different kinds of 'feminisms,' and they may be liberal or socialist feminists. But the women I interviewed were committed to struggling to gain equality for themselves and for women from their communities, and they were cognizant of how their personal lives were structured by the racism of the larger society. Ideological commitment to liberal- and socialist-feminist theories was secondary to the need to find pragmatic solutions to the issues confronting them. The struggles, rather than the intellectual debates, were significant for them.

DEFINING RACISM

One of the themes of this book is that a racist ideology has pervaded feminist theories and practices, and that the struggle against racism has informed the organization of community-based groups. Racism, both interpersonal and systemic, articulates with other systems of domination, but for analytical clarity I discuss racism separately in this section.

Beliefs about what race is have evolved from allegedly scientific doctrines attempting to link social differences to biological, genotypical, or phenotypical characteristics to the contemporary understanding of race as a social construction (Anderson 1991, 8–20; Miles 1989, 11–40). Race is socially constructed in the sense that the dominant group in a society that is characterized by unequal social relations selects certain physical traits and attributes significance to them. These physical traits – such as skin colour, shape of eyes, and hair texture – are then associated with some moral, psychological, or social norms and values. Over a period of time, the association of physical characteristics with a set of values comes to be seen as natural, normal, and inevitable. The correlation between the physical traits and their encoded attributes does not have to be scientifically established, and indeed proof is irrelevant. The association between the physical traits and the norms and values derives its strength from the wide acceptance of belief in race (Li 1990, 5–6). The content of these socially constructed concepts changes over time. For example, in the early part of the 1900s male Chinese in Canada were stereotyped as cheap or 'coolie' labour, but in the 1990s they are often thought of as wealthy businessmen and owners of 'monster homes' (Cannon 1989).

Evelyn Kallen defines racism as 'a set of beliefs, policies and/or practices predicated on the erroneous assumption that some human populations are innately superior to others. Following from this premise, the races of humankind are ranked in accordance with the presumed calibre of their group characteristics' (1982, 22). Robert Miles explains that there are two distinguishing marks of racist ideology. First, it uses some biological 'characteristic(s) as the criterion by which a collectivity may be identified. In this way, the collectivity is represented as having a natural, unchanging origin and status, and therefore as being inherently different.' Second, it attributes to the group 'additional, negatively evaluated characteristics,' biological or cultural, and describes the group as a danger to other groups. 'Such a naturally defined collectivity constitutes a problematic presence: it is represented ideologically as a threat' (1989, 79).

'Racial prejudice' refers to racist attitudes, beliefs, and images (Anderson and Frideres 1981; Kallen 1982; Mackie 1985). Like the ideology of racism, prejudice is 'antipathy accompanied by faulty generalizations' (Pettigrew et al. 1982, 3). Philomena Essed delineates four characteristics of racial prejudice: 'feelings of superiority,' 'perception of subordinate race as intrinsically different and alien,' 'a feeling of proprietary claim to certain areas of privilege and advantage,' and 'fear and suspicion that the subordinate race wants the prerogatives of the dominant race' (1991, 45).

In Canada racism has, sometimes explicitly and at other times tacitly or unconsciously, influenced legislation and feminist practices. Racism establishes criteria for excluding or including groups of people in discourses, organizations, and practices and for allocating resources and services. Racism has been manifested in Canadian policies and laws that categorize groups of people. For example, immigration policies restricted the entry of Asians in the early 1900s when Chinese, Japanese, and South Asians were characterized as being unable to assimilate into Canadian society or to compete in Canada's capitalist economy. The entry of individuals from these groups into the country was described as posing a 'problem' for Canadian society (Satzewich 1991, 123–45).

The entry of racialized women was also represented as a 'problem.' In the early 1900s Chinese men were suspected of wanting to bring women from China to Canada to work as prostitutes (Chan 1983; Yee 1988). At the present time, Chinese and South Asian women are assumed to belong to cultures that make it difficult for them to adapt to white Canadian norms (Royal Commission on the Status of Women 1970; Parmar 1986). This view serves to rationalize their exclusion and marginalization from social resources and opportunities. Black women from the Caribbean have been constructed as promiscuous and therefore a threat to the standards of Canadian morality. This 'problem' was used as an excuse to restrict their entry to Canada in the 1950s (Satzewich 1991).

The dominant group in a society exercises the power to label and define people, and these definitions construct relations between them. Although race is a consequence of constructed dominant/subordinate relations, the ideology of racism may become part of our everyday understanding and common sense (Lawrence 1986). Philomena Essed defines everyday racism as 'systematic, recurrent, [and] familiar practices' (1991, 3). Some feminist practices can be characterized as everyday racism. They include claiming to speak on behalf of all women, asking racialized women to participate in 'our' organizations, and assuming leadership roles in the 'mainstream' women's movement. Everyday racism is often automatic and unconscious; even if one does not deliberately intend to discriminate, if the effects of one's act result in unequal treatment of a member of a racialized group, that counts as racial discrimination (Kallen 1982; Mackie 1985; Driedger 1989).

'Discrimination' refers to behaviour or acts predicated on racial prejudice (Anderson and Frideres 1981; Kallen 1982; Mackie 1985). Discrimination leads to unequal, illegitimate, and disadvantageous treatment (Driedger 1989, 350–4). For example, women from Asia, Africa, and the Caribbean may experience discrimination in gaining access to services from state agencies. Discrimination can be individual, institutional, or systemic. Individual discrimination can occur between two residents in a shelter for women or between a white counsellor and a Chinese or a

South Asian woman. Institutional discrimination is embedded in rules and regulations which result in excluding some groups of people (Kallen 1982, 35). An example is the refusal by institutions and employers to accept educational qualifications or work experience acquired in Third World countries on par with those obtained in Canada. Structural or systemic discrimination is found in a society that 'excludes substantial numbers of members of particular ethnic collectivities from significant participation in its major institutions' (Kallen 1982, 36).

There is wide divergence of opinion on the functions of racism in a capitalist society. Marxists view the state as an instrument of the ruling class that facilitates the accumulation of capital and the growth of profits. Racism, by defining some people as inferior, justifies paying them lower wages, which exploits them further since the extraction of additional surplus value from their labour leads to higher profits for capitalists (Basran 1983, 7; Solomos et al. 1986). B. Singh Bolaria and Peter Li applied this analysis to the immigration of Chinese, Japanese, South Asian, and black people to Canada, and found that racist ideology segregated them into the lower segments of the labour market (1988).

Robert Miles argues that racism has a history that predates the development of the capitalist mode of production and is therefore not just a consequence of capitalist class relations (1989, 100). Moreover, in the early 1900s, the Canadian government restricted the entry of cheap labour and thus acted in apparent contradiction to the interests of the ruling class. Alan Simmons and Kieran Keohane argue that one of the functions of the state is to manage conflicting social relations (1992, 426–7). The formulation of immigration policies balanced the needs of the capitalist class against the demands and pressures of other interest groups, such as labour unions (Satzewich 1991). And state policies responded to the beliefs, attitudes, ideologies, and sentiments of the society at large. For example, in 1942 the government interned Japanese Canadians because of a widespread but irrational fear that they posed a threat to national security, a fear fuelled by racist sentiments (Berger 1982, 93–126). Most scholars now agree that race cannot be reduced to class and must be seen as having its 'own complex and historically specific modes' (Stasiulis 1990, 279).

My discussion of racism in feminist theory and practice refers to the ethnocentrism of white feminists and to the exercise of power based on race privilege. Ethnocentrism is the 'tendency to view all the peoples and cultures of the world from the central vantage point of one's own particular ethnic group and, consequently, to evaluate and rank all outsiders in terms of one's own particular cultural standards and values' (Kallen 1982, 26). Ethnocentrism was most evident in feminist theories and practices up to the 1970s. Feminists saw their own experiences as representing the norm for all women and maintained that gender alone oppressed women. In the 1980s this narrow view was challenged by women from Asia, Africa, and the Caribbean, who identified the multiple sources of women's oppressions. But more subtle ethnocentric biases remained hidden in the language of feminists – for instance, the binary terminology of 'white/black,' 'Western/non-Western.' And white, middle-class feminists have exercised the power to identify problems and propose solutions, projects, and programs.[5]

The recognition of differences in the sources of women's oppression and in the beliefs and political ideologies among women did not eliminate conflicts among feminists. Debate focused on whether feminists were 'different but equal' or 'different and unequal' to each other. While white, middle-class feminists insisted that they were 'different but equal,' women from Asia, Africa, and the Caribbean argued that they were in fact treated as 'different and unequal' by the women's movement. They complained that white feminists used privilege in everyday interactions and set the agendas for debates and discussions.

This exercise of power and privilege is based on both race and class. Women from Asia, Africa, and the Caribbean find white, middle-class feminists in the role of 'gatekeepers' in organizations that have emerged to take up women's issues. The power to include, exclude, or marginalize individuals and groups most frequently belongs to white, middle-class women. The Royal Commission on Violence Against Women (1993) included racialized women, but the National Action Committee on the Status of Women, at the behest of its racialized executive, argued that the women on its board were appointed by the state and were not truly representative of the organizations of racialized women.

Women from Asia, Africa, and the Caribbean have formed autonomous organizations committed to resisting the consequences of racism. Although they struggle against class, race, and gender oppression, their practices prioritize activities that resist racism. Community-based organizations of women from Asia, Africa, and the Caribbean have criticized state agencies for discriminatory treatment in mainstream social service agencies, and they have argued that their own community groups should provide services. There is disagreement about means and objectives among the community-based groups and between women within these groups, but they are all committed to antiracism.

2

The Experience of Race and Gender Discrimination

Ethnic history belies portraits of Canada as a country settled by northern European immigrants by celebrating the achievements of many other groups. Women's history documents the social and political achievements of Canadian women and their contributions to the intellectual and political debates of their times. Women from Asia, Africa, and the Caribbean have become active, participating subjects in both Canadian ethnic history and Canadian women's history. Accounts of their achievements have contributed to the dignity and self-esteem of members of the group. However, these accounts are limited if they do not explain how race, class, and gender create and perpetuate inequalities.[1]

Consciousness of the integrated nature of race, class, and gender discrimination created the impetus to document the history of women immigrants from Asia, Africa, and the Caribbean. Women from Asia, Africa, and the Caribbean who came to Canada in the early 1900s have left few accounts of how they experienced race, class, and gender oppression. Their experiences must be reconstructed from accounts of dominant groups – from male historians and the records of volunteer and benevolent societies. Women from Asia, Africa, and the Caribbean are now interpreting the experiences of their foremothers from oral histories of second-generation women.[2] These histories give a voice to women from Asia, Africa, and the Caribbean and form an integral part of Canadian history.

This first part of this chapter defines the subject – women from Asia, Africa, and the Caribbean – and comments on methodology; the second part analyses the intersection of race, class, and gender in the lives of these women. These integrated oppressions create a commonality of experience but do not necessarily create political consciousness of class, race, and gender oppression or lead to political solidarity among the women. Topics discussed in the second part of the chapter include immigration history, paid employment, and the absence of Asian, African, and Caribbean women from feminist practice of the first wave (1880–1920). This chapter aims to demonstrate that racism prevented the first wave from addressing the problems these women faced.

DEFINING THE SUBJECT

Women from Asia, Africa, and the Caribbean come from diverse cultures and different socioeconomic groups, and they have varying degrees of consciousness of race, class, or gender oppression. Unity may sometimes be imposed on them as a result of a common labelling or a common positioning vis-à-vis another group of women, but their differences prevent them from forming one homogeneous category. Gender and race discrimination takes different forms in different historical and material contexts, but at particular moments in history, it is possible for many divergent groups of women to come together in collective response to an ideology, in assertion of their rights, or in opposition to a prevailing belief system.

This study focuses on the experience of women who came to Canada from Asia, Africa, and the Caribbean, but not because they fall into some natural category, least of all one grounded on arbitrary geographical divisions. It is not my intention to impose a false unity upon very diverse groups of women, or to imply that other immigrants (e.g., from Latin America or from southern or eastern Europe) or native Canadians have not also suffered from the oppressions of race, class, and gender bias. The study focuses on the experience of women who have come to Canada from regions that have been particularly marked (albeit in different ways) by the effects of foreign (especially British) colonialism and imperialism. It aims to demonstrate how racism affects the construction of historical knowledge and the organization of social relationships and how the intersection of gender, class, and race deepens inequalities.

The phrase 'women from the Caribbean' obscures the range of different cultures that exist on the islands and continental coasts of that region. Women from the Caribbean may trace their cultural roots to India, Africa, Europe, or – as a result of cross-cultural marriages – to more than one of these places. These women do not constitute a homogenous group. Their identity is constructed from gender, class, colour, ethnicity, age, occupation, and sexual orientation. But these factors are not equally significant in their countries of origin. Ethnic identity, for instance, is a significant factor in the politics of some of the countries but not of others. It is important in Trinidad and Guyana but not in St Lucia. Sometimes class and ethnic categories overlap and create political tension. Women's cultural roots as well as their sense of ethnicity may thus differ on their arrival in Canada. These points further diversify the group 'women from the Caribbean.'

South Asian women form a segment of a larger group of women from Asia and Africa. Analysing this group reveals numerous differences among them. South Asian women may come from India, Pakistan, Sri Lanka, Bangladesh, Uganda, Tanzania, South Africa, or elsewhere. They may be first-generation immigrants from their country of origin, daughters of immigrants to Britain, or granddaughters of immigrants to Africa or the Caribbean. Even within a specific group there may be additional differences. For example, women who come from India may be Hindus, Sikhs, Muslims, or Christians. Each of these religions has its own view of women and has constructed somewhat different gender roles within the family, educational institutions, and the workforce. There may be additional differences among them – for example, different degrees of commitment to tradition, Westernization, or modernization. They may come from rural or urban backgrounds, and they differ from each other in caste, region, age, sexual orientation, and time of arrival in Canada.

A study of a smaller group of women would no doubt explore more fully their particular situations. A specific, localized subject would conform to one feminist methodology which contextualizes a particular subject in order to avoid errors of the grand 'meta-narratives' of the past (Code 1991; Cancian 1992). For example, a discussion of Sikh or Chinese women living in Richmond, British Columbia, between 1906 and 1945 could illustrate many aspects of their culture, the prevailing social structure in Richmond, and the roles of class, culture, and gender in constructing a specific identity for them. One could see whether the white, middle-class women in the neighbourhood were from Britain, Ukraine, Scandinavia, whether they were Catholic or Protestant, and recent or assimilated immigrants. And one could investigate who excluded or discriminated against whom and why.

But too narrow a focus has disadvantages of its own. As Nancy Hartsock notes, for feminists to invoke 'the ideal of endless difference' would be to deny women any unity based on common condition and similar experience (1990; see also Hawkesworth 1989). And it would fail to show how social power is exercised in the larger society, how gender bias and racism operate as principles of social organization, and how ideas of race permeate a society, even infecting some feminist analyses and politics.

Study of the more diverse group of women has the research objectives of showing, first, how white feminist theory, despite assertions to the contrary, subordinates the experience of class and race prejudice to gender discrimination; second, how racial identity distinguishes the experience of women within feminist practice and undermines feminist solidarity; and, third, how feminist consciousness has nonetheless played a positive role in addressing the oppressions experienced by women who are identified by race. In Canada, state practices – such as immigration policies and social welfare legislation – have placed women from Asia, Africa, and the Caribbean in similar positions and thus have constructed a common identity for them. This study aims not to perpetuate that categorization, but to deconstruct it.

Race bias in immigration policy in the early 1900s excluded or restricted the immigration of women from China, Japan, South Asia, and the Caribbean (Li 1988a; Adachi 1976; Calliste 1989; Satzewich 1991). The bias was rationalized in different ways for each of the groups, and a separate immigration policy was designed to restrict the entry of members from each of these groups. These immigration policies had implications for the families and communities of those groups: the Chinese and South Asians in Canada were an all-male community, while the Japanese were a family-oriented group. More black females were admitted from the Caribbean than black males. Racism provided a common denominator, yet there is no evidence to indicate that the victims engaged in any common struggle. The struggles of the Chinese and South Asian men shared a common objective – to gain the right to bring their wives to Canada – but their efforts ran along parallel lines and the groups did not make common cause. They sought entry for women of their communities by appealing to humanitarianism and the injustice of being denied a family life, but they did not assert their equality with other ethnic groups or make an appeal based on human rights (Jensen 1988, 127–8; Raj 1980).

A common political platform of opposition to racial discrimination did emerge in the late 1960s and 1970s. This period saw the growth of several social movements of oppressed groups demanding equality with members of the dominant groups: blacks in the United States, French Canadians and other ethnic groups in Canada, and women in both countries (Ubale 1977; Head 1975; Pitman 1977; Black 1988, 1992; Bégin

1992; Fleras and Elliott 1992). These movements created a consciousness of human rights in diverse groups of people. It also created a unity among women from Asia, Africa, and the Caribbean.

Feminism raised consciousness of gender oppression and, over a period of time, provided a language for conceptualizing and asserting equal rights for women of other races and classes. Consciousness of gender oppression led to the emergence of women's groups whose membership was derived from a diverse mix of ethnicity, race, and class. While mainstream women's organizations tended to be dominated by white, middle-class women, others (often referred to as 'immigrant women's associations') drew their membership from working-class women and those who belonged to stigmatized minority groups. Such organizations brought working-class women from Asia, Africa, and the Caribbean together with working-class women from Portugal and Greece. This coming together reinforced a commonality of interests and created consciousness of shared experiences and common goals. Race, ethnicity, and class oppression divided them from mainstream women's organizations and created a community of women with similar experiences. The imposition of other labels – such as 'visible minority women,' 'Third World women,' or 'immigrant women' – on these diverse groups of women created a unity among them. This unity was structured not only by characteristics shared by them, but by their distinction from white, middle-class women. Ironically, the arbitrary categorization of women from Asia, Africa, and the Caribbean placed them in a position to attack the race, class, and gender biases that produced it.

FEMINIST HISTORICAL METHODOLOGY

A historian of women from Asia, Africa, and the Caribbean faces many difficulties. The oppressed must be the subjects of their history, and the history must give voice to their experiences. But it is difficult to document the responses of the first generation of women from Asia, Africa, and the Caribbean to the situations they encountered in Canada during the first half of the twentieth century. Unlike some of their European counterparts, most women in these groups did not keep diaries, write books, or even serve as record-keeping or minutes-taking members of government or voluntary organizations.

Women from Asia, Africa, and the Caribbean are now engaged in documenting, from oral history accounts of second-generation women, how race, class, and gender structured the lives of their forebears (Brand

1991; Chinese Canadian National Council 1992; Shibata 1980; Ayukawa 1987, 1991; Nipp 1983; Yee 1987). And they are editing letters and diaries left behind by first-generation immigrants (Oiwa 1991; Kitagawa 1985). These histories give a voice to women from Asia, Africa, and the Caribbean and provide some answers to questions of how they experienced oppression and exploitation, what priority they gave to different struggles at different periods of time, how they established solidarity with white Canadian women, and what their goals and objectives were in forming different kinds of women's groups to serve their needs and aspirations.

The history of women from Asia, Africa, and the Caribbean can also be documented with fragments that appear in other accounts of immigrant groups (Broadfoot 1979; Chan 1983; Con et al. 1982; Adachi 1976; Buchignani and Indra 1985). In these accounts women are viewed primarily as adjuncts to male immigrants and confined to traditional gender roles. Histories of volunteer and benevolent societies, which were established by males in some of these groups, indicate how the men struggled to bring their wives to Canada or how they attempted to stop the sexual exploitation of women from their own communities (Chandrasekhar 1945; Lai 1972). The accounts of missionaries and debates of state officials about women from Asia, Africa, and the Caribbean reveal how institutional biases of race, class, and gender oppressed the women. Missionaries have documented their attempts to 'save' Chinese and Japanese women from sexual exploitation (Women's Missionary Society n.d.; Platt 1908; Valverde 1991a; Van Dieren 1984; Nipp 1983). Government debates on immigration policies reveal how race, class, and gender biases functioned to exclude women from Asia, Africa, and the Caribbean from gaining entry to Canada (Reid 1941; Morse 1936; Wagle 1990; Daenzer 1991; Calliste 1989; Satzewich 1991).

Accounts by women from Asia, Africa, and Caribbean begin by noting the absence of their forebears from conventional accounts of Canadian history (Nipp 1983; Brand 1991; Oiwa 1991; Kogawa 1981; Chinese Canadian National Council 1992). This chapter asks what the absence of these women tells us about feminists of this period and about the women's movement. What was the prevailing ideology that justified or rationalized this exclusion? Racist ideology and immigration policy structured the conditions of women's lives from Asia, Africa, and the Caribbean. Did they unquestioningly accept their lot, or did they resist? Did these women attempt, individually or collectively, to transform the conditions of their lives?

The following part of this chapter uses the narrative approach to examine the lives of women from Asia and the Caribbean. It documents how race, class, and gender biases constructed their social identity, and how these biases were reflected in the social relations among women and in the feminist discourse of this period. These biases provide material for further analysis of the processes that reconstructed their identity in the 1970s and 1980s. The chapter shows how power and knowledge came together in constructing an identity for 'immigrant woman.'

IMMIGRATION: THE FIRST PHASE

During the early part of the twentieth century, a racist ideology was widespread in Canada. According to this ideology, it would be difficult for Asian and black immigrants to assimilate Canadian norms; they had a low potential for 'adaptability' to the Canadian climate; and Canada ought to be preserved as a 'white man's country.' The ideology was most explicitly enunciated in British Columbia, where immigrants from South Asia, China, and Japan had settled (Ward 1978, 1989; Roy 1989a, 1989b; Creese 1988–9, 1992).

Race bias appeared in much legislation, particularly in the areas of immigration policy and employment practices. Immigration policy prohibited or restricted the entry of members of these groups, and legislation restricted the employment of Asians in several sectors of the economy (e.g., government projects) and imposed conditions under which they were permitted to operate businesses (Berger 1982; Sunahara 1981; Anderson 1991).

The impact of such legislation on women was different from its impact on men. Racist sentiments in British Columbia aimed to exclude Asians from entering Canada, but many males gained entry as cheap labour. Although Chinese, Japanese, and Indian women engaged in paid and unpaid work, their status as workers seldom gained them entry. They were admitted only as spouses. Immigration policy made it impossible for the wives or children of men from India and China to come to Canada and gave only limited access to wives from Japan. It excluded South Asian and Chinese women from Canada before the First World War, and later granted entry only to wives and children of immigrants already in Canada.

In 1908 Minister of Labour Mackenzie King conducted an inquiry called 'Immigration to Canada from the Orient and Immigration from India in Particular.' He noted in his diary that 'we should endeavour to keep our country as pure in the matter of race as possible' and justified the exclusion of Indians by arguing that 'they were not suited for the railways, for hard work, or for our climate.' He tried to defend these views with high-minded principles:

The thought that has come to me during the last few days is that, as between Asia and Canada, we should declare India for the Indians and Canada for the Canadians, pointing out that the aim of India should not be to make Canada a black or a yellow Canada, but to develop within each race itself an attitude which will make the whole Empire one and indivisible, and lead to advantages which accrue through alliances ... This would seem to reconcile the teachings of Christianity with the doctrine of exclusion or what might be more properly termed, reservation of countries for inhabitants for which it is intended by nature. (Quoted in Wagle 1990, 15–17)

However, politicians were constrained from acting on such sentiments in a straightforward manner. The British Foreign Office discouraged the government of Canada from acting in any way that would cause difficulty for the British government in India or provoke agitation or unrest there, but after 1908 the British government refrained from interfering (Wagle 1990, 7; also Singh 1977, 168–92). The British government did not support the struggles of Indians to gain entry to Canada, and later aided only spouses who wished to immigrate.

In British Columbia where racist passions ran particularly high, legislation was enacted to exclude South Asians. A literacy test was introduced in 1907, but it was challenged by South Asians and disallowed by the courts (Jensen 1988, 59–65). Although the Liberal government in Ottawa was often unsympathetic to the racist sentiments of British Columbians, in 1908 it passed legislation that required all South Asians who wished to settle in Canada to come by a continuous journey. Since no such transportation was available, this effectively halted all immigration from the subcontinent for several years and prevented wives from joining their husbands (Johnston 1979, 4–5; Buchignani and Indra 1985, 36–47).

South Asians struggled against such legislation. They took their 'complaints about Canadian immigration laws to the imperial council and petitioned the government at Ottawa to allow their families to be admitted' (Jensen 1988, 127–8). When these efforts failed, they tried to put the law to the test. In 1911–12 two South Asian residents attempted to bring their wives to Canada after visiting them in India. Although the men were readmitted, the wives could not claim automatic entry by virtue of their spousal status. The exclusion of South Asian women was supported by the Women's National Council, an organization representing 400 women in Vancouver, and the wives were issued deportation orders (Johnston 1979, 13).[3] However, after vigorous protests by South Asian organizations, the deportation orders were rescinded and the women were allowed to stay – as 'an act of grace without establishing precedent' (Jensen 1988, 128). The *Komagata Maru* incident of 1914, in which a ship carrying Indians was refused permission to land in Vancouver harbour, marked the end of immigration from South Asia for some time (Johnston 1979; Morse 1936; Reid 1941).

The exclusion of women placed Indian men in an unenviable position. Public opinion criticized them for not following conventional family norms, and yet they were prevented from bringing their wives to Canada (Ward 1978, 83–4). The *Colonist* declared:

Their habits of life are unsatisfactory. They do not bring their wives with them, and will not make homes and rear families. They are totally unfitted for a white man's country ... For the Sikh in his home we have every respect; for the Sikh in Canada there is no proper place, and it is a great unkindness to a well-meaning people to bring him here. (Quoted in Ward 1978, 83–4)

The attempts by Indian men to bring their wives to Canada were viewed sceptically. H.H. Stevens, a Conservative member of Parliament and an avid opponent of immigration from India, claimed:

[Hindu] agitation for entry of wives for those now here is a subterfuge and was only taken up when it was found to be a good ground for appeal to the sentiment of Eastern Canada. This is an effort to break the immigration regulations in principle. If the privilege to bring in wives is allowed it will result in large numbers of women being brought in for immoral purposes under the guise of 'wives of Hindus here.' British Columbia is opposed to Asiatic immigration, because from experience they know they will not assimilate. It results in a large male population with much immorality, where there should exist a large community of white families. (Quoted in Wagle 1990, 24)

Sunder Singh, an Indian male, replied in a pamphlet entitled 'India's appeal to Canada: or an Account of Hindu Immigration to the Dominion':

But Christian Canada denies home-life, the birthright of each human being, by shutting out the wife of the Sikh, who is a fellow citizen of the Empire. The right of a husband living with his wife is the most sacred human institution, and anything done to impair it goes at the very root of all principles of morality and social welfare. Further, the ideals of Sikh home life are highly spiritual and monogamous. (Quoted in Wagle 1990, 24)

Racist views were also voiced about the predominantly male Chinese communities (Woodsworth [1909] 1972, 145). Racism made interracial marriages all but impossible (Roy 1989a, 18; Cheng 1931, 138–59). 'The prospect of Chinese men marrying white women was so horrendous that, when one British Columbian editor learned of two such cases in Halifax, he suggested that perhaps the 'brides were better off in their coffins.''' And a journal observed that 'it is when we contemplate these unnatural unions that we find the kernel of the Asiatic problem – the mixing of the races. Race mixture is the essential danger of the Asiatic occupation of the country for race mixture means race deterioration' (Roy 1989b, 18).

The distaste of the time for any cross-cultural communication between Chinese men and white women was institutionalized by the law, which prohibited white women from working in Chinese restaurants. A prosecutor concerned with enforcing this law suggested that, if 'the Licence Inspector makes a personal visit to one of these places and finds loose conduct, such as a white waitress sitting down with a Chinese,' he could lay a charge. This scenario was insufficient to lay a criminal charge but would suffice to cancel a licence: 'no outward crime is being committed but the chances are that procuring may be well under way' (quoted in Anderson 1991, 161). Statistical evidence of intermarriages is scarce, but of the 22,000 Japanese who were removed from protected areas in British Columbia, only 22 were exempt as partners in marriage with whites (Ward 1989, 271).

Racist sentiments excluded the entry of Chinese women to Canada. The cultural norms of wealthy Chinese families fuelled racist fears of immorality and reinforced the arguments for the exclusion of all Chinese. Some wealthy Chinese merchants followed the traditional norm of having a 'secondary wife' or a concubine, and this practice was widely used as evidence of the low morals of all Chinese men. Further, wealthy Chinese merchants often employed a *Mui Tsai*, a domestic worker who had special status within the family. She might be included in the bride price of a newly married wife as compensation for having to live overseas. She received food, shelter, and clothing, but no wages. The family for whom she worked had an obligation to find her a husband; once married, she was free to leave. Dora Nipp argues that becoming a *Mui Tsai* was often the only means for a poor girl to survive and represented her best expectations (1983, 38–41). But this practice was largely misconstrued by Canadian public opinion, which portrayed the women as debased 'slave girls' who were being brought into Canada for prostitution.

Legislation made it difficult, if not impossible, for Chinese women to enter Canada. In 1885 the Royal Commission on Chinese Immigration heard claims that Chinese women were being brought as prostitutes into San Francisco from poverty-stricken provinces in China. In 1886 a head tax of $10 was imposed on the Chinese, and this was gradually increased to $500 by 1903 (Li 1988a, 23–42). Although the tax did not distinguish between men and women, it was prohibitively expensive for most Chinese males in Canada, who were primarily employed as 'cheap labour' on the Canadian Pacific Railway. The head tax effectively kept the women out.

Chinese merchants were often exempt from regulations that applied to wage-workers, and they were allowed to bring their wives (Yee 1988, 40–5). Sometimes owners of restaurants and laundries passed themselves off as merchants and brought their wives to Canada. A Canadian-born Chinese man familiar with the Chinatowns of the 1930s notes: 'In the restaurants there were women from Hong Kong, brought over by businessmen, men who owned grocery stores, labourers. The women lived with these "husbands" but they were brought over to work as waitresses and whores' (Yee 1988, 95). Such a situation was a consequence of legislation that prohibited white women from working for Chinese men and of racism, which made social interaction between them difficult (Adachi 1976, 93; Roy 1989b, 288–9).

An unintended result of the head tax was the admission of Chinese prostitutes who were 'owned' by their male procurers. Prostitutes were considered financial assets by Chinese males and could be expected to pay off the cost of their head tax with their earnings. Young girls were imported by Chinese merchants and were later sold into prostitution, bringing these merchants large profits from the 'sexual needs of Chinese workers and the curiosity of white pleasure seekers' (Chan 1983, 81; also Valverde 1991a, 87). At least 100 to 200 Chinese women were imported annually from 1887 until the beginning of the twentieth century (Platt 1908, 106).

The existence of Chinese prostitutes fuelled racist sentiments. *Missionary Outlook*, a publication of the Methodist Church of Canada, noted in

1943: 'In 1886–1887, the [Methodist] Church in Victoria was awakened to the monstrous fact that Chinese girls were being bought and sold by white men and Chinese for immoral purposes. Canadian law does not permit the buying and selling of women, but with diabolical ingenuity, by trickery and cunning, this horrible practice was pursued' (quoted in Nipp 1983, 38). White prostitutes in Victoria outnumbered Chinese prostitutes by 150 to 4 in 1902, but it was the Chinese who were condemned for their immoral behaviour (Chan 1983, 80). Racists portrayed all Chinese women and girls as prostitutes who undermined the morals and health of white community. The desire to maintain Canada as a 'white man's country' further created resentment towards Chinese women, who, it was feared, would increase the Chinese population (Adilman 1984, 56; Van Dieren 1984, 80).

Historians of Chinese immigration have usually argued that racist sentiments in British Columbia were instrumental in keeping Chinese women out of Canada. But Dora Nipp notes that conditions in China, particularly the attitude of the government and Chinese cultural mores, also made it difficult for women to emigrate. For financial reasons, the Chinese government was determined to prevent women from following their husbands. When an emigrant sent remittances home, these were taxed to help support the village. If an emigrant returned to re-establish himself in the village, he had to make additional payments. Women had the responsibility of following the rituals of ancestor worship, burial rites, and care of the elderly, which kept them tied to the village. The departure of the woman would have severed the ties of the family to the village. And, given the insecurity of life in British Columbia, Chinese males were reluctant to bring their wives to Canada (Nipp 1983, 15–18). Sing Cheung Yung, a Nanaimo market gardener, explained: 'I have been here twelve years. My wife and two children are in China ... I would like to bring my wife and children here. She don't want to come. The people in this country talk so much against the Chinese that I don't care to bring them here' (Chan 1983, 50).

It is difficult to estimate the number of Chinese women in British Columbia because there are discrepancies between the number of Chinese women who arrived in Canada and the number who became residents. The practice of having more than one wife further complicates attempts to arrive at figures. Some estimate that in 1902 there were only 92 wives among 3,263 Chinese in Victoria, 61 of whom were married to merchants, and 28 to labourers. In Vancouver there were 2,053 Chinese men and 27 Chinese women; 16 women were wives of merchants, 8 of labourers, 1 of a minister, and 2 of interpreters (Li 1988a, 58–9; Con et al. 1982, 26). Although some women came later, the Chinese remained primarily an all-male community until the 1960s (Li 1988a, 97).

There are few, if any, records of the immigration of Japanese women prior to 1907. Japanese immigrants, like Indian and Chinese immigrants, were the targets of racial hostility, and in 1907 the news that a ship carrying 1,189 Japanese had arrived in Vancouver triggered the worst race riot in British Columbia's history. However, the advantage of maintaining cordial political relations between the British and the Japanese governments led the government of British Columbia to take a moderate stand against Japanese immigration. The Gentlemen's Agreement of 1908 between the Canadian and Japanese governments restricted the immigration of more men from Japan but allowed residents to bring in their wives and children. Because many of the Japanese workers were unmarried, they arranged, with the help of relatives in Japan or through the Prefectural Association matchmakers, to marry 'picture brides' (Adachi 1976, 87–108). The women chose these alliances to escape poverty or to help their families (Ayukawa 1987, 14). In 1908, 566 women arrived, and between 1909 and 1929 their annual numbers, ranging between 153 and 530, usually exceeded those of men (Ujimoto 1988, 132). A woman of Japanese origin describes the experience of her mother, who came as a picture bride: 'The girl looked at the man's picture and I'm not sure if she had much to say in the matter and the man looked at the girl's picture and then documents were signed at the Japanese consul's place in Vancouver ... There was no wedding. You didn't have to have a wedding to get married ... You just [had] to agree and sign' (Broadfoot 1979, 18). In 1929, as a result of the revised Gentlemen's Agreement, the Japanese government agreed that the picture-bride system would end and annual immigration from Japan would not exceed 150. Between 1929 and 1940 the number of new female immigrants was fewer than 50 a year (Ujimoto 1988, 132–7).

In the early 1900s, blacks from the United States attempted to immigrate in response to Canadian advertisements for agriculturalists to settle the western provinces, and they usually met with some resistance. Nevertheless, some blacks were able to immigrate to the Prairies and to Ontario (Winks 1971, 300–37). In addition to these immigrants, there was a small community of black Loyalists and refugees who had settled in Nova Scotia in the late 1700s (Henry 1973). It is difficult to analyse the experience of the blacks in this period because they represented less than 2 per cent of Canada's population and were widely dispersed throughout the country. Although they experienced racial discrimination, laws varied from place to place, and this lack of uniformity inhibited the emergence of any strong sense of community or common interest (Winks 1971, 300–37). Women formed part of the black population, but there is little evidence to indicate the conditions of their lives. The only identifiable group among them is the women who immigrated from the Caribbean as domestic workers. They encountered both sexist and racist discrimination.

Women from the Caribbean were needed as domestic workers because European immigrants and Canadian women preferred manufacturing and service-sector jobs to domestic work. The first Caribbean Domestic Scheme recruited approximately 100 women from Guadeloupe in 1910–11 to fill the demand for cheap labour in Quebec. But during the recessionary period of 1913–15, they were deported because government agencies feared that they were likely to become a public charge (Calliste 1989). In the period between 1922 and 1931, 74 per cent of the 768 Caribbean blacks who immigrated to Canada came as domestics. These women were required to be single and between the ages of twenty-one and thirty-five. Women who were single parents were barred from entry because it was feared that they would become pregnant again. The women were evaluated positively as domestic workers but in a racially biased manner. Their gender and race, it was believed, made them 'fond of children,' they were expected to 'know their place,' and public opinion held that they could stay provided they 'remain in the country as servants' (Calliste 1989, 135). Such attitudes were different from those displayed towards single women who came from Britain to work as domestics. Domestic work for British immigrant women was viewed by middle-class Canadian women as temporary; they were expected to marry eventually and raise families in Canada (Barber 1985).

The goal of restricting immigration of women from Asia and the Caribbean was to limit the growth of their communities. The Chinese Immigration Act of 1923 was passed in response to concerns of the Department of Immigration that Chinese women were being brought into Canada illegally as labourers. Members of Parliament and senators believed that it was necessary to curb the population growth of the Chinese immigrants and thus to exclude women (Adilman 1984, 61). Excluding women meant that families could not be established and that the natural increase of members of the Asian communities would be limited. There is no documentary evidence that interracial marriages took place in any numbers. However, despite racist wishes that the communities would gradually fade and disappear, the number of female immigrants from China and South Asia slowly expanded in the period following the First World War. Although the Chinese Immigration Act of 1923 prohibited all immigration from China, a federal order-in-council in 1930 allowed the wives of Canadian citizens and their children under eighteen to enter Canada from China (Con et al. 1982, 135–47; Yee 1988, 107).

Throughout the 1920s and 1930s, South Asian men struggled to have restrictions on the immigration of women removed. But social hostility meant that, even when the law allowed women to enter Canada, only a small number took advantage of it. For example, there were 900 to 1,000 South Asians living in Canada in 1924, but by 1941 only 180 wives had immigrated to Canada (Johnston 1979, 95; also Cheng 1931, 156). Similarly, the ratio of Chinese males to females decreased slowly in this period, but the Chinese remained essentially an all-male community. Only the Japanese had a more or less settled community and family life.

WOMEN'S PAID WORK

Women from China, Japan, and South Asia came to Canada primarily as dependent spouses; they were not allowed to enter as 'labourers' (Adilman 1984, 61). Although categorized as dependants, most did wage work in addition to traditional 'women's work' within the home. Those women whose spouses had small businesses provided crucial support with their free labour, which enabled those businesses to survive and flourish. Women from China, Japan, and South Asia lived isolated lives, and their interactions were almost wholly confined to members of their own communities. Language was an obvious barrier to communication with either white Canadians or other ethnic groups. And a large percentage of these women were married to poor men and could not afford the luxury of being full-time housewives.

Some of the women from Japan were from middle-class families and had some education. Most others had been poor in their countries of origin. Some had experience working on the land. The Chinese women found work as maids or in canneries; some clerked in grocery stores or sewed for Chinese-owned businesses (Yee 1988, 99). A Chinese woman who became a maidservant at the age of ten in 1900 recalled:

Yip Yen's family brought me over, but they gave me to Yip Yen's brother's second wife ... I got up at seven in the morning to light the stove in the room. They would still be sleeping. The stove burned coal, so I had to rake out the ashes ... When she got up I made her toast and tea and coffee. Then I washed the dishes. I cooked the rice, I scrubbed the clothes and the floors. After she ate her fill of dinner, she'd go out to play dominoes with the Jung Kee lady and leave me working. There used to be seamsters in Chinatown, and she brought home clothing for me to work on: feather stitching, buttonholes, butterfly buttons – I did everything. I worked from morning to night without stopping. (Yee 1988, 45–6)

Japanese women worked alongside their men in the market gardens and in the fields. They also worked in canneries or as cooks at logging camps and mining camps, as houseworkers, or as clerks for small storekeepers (Shibata 1980). The women were paid little for their work, less than men or white Canadian women. One picture bride who came to Canada in 1911 ended up travelling with her spouse to several logging camps where she cooked and cared for the entire gang of workers. Her impressions were recorded by a Nisei woman:

The next location was even worse. There she had to cook three meals for twenty-seven people. The water had to be hauled from the river ... at night ... to wash twenty-two kilograms of rice. She rose at 4:00 a.m. to cook this rice, to make the miso soup, and to pack the lunches. At 6:00 a.m. the men woke up, ate and went to work. Then she had to clean all the cabins, in which three to four men each lived, to clean about forty kerosene lamps, and to fill them up. Then she made lunch for about six of the men who returned for it. Her next chore was the laundry, and then she prepared the supper ... For cooking, she was paid $1.00 per person per month and the same for the laundry ... [However,] she never received a penny for her efforts because her husband took all her pay. (Ayukawa 1987, 19)

There is little evidence of the work that South Asian women did outside the home. Compared to Chinese and Japanese immigrant women, they comprised a much smaller group. The discrepancy between the number of wives and the total number of women immigrating is explained by James Chadney: 'It can be safely assumed that the majority of these women were destined to be brides of adult males already in Canada' (1984, 37). The South Asian women did not work outside the home perhaps because, unlike the Chinese, South Asians did not own the kinds of businesses that could employ their women – such as restaurants, market garden, corner grocery stores. South Asian men were primarily employed in the lumber industry, which provided very limited

opportunities for female employment. Employment as domestic workers was regarded as demeaning by South Asians.

Some second-generation Chinese and Japanese women were forced
into the same kind of work their mothers had performed because of poverty and racial discrimination. A Canadian-born Japanese woman recalls
her own introduction to farm work:

Work? On a farm? Peasant work? I? ... I saw the Japanese women in khaki cover-
alls, floppy straw hats tied under the chin with thin towelling, their dirt-stained
fingers showing through the holes purposely cut in the discarded lengths of
winter stockings they used to cover their arms from the sun and mosquitoes. I
saw them on their knees, weeding, or squatted between rows picking straw-
berries, or peas, or reaching up between the shaded dew-lamp rows of rasp-
berries, pole beans. I heard the early morning truck call around for the straw-
berry pickers. (Kitagawa 1985, 279)

From 1923 onwards Chinese women began to enter the industrial
workforce, but their total numbers remained low. They worked primarily in three industries: in the manufacture of food products; in laundries (cleaning and dyeing); and in garment making (Adilman 1984, 69).
Some second-generation Chinese and Japanese women were able to
obtain an education and to train as teachers, secretaries, and nurses, but
they found employment primarily within their own group. This was the
experience of both males and females, but the women's situation was
exacerbated by sexist bias. Among the Nisei, only three women found
work as nurses in institutions operated by the Japanese. In exceptional
cases, a teacher was hired in areas where students were predominantly
from a Japanese background. In the municipality of Maple Ridge, a substitute teacher was 'barred from working when a delegation of irate
white parents and Canadian Legion officials demanded her dismissal.'
Although the school trustees insisted that she was 'a fine Christian girl,'
they gave in to the argument that her appointment might set a precedent for hiring 'a teacher with Buddhist persuasions' (Adachi 1976,
172).

Chinese immigrants had similar experiences. A Canadian-born Chinese woman recalls:

My sister Aylene wanted to become a nurse. She finished high school and
tried again and again to get into nursing school, but they wouldn't take her. My
dad tried all the well-known doctors. No dice. My other sisters wanted to get in
too, but they couldn't. After that they took up stenography. But it was hard to

get into an office also because they said, 'We're doing white people's business. Why would we hire Chinese?' (Yee 1988, 67)

RACE IN FEMINIST THEORY AND PRACTICE

The racist biases of first-wave feminist theory and practices are now widely acknowledged. Mariana Valverde's 'When the Mother of the Race Is Free' documents how feminist thought from 1880 to 1920 incorporated the arguments for eugenics based on 'scientific racism' and the more conventional assumptions of the moral and cultural superiority of white, Christian nations. She notes: 'The fact that purity was equated with whiteness, and hence indirectly with European culture, made it difficult if not impossible for Canada's women of colour to identify with the brand of feminism elaborated by the WCTU (Woman's Christian Temperance Union), and in general by the overwhelmingly Protestant women of first-wave Canadian feminism' (1992, 20).

Feminism of this period had absorbed the racist ideology of the times and reproduced it when advocating women's rights. White feminists thought that, as 'mothers of the race,' they were responsible not only for the propagation of the species but also for the regeneration of the 'race.' Valverde notes that, although they used the word 'race' to mean 'the human race,' their arguments implied that they were thinking primarily of Anglo-Saxons (1992, 5).

Accounts such as those of Valverde leave unexamined the significance of the ideology of 'racial and imperial power' for the everyday experiences and life chances of women from Asia, Africa, and the Caribbean. We do not know exactly how the feminist ideology intersected with the lives of women from Asia, Africa, and the Caribbean to oppress and exploit them. Chinese prostitutes during the late nineteenth century are discussed, and there are some references to destitute Japanese women, but all other women remain mute and invisible in these accounts. The accounts by white women of the 'women's movement' refer to their own experiences, and there is no discussion in these accounts of how white women interacted with women from Asia, Africa, or the Caribbean.[4]

Feminists of this period seldom recognized ethnic differences among immigrant women and articulated the general racist bias of their society. They basked in their roles as the watchdogs of the morality and virtue of the nation, and their struggles for enhanced social and political rights showed class and race biases (McClung [1915] 1972; Strong-Boag 1976; 1986; Cook 1974). Many examples occur in the writings of Nellie McClung, particularly in her novel Painted Fires (1925), which portrays all its characters in a stereotypical manner. The upper-class 'Canadian women' in the novel attempt to do good works by befriending helpless young European immigrant women. The central character is a Finnish immigrant woman who idealizes the 'English.' Upper-class Canadian women are primarily of British origin, and they are portrayed as representing the Canadian norm which others seek to assimilate. The Chinese in *Painted Fires* are restaurant owners and drug dealers. They are portrayed as a threat to the morals of white women, and any association of white women with them is assumed to be only for illegal purposes, a confirmation of the women's disreputable ways.[5]

McClung was patronizing towards women of other races. She argued: 'It seems a fitting thing that women should use their new political power to make motherhood easier, to rob colonization of its fears and dangers, to give the lonely woman on the outposts of civilization the assurance that she is part of a great sisterhood and is not left alone to struggle with conditions which may prove too hard for her!' (quoted in Cook and Mitchinson 1976, 321).

Emily Murphy, the well-known suffragist and first woman magistrate in Edmonton, undertook a study of drug abuse in Canada and published it as *The Black Candle* in 1922. The book reproduced the prevailing racial stereotype of the Chinese as drug dealers supplying the habit of white women. As Brian Anthony and Robert Solomon say in their introduction to a reprint of *The Black Candle*, Murphy created 'a series of women-seducing villains, primarily non-white and non-Christian, who threatened the Anglo-Saxon way of life. Driven to insanity and crime by hopeless addiction, these cunning "dregs of humanity" more than deserved the harshest penalties.' Her ability to 'blend statistics, anecdotes, [and] popular racial bias ... gave her writing wide public appeal' (Murphy [1922] 1973, 3).

Other suffragists also reproduced the class biases of society. One wrote:

Turn to the demoralized sight, the racked and poverty-burdened woman dwelling in a city tenement, with her brood of ill-nurtured, sickly children. All trace of that softness and feminine delicacy, and the reflective deep-souled mother-love of the Madonna obliterated in this poor, hard-used mortal. Teach her hygiene when there is no fresh air to be had, and barely a blink of the sun, not a mouthful of unpolluted water to drink, nor sufficient bread to eat, because taxes are too high, wages too low, and liquor too near her husband's temptation. (Quoted in Cook 1974; xvii)

Popular racial biases against 'Orientals' and 'European immigrants' were manipulated by white feminists to promote their own struggles. Examples of their attitudes appear in their arguments for female suffrage. By 1905 Augusta Stowe-Gullen had 'begun to master anti-immigrant innuendo.' She argued that if naturalized Poles and Italians could vote, 'surely, women could vote as intelligently as these classes' (quoted in Roberts 1979, 23). Some agrarian reformers thought it would be an 'outrage' to give the vote to European immigrants, 'the lowest-browed, most imbruted foreign hobo[s] that choose to visit our shores,' while denying it to 'the highest-minded, most cultured native-born lady of Canada' (quoted in Cook 1974, xvi).

Feminists often contrasted 'untutored' and 'unlettered' European male immigrants with 'Canadian' women, and appealed to fears of the erosion of race and class privilege to win support for women's suffrage. The suffragists argued for extending democratic rights to themselves but insisted that such rights not be extended to immigrants. Without apology, they argued that the female franchise was needed to offset the increased numbers of illiterate immigrants and paupers (Bacchi 1983, 50–5). The platform of the National Council of Women of Canada for the vote included some demands on behalf of working-class women, but the specific needs of women from Asia and the Caribbean were ignored (Cook and Mitchinson, 1976, 324–7).

Flora MacDonald Denison represented a more 'radical side of suffrage and reform.' She had little sympathy for the temperance movement and even less for organized Christianity (Gorham 1979, 47–8). She worked as a dressmaker and journalist and even established a small business. Her biography attests to her interests in the conditions of women in the sewing trades and in the rights of women to obtain divorce, practise birth control, and vote (Gorham 1979, 47–70). Her biography suggests that her work was primarily with working-class women, but mostly those of British descent.

Although many European women – Ukrainian, Jewish, and Finnish women, for example – were stigmatized at the time, they joined the Canadian Socialist League and the Socialist Democratic Party of Canada in the early 1900s. These women were from working-class backgrounds and some, like Helena Gutteridge, even took on leadership positions and connected class oppression with gender. Generally, however, the socialist parties supported a maternal feminist ideology, similar to that of the liberal feminists, which idealized the home, women's place within it, and their nurturing characteristics (Kealey 1984; Sangster 1989). The

Canadian Socialist League emerged from social reform groups, and many women who were active on the left had a history of work with these groups. But Janice Newton disagrees with historians who have interpreted the maternal feminist ideology of socialists as indicative of a middle-class bias. She explains that 'domestic concerns largely shaped women's lives, even the lives of working-class and women who worked for pay' (1992, 120).

The literature does not report any mention of Chinese, Japanese, or South Asian women within these parties (Kealey 1984; Sangster 1989; Newton 1992). However, other than the Co-operative Commonwealth Federation, none of the socialist parties in the west spoke out on behalf of racialized men either until after the 1930s.

Until the 1930s, the labour movement showed ambivalence in supporting women's issues. It sometimes argued for a 'family wage,' which implicitly identified the home as the proper place for women. It supported legislation to protect women as the 'weaker sex,' and its concern with low wages, long hours, and poor working conditions focused on the 'moral' well-being of women (Creese 1992, 373). Although women who worked for pay were integrated into labour politics to this extent, there is no evidence that women from Asia, Africa, and the Caribbean were part of labour politics or members of unions. There were very small numbers of Chinese, Japanese, and South Asian women in Canada at the time; most were in British Columbia and they frequently worked alongside their spouses (e.g., on farms and in restaurants). Although some Chinese and Japanese women worked for pay, there is no documentation to indicate that they worked in unionized situations (Adilman 1984). When racism in the labour movement is discussed, it refers primarily to what male Asian workers confronted (Creese 1988–9).

Feminist ideology and practice were part of a racist culture, and they reproduced that culture. Since white feminists were excluded from all positions of power and authority, what they said and did was of little relevance to the circumstances under which non-white women were admitted into Canada or, once here, to the hardships of their everyday experiences in Canada. Employers were mainly males, and feminist thought and activity were in their incipient stage and had little impact on public policy.

Women from Asia and the Caribbean were victimized by white Canadian culture and by men of their own communities. But there was no ideological or organizational base that could help them identify their oppressions or assert their rights. The intersection of gender, race, and class provided some similarity of experience for these women, but there is little evidence that there was any cross-cultural interaction among women from these groups. Chinese, Japanese, and Indian women seldom encountered white women as equals. White women interacted with women from Asia or the Caribbean either as employers or through mission- or church-related work (Platt 1908; Van Dieren 1984; Mitchinson 1977). Such interactions reinforced the dependent status of the women from Asia and the Caribbean and the superiority of white women.

Racism and classism constructed the reality of women from Asia and Caribbean. The early history of Asians and blacks reveals that their communities were often physically isolated by the racial biases of the larger society. Lack of a common language further isolated them from white communities and from other racial groups. Work, paid and unpaid, absorbed all their energies. Sometimes, as in the case of Japanese women, their paid work with men from their own communities in logging camps, farms, and canneries added to their social and physical isolation from other white communities. Wives of Chinese merchants had some leisure time, but they remained at home absorbed in their domestic routine. This situation was accepted by the women as normal and natural. Neither white women nor women from Asia and the Caribbean contested the divisions or attempted to overcome them.

The struggles of South Asian, Chinese, and Japanese men to enable women from their communities to immigrate reinforced solidarity between men and women within the group. The internment of the Japanese in 1942 illustrates how the shared experience of racism reinforced bonds of community and solidarity between men and women. But external threats to their safety and the need to survive the ordeal of internment often produced a reversal of gender roles within the family. When families were split up, women had to learn how to survive on their own.

Nisei women were politically active. During the internment, they attempted to resist the dispersal and deportation of the Japanese by challenging provincial and federal governmental authorities. After 1945 they were active in the debate, conducted through various Japanese newspapers in Canada, over the future direction of the community (Kitagawa 1985; Adachi 1976; Kogawa 1981; Sunahara 1981). Racism created solidarity between men and women; gender discrimination was a secondary consideration.

The experience of racial discrimination strengthened the women's adherence to the culture of their country of origin. A Nisei woman describes the women of her mother's generation: 'Without nonsamurai village values, female relatives and long-standing neighbours, they were all on their own. Facing ostracism by mainstream white society, their only support came from the Japanese Consulate – the official representative of Japan's national ideology. Unsurprisingly the immigrant women bolstered their confidence by becoming very Japanese' (Ayukawa 1991, 4). Traditional Chinese and Japanese cultures assigned subordinate roles to women and encouraged submission to male authority. White feminists did not provide support to the women from Asia in challenging these roles. Chinese women responded to 'the hostile and aggressively assimilative colonial society' by adopting rigid Confucian ideals which had already become dated in China: 'As the coveted wi[ves] and respected mother[s], these women led carefully ordered lives. Yet, while serving as a haven from the unwelcoming host society, "home" gradually became a cage from which these women rarely emerged. Isolation and loneliness were the price paid for their obligation to husband, children, and community' (Nipp 1983, 88–9).

We do not know whether Asian and black women internalized the negative assumptions that white feminists held about their cultural traditions, but oral history accounts by the second-generation daughters of Chinese and Japanese women express their respect and admiration for their mothers' unending labour of love for their families. Chinese or Japanese women who lost the support of their spouses through death or desertion struggled against all odds to keep their families together in an assimilationist and racist society. Sometimes destitute Chinese women resisted going back to China, fearing that their female children would be sold by their kinsmen: 'Because my father died I had to go to work. My mother couldn't go back to China. Where would she get the money? What were we going to eat if we returned ... water? Even when father wanted to send us all back, mother wouldn't go. She was afraid he would sell the girls ... and we'd be split up. Then she wouldn't know where we were ... I had to baby sit. I worked 15 hours a day' (Nipp 1983, 82).

Chinese prostitutes and destitute Japanese women were most susceptible to the evangelical zeal of the feminists and the missionaries, but even they sometimes preferred the hardships of the larger society to accepting the ministrations of white, Christian women (Van Dieren 1984). The Women's Missionary Society's annual reports described the unwillingness of prostitutes to stay in the Rescue Home for Chinese Girls: 'A Chinese woman sought refuge with us. We made her welcome and tried to induce her to stay, but after three days, she preferred to

return to the dark life which had already claimed six years of her existence ... We had charge of a Chinese woman for nearly three weeks but
she is unimproved in her life, as she is an inveterate gambler and prosti-
tute' (quoted in Van Dieren 1984, 84).

Many white women in Canada became committed to feminism
through their experience in social reform movements like the Woman's
Christian Temperance Union (Mitchinson 1977; Roberts 1977; Cramer
1992, 56). For example, before she became a suffragist and political activist, Nellie McClung was involved in social reform work. She was also
involved in Winnipeg's All Peoples' Mission, which was run by the Rev-
erend J.S. Woodsworth and catered to the needs of new immigrants
(Errington 1988, 51–79; Strong-Boag 1986, 182). The similarities in the
values of mission women, social reformers, and feminists may have
stemmed from the close association among these women. They were
united by the 'social gospel.' Ramsay Cook observes that 'suffragists
were a part of a more general, middle-class reform movement that was
concerned to remove a wide range of injustices and evils that afflicted
the country. The most obvious features of this broad reform movement
were its Protestant ethos (though the Roman Catholic church was certainly not unmoved by social questions), ... [and] its predominantly
Anglo-Saxon nationalism' (1974, xvii–xviii).[6]

Mission work and church activity on behalf of women from other cultures and classes seldom showed a sensitivity to the culture of those
women. Home and foreign mission societies of various denominations
attracted well-off, educated 'Canadian' women. The work of the mission
women on behalf of women from other classes and ethnic groups was
driven by their zeal to convert them and to bring them the benefits of
Christianity. They marked their success by the services they performed
for other women and by the rate of conversion (Mitchinson 1977, 72).
Converted Chinese and Japanese women were perceived as useful in
opening the doors of other families, both in Canada and overseas, to the
ministrations of the missionaries. When Chinese men obstructed the
work of the missionaries for the Rescue Home for Chinese Girls, they
were portrayed by the missionaries as merely desiring to exploit the
women sexually and economically (Platt 1908; Van Dieren 1984; Nipp
1983, 38–66; also Woodsworth [1909] 1972, 142–53). The ethnocentric
values of the missionaries are obvious in the following comment: '[I]t is
certain that if we would preserve the moral and religious standard of
our own people, either the Chinese must be excluded, or they must be
helped and taught and governed. The Chinese bring with them their

own superstitious beliefs and heathen form of worship, their degraded family life, and their own standard of morality, or, to speak correctly, of immorality' (Platt 1908, 115).

The mission women never considered the objects of their activity as social equals, and there was little sympathy based on gender. The work of the Rescue Home for Chinese Girls is a case in point. The Rescue Home was established in 1886–7 in Victoria, B.C. Its initial purpose was to rescue prostitutes, and later its work was expanded to include rescuing Chinese girls who had been brought into Canada to work as domestics but who, missionaries argued, were treated no better than slaves. The rescued women were first provided with shelter and food. Then they were recruited to undertake further mission work among the women and children of Chinatown, or marriages were arranged for them with Christian Chinese men. The mission women derived immense satisfaction from the work of rescuing Chinese women. But their attitude is revealed in the following journal entry: 'No mother ever mourned over a child more than I did over Soy King. We have named her Dorothy, for was she not a gift from God?' (Platt 1908, 114).

Work with immigrants and the poor provided benefits to women who desperately needed support, but it also provided opportunities for mission women, social reformers, and feminists to extend their roles in socially acceptable ways. And it provided an opportunity for talented, educated, ambitious, or aggressive women to exercise power and authority over women from other cultures (Mitchinson 1977; also Brouwer 1991). This power was derived from their position as representatives of a 'superior race and culture.'

First-wave feminist ideology enunciated for the first time the general oppression of women based on gender. But it assumed that the roles, values, and ideals of middle-class, Anglo-Saxon women were universal and that the conditions of the lives of women from different classes and ethnic groups were similar to their own. Although it raised the issue of oppression based on gender for all groups of women, it generalized from the experience of middle-class women and raised social consciousness only about their situation and concerns. In using middle-class, Anglo-Saxon experience and norms to measure the oppression of women, liberal feminist theory ignored the ways in which racism shaped the very different experience and social reality of women from Asia and the Caribbean.

It can be argued that an all-inclusive movement based upon the universal categorization of women was necessary before the oppression and exploitation of specific groups of women could be recognized. There may be an important 'demonstration effect' here: rights claimed successfully by one group of people give rise to claims by others (Abella 1984, 1–18). Women from Asia, Africa, and the Caribbean could more successfully pursue their own interests once oppression based on gender had been commonly acknowledged.

Moreover, the women's movement was more diverse than has been previously thought. Working-class women became conscious of their oppression, women's issues were debated within left-wing organizations, and middle-class women worked with working-class women (Strong-Boag and Fellman 1986; Burnet 1986; Sangster 1989; Creese 1992). But class differences were not addressed by the movement's ideology, which continued to romanticize and glamorize the maternal role of women within the home and family. The ideology enunciated about women's role in society accepted the distinctions between the public and private spheres found in the experience of middle-class women. Their power to define what constituted femininity and proper feminine behaviour tended to silence all other women.

The absence of women from Asia, Africa, and the Caribbean from the first-wave women's movement was an inevitable consequence of a racist culture whose values were absorbed and reiterated by white feminists. The absence of women from China, Japan, and India reflected the physical and material separation of white, middle-class feminists from them. Feminists of this period asserted their moral superiority over women of 'lower classes and lower races.' They advocated rights for themselves by highlighting their distinct value system and their 'womanly' talents. They focused on their own sexual, political, or economic oppression and exploitation but failed to consider the greater problems facing Chinese, Japanese, and Indian immigrant men and women.

The absence of women from Asia, Africa, and the Caribbean from feminist theory and practice of the first wave became politically significant during the second wave which began in the late 1960s. Their absence supported their arguments that racism existed in feminist theory and practice. Consciousness of their differences from white, middle-class feminists marked a stage in the political awareness of women from Asia, Africa, and the Caribbean and lay the basis for solidarity. The growth of political solidarity among women from Asia, Africa, and the Caribbean, through feminist dialogues and state-sponsored activities, is the subject of the following chapters.

3

Race, Class, and Feminist Theory

The integration of feminist ideas into academic disciplines, the policies of state agencies, and the practices and programs of volunteer groups provides some measure of feminist success. Feminist theory has encouraged women to identify, question, and resist oppression by the practices and discourses of dominant groups. But feminist theory is constantly being challenged by new insights from feminist critics and by the intellectual currents of society at large. Debates within the women's movement, and without, require that feminists continually re-evaluate their concepts and reformulate their theories. This process has moved feminism from a narrow focus on combating gender bias to more dynamic programs with broader goals and objectives.

In the 1970s, racism in feminist theories was detected in the apparently universal category of 'woman.' Feminists from Asia, Africa, and the Caribbean, in Canada and elsewhere, argued that mainstream feminism focused on the oppressions of white, middle-class women, although it claimed to address the concerns of all women.[1] That assump-tion represented an exercise of race and class privilege; it oppressed women who did not belong to this group by imposing a norm upon them. In the 1980s, feminists of all persuasions acknowledged the multiple and integrated nature of the oppressions of race, class, gender – as well as of age, sexual orientation, and disability.[2]

Despite the growing consensus among feminists that feminist theory in the 1970s and early 1980s was racially insensitive, there is some question whether feminism has integrated race analysis into its theories or has become antiracist in its practices. White, middle-class feminists assert that problems of racism within the women's movement have been resolved, but women from Asia, Africa, and the Caribbean argue that 'white women just don't get it.' While white feminists acknowledge the integrated nature of race, class, and gender oppression, they seldom incorporate this insight into their theories.[3] Deborah Rhode comments on the difficulty white feminists confront in 'addressing issues that could expose our unconscious racism, homophobia, or class biases.' She explains:

The dilemma is that either talking or not talking about differences these days can get one in trouble. Yet all too often we seek to escape the dilemma by acknowledging without really addressing differences ... In seeking to avoid parochialism, we often compound it; a common strategy is what Marilyn Frye describes as a retreat into autobiography – stringing suitable adjectives before the noun 'woman' (speaking as a middle-aged, middle-class Anglo ...). Or we assume the existence of some illusory 'generic woman' and add qualifying tag lines to every other paragraph such as 'and all this is worse for women of colour.' (1991, 37)

The differences between white feminists and feminists from Asia, Africa, and the Caribbean have created an emotionally charged atmosphere which has led to discouragement on both sides (Bunch 1990, 49–56).

However, the cumulative impact of the debate has been positive and constructive. It has encouraged feminists to reconsider some of their initial rallying cries – for example, 'sisterhood,' 'the personal as political,' 'common oppressions,' 'men as the enemy,' and 'women as victims.' Feminists now see the need to question assumptions encoded in terms such as 'we' and 'woman,' which have tended to refer only to white, middle-class women. They see the need to re-examine the experiences from which their theories are derived and the practices that their theories recommend rather than to claim that their theories are unbiased, neutral, or universally applicable to all women. White feminists in Canada now admit that they speak as white women and that their discussions usually refer to a specific group of the population – English Canadians.

The exposure of racism in feminism has been particularly difficult for white, middle-class feminists even though they espouse principles, ideals, and norms that repudiate the power structures of society. Feminists are critical of individuals and institutions that exercise 'power over' others. They want women to acquire the 'power to' achieve their own goals. Feminists note that as individuals or groups become empowered, they 'experience a growth and development of their sense of autonomy and a trust in their own abilities' (Lips 1991, 6–10). But in concentrating on their own goals, including gaining greater access to society's resources, they have often overlooked the needs of other, less organized groups and have thus rendered them invisible.

White feminists disclaim any interest in exercising 'power over' any group, but it is difficult for them to disentangle themselves from the power structures of race and class that are embedded in society. Women from Asia, Africa, and the Caribbean resent white, middle-class feminists exercising the power to define feminism and to identify the sources of women's oppression.

BIAS IN FEMINIST THEORIES

The presence of racism in feminist theory challenges feminists' assertions of the primacy of gender oppression in male-dominated society and undermines their goals of social transformation. White feminists have sometimes interpreted the problem of racism in feminism as a moral one, whose solution lies in changing personal attitudes and behaviour. But this interpretation does not explain why biases persist. Racism in feminism is difficult to resolve because racial and ethnic stratification is an integral part of institutional structures, and these determine the social, political, and economic realities of Canadian women. The differences in power and privilege among women are obstacles to creating a common understanding of how race, class, and gender oppress women from Asia, Africa, and the Caribbean.

Feminist theoreticians have emphasized the significance of everyday living as an important guide for theory making. Dorothy Smith, a white feminist, has argued that our everyday reality is constructed by the larger social organizations of society. They structure our day-to-day experiences (Smith 1987). To overcome the racist biases of society even at a personal level, white feminists must question the practices that surround them and support their own privilege.

Many practices identified as racist by women from Asia, Africa, and the Caribbean are accepted by white women, along with the rest of society, as natural and normal. This situation makes detecting and eradicating racist practices difficult. Racist biases infect the very language, even the language in the assertions that feminist theory must take into account differences among women, such as 'we need to hear the many voices of women,' and that 'feminist theory must include more of the experiences of women of different races and classes.' In these statements, the assumption is that women from Asia, Africa, and the Caribbean are outsiders and white, middle-class feminists have the power to add the perspective of 'other' women to their discourse. Elizabeth Spelman, a white feminist, has argued that such assertions do nothing to dislodge white women from their privileged position (1988, 162–4). White women determine the conditions under which 'entry' is to be granted and the 'differences' among women will be settled.

Treating racism within feminism as a moral problem has generated feelings of guilt and anxiety. It has also led to accusations that women from Asia, Africa, and the Caribbean are 'laying a guilt trip' on white women, who, after all, were not personally responsible for racism, colonialism, and imperialism, but who were attempting to educate themselves to be antiracist in their practices and to understand how race and class differences affect women's experiences. Ann Russo, a white feminist, says: 'I think that many white feminists may feel genuinely bad about racism, but do not know what to do – our guilt and feelings of hopeless responsibility lead many of us to passivity and/or defensiveness, both of which maintain our position of power' (1991, 308). And Kari Dehli, another white feminist, objects: 'However real our feelings of guilt may be, to shift the discussion of racism in the university or the women's movement to white women's pain in dealing with our feelings, centres white women while marginalizing those who are subjected to racist practices. Focussing on individual feelings of guilt also tends to reduce questions of racism to matters of attitude, while ignoring social relations and practices of racism and how they might be taken up politically' (1991, 51).

Race, class, and gender hierarchies in social institutions determine what is known, how it is known, and who knows it. The emphasis on gender and the subordination of race and class analysis reflect not merely individual biases but institutional structures. The problem lies in systemic racism, for example, in the structures of academic institutions from which feminist discourses usually emerge. The priority given to gender in the discourse of white, middle-class Canadian feminists reflects their position in such institutions. Conversely, the absence of literature that documents the experiences of women from Asia, Africa, and the Caribbean reflects their absence from institutional structures.

Feminist discourse is primarily constructed by academics in Canadian universities. Like most institutions of higher education, Canadian universities are overwhelmingly white, male domains. The percentage of female faculty is low. Visible minorities are even less well represented on campuses than white women are (Backhouse 1990, 38). And female faculty members from Asia, Africa, and the Caribbean are virtually non-existent. Women students from Asia, Africa, and the Caribbean experience alienation and marginalization in the classrooms of white, male professors and even in women's studies programs, where Eurocentric interpretations and analyses of required readings dominate (Carty 1991). A South Asian woman recalls her experience: 'Often I was the only non-white student in these classes. Other students would talk among themselves with ease and were willingly responded to by the professors even when there were disagreements. I looked for reasons for their sense of a shared reality. It was in their ... whiteness ... and their political commonality. They carried on discussion as if I was not there' (Bannerji 1991, 69–70). The lack of faculty and students from visible minorities creates a self-perpetuating cycle. The low number of students translates into few faculty, and the result is the perpetuation of the Eurocentric biases of individuals and institutions. At the present time, there are no data bases that maintain statistics on visible minorities or on visible-minority women, although it is expected that this situation will change.[4]

Frances Henry, a white feminist, notes that few social scientists have shown an interest in research on race relations or inequality created by race, and there is a 'notable lack of advocacy research.' Only four academics – two sociologists and two anthropologists – made submissions to a task force examining the participation of visible minorities in Canadian society which was appointed by the federal government in 1983. Uncovering, documenting, and analysing racism is 'risky business' which would tarnish the image and shatter the myths Canadians have lived with for generations. Such a state of affairs is consistent with the image projected by the Canadian government of a country in which people of different cultures live in harmony, tolerance, and understanding (Henry 1986, 7). Women from Asia, Africa, and the Caribbean are now struggling to tell their own histories, identify their oppressions, and represent themselves. Their exposure of racism in feminist theories and practices is an act of resistance that symbolizes the struggle of women from Asia, Africa, and the Caribbean against racism and sexism.

THE 'GENERIC WOMAN' OF THE 1970S

Feminism was conceived as a project to liberate women from gender discrimination in a male-dominated society and to organize struggles to gain equal rights and opportunities for women.[5] Liberal feminists emphasized the principles of individuality, equality, autonomy, and self-fulfilment for women. They argued that gender defined and structured women's location within institutions (such as the family, labour force, schools). The sexual division of labour restricted women to dependent roles as wives and mothers within the 'private sphere.' Gender ideology ensured the participation of women in their own subordination and maintained the status quo of female dependence and male dominance.[6]

During the 1970s, the feminist discourses of white, middle-class women did not refer to the experiences of women from Asia, Africa, and the Caribbean. An analysis of the subject index of the *Canadian Newsletter of Research on Women* (March 1978), which lists all the 'recent research reports and publications, Canadian theses and major articles' from 1971 to 1977, revealed that publications primarily concerned white, middle-class, English-speaking, Canadian women. Of the 2,274 entries listed in the subject index, only 2 per cent focused on women who were not English Canadians. Eight of these entries focused on immigrant women, one on minority groups, nine on native people, and twenty-seven on French Canadians (Siu 1979, 6). Only one per cent of the articles addressed the 'women's movement' (defined as 'the collective actions of women which aim to effect changes in the present status of women'); the rest analysed occupations, family, and sex-roles (Siu 1979, 1–7).

According to this analysis, women's movement studies focused on 'middle-class movements, especially on the woman suffrage movements, with peripheral interest in the struggles of working class or farm women.' A few studies referred specifically to 'working-class women's struggles (Kidd 1974; Klein and Robert 1974; Revolutionary Marxist Group 1975; and Roberts 1976) but farm (rural) women were ignored.' The studies concentrated on the struggle of English Canadians and ignored the struggles of other ethnic groups. Of the fifty-four studies on the women's movement, only one 'dealt explicitly with the struggles of Indian and black women (Teather 1976, 338–41) and only a few with French-Canadian women' (Siu 1979, 4).

The subject of research conducted in the 1970s was supposed to be the 'generic woman,' but most of it described the experience of white, middle-class women, which was presented as the female norm.[7] In her article 'Women as Personal Dependents: A Critique of Theories of the Stratification of the Sexes and an Alternative Approach,' Margrit Eichler disputed the characterization of women as a minority or a caste.[8] In contrasting blacks and women as minorities, Eichler did not examine the particular situation of black women. She wrote as if all blacks were men and all women were white. All others were absent. She concluded that women were potentially occupants of two statuses: 'an independent one, in which they are ranked on the same basis as men, with an additional factor, femaleness, included and a derived one, in which they are ranked on the basis of the male they are attached to. On the basis of this double status ... women must be differentiated into those who are economically independent and those who are not' (1973, 52). When she discussed women as a class, she did not bring race into her analysis of dominant-subordinate relationships.

Feminist writings in the 1970s attempted to use Marxist concepts to analyse the paid and unpaid domestic work of women. But they perceived women as a unitary, undifferentiated category and attached significance only to class. They applied the concept of 'production relations' to women's work within the home and extended it to the daily and generational reproduction of labour power. Few of the studies included an analysis of race or the ways in which it intersected with women's paid and unpaid work (Guttel 1974; Fox, 1980; Armstrong and Armstrong 1977). In their analysis of women's work, Pat Armstrong and Hugh Armstrong used the broad terms 'women' and 'men' without making any distinctions on the basis of race: 'Women and men do different work, frequently in different places. These separate and segmented experiences of women and men help to create different visions of life, different ideas about themselves, different consciousness. They do not arrive at their first jobs unconscious, but they do further develop their consciousness on the job' (1977, 202). There is no discussion of how race further segmented the workforce or how racial identity intersected with gender to create a specific kind of consciousness.[9] When women's domestic work was discussed, the paid domestic work of women from Asia, Africa, or the Caribbean was not examined.[10]

When discussing specific issues, white feminists concentrated on gender and excluded race and class from their analyses. For example, Lorenne Clark and Debra Lewis, in *Rape: The Price of Coercive Sexuality*, asserted that their perspective was feminist and that they 'felt that all women, regardless of background, education, or work-orientation, would be familiar with at least some recent feminist writing on rape, and would therefore be able to approach the results of the study from a common framework' (1977, 16).

The research sample of Clark and Lewis was derived from the Metropolitan Toronto Police Department records of rape cases reported in 1970. They were given access to the general occurrence reports, which are 'standard forms filled out by the police officers for each reported offence' (1977, 31–2). These reports gave the age, sex, nationality, occupation, and marital status of the victim, but for the offender the reports specified age, sex, *colour*, height, weight, and so on (199). The authors reproduced this bias in their research instrument. They asked for the victim's national origin (Canadian, American, British, Greek, Italian, Portuguese, Chinese, West Indian), but they asked for the offender's age, sex, *colour*, occupation, and *place of birth* (201–2). The research treated women as a single category and disregarded racial differences among them. The authors found that 'the rape victim's background and character strongly influenced the way in which the report was classified by the police.' It was 'very clear from [the] data that the primary determinants of police classification are variables which describe the victim, not the attacker' (76).

The authors did not investigate the extent to which the racial identity of the victim affected how the police responded to the complaint, and they did not.even analyse the nationality of the victims. They sidestepped the issue by simply asserting that country of origin was not a distinguishing feature and that three-quarters of the rape victims were 'English-speaking and born in Canada' (78). In contrast, they produced two tables (12 and 13) that analysed racial origin and place of birth for the offenders (97).[11]

Feminists during the 1970s vigorously pursued the thesis that sex-role socialization (later referred to as 'gender role') was a major contributor to women's subordination and inequality. They noted that the socialization of women encouraged them to voluntarily adopt traditional gender roles and 'feminine' characteristics, despite the societal evaluation of them as less valuable than those of males. Feminists reiterated the arguments made much earlier by Mary Wollstonecraft (1792) and John Stuart Mill (1869), who had described the role of gender socialization in maintaining the subordinate position of women. Feminist literature on socialization and feminist political struggles revealed how institutions such as the family, schools, and mass media socialized women to adopt gender roles that were implicitly inferior, less rewarding, and less powerful than those available to men. They demonstrated the biases in school texts that associated femininity with passivity and dependence and described feminine roles as nurturing and supportive. Mass media, they argued, denigrated women and portrayed them as 'sex objects,' and exploited them to serve the needs of capitalism (Wilson 1982; McDaniel 1988; Pyke 1976).

The theories of gender-role socialization seldom distinguished between the experiences of working-class women and those of middle-class women, or between the experiences of women of northern or western European descent and those women of southern or eastern European descent. In reading Marlene Mackie's *Exploring Gender Relations: A Canadian Perspective*, for example, one cannot help but note that her discussion of women refers only to white, middle-class women of British descent. Mackie does not completely ignore the differences of class and ethnicity, but the differences of class and ethnicity are considered as tangential variables, although different classes and cultures may socialize their children to adopt different values. She writes: 'No one has even begun to untangle the ways in which gender socialization is influenced by the interacting effects of ethnicity, social class and region. Unfortunately, too, systematic information is sparse concerning the nuances of gender socialization in nearly forty different ethnic groups' (1983, 143). Mackie's discussion of gender socialization reflects the stratification of society: anglophone, white, middle-class experience is the norm and the rest is 'other.' There is no discussion of race or of how that may influence socialization.

Gender roles are learned in a social context that is stratified along lines of class, race, and ethnicity. Children learn not only to be female or male but also to be the kind of male or female appropriate to their race and class. Analyses that focus on gender in socialization theories, on female stereotypes, or on images of femininity treat gender in isolation from race and class. No reason is given to explain why gender is more significant than ethnicity, race, or class in developing an individual's sense of self or social identity.

Joyce Ladner has demonstrated that many theoretical categories derived from the experience of white females are not applicable to the lives of young black girls. The lives of black women are conditioned by 'poverty, discrimination, and institutional subordination' (1987). Their values and expectations are markedly different from those of their white counterparts, and are imbued with a consciousness of race. Black feminists note that black mothers consciously socialize their children to racial hierarchies in addition to creating an awareness of 'male dominance' and 'gender role expectations.' Black mothers inculcate a sense of race consciousness in their children, hoping thereby to prepare them for a society in which race hierarchies exist. Patricia Collins notes:

Black mothers of daughters face a troubling dilemma. On the one hand, to ensure their daughters' physical survival, mothers must teach them to fit into systems of oppression ... Black daughters learn to expect to work, to strive for an education so they can support themselves, and to anticipate carrying heavy responsibilities in their families and communities because these [values] are essential to their own survival and those for whom they will eventually be responsible. [On the other hand] mothers also know that if their daughters uncritically accept the limited opportunities offered black women, they become willing participants in their own subordination. (1990, 123)

White families may not consciously teach their children about the privilege that is attached to their race but, as Elizabeth Spelman notes, that is the message they convey:

My mother was white, and a Christian, but she didn't tell me not to play with Black children or with Jewish children ... However, that doesn't mean my mother's mothering was not informed by awareness of her family as white and other families as Black, or her family as Christian (nay, Episcopalian) and others Jewish. My brothers and sisters and I may have learned different lessons about the difference between being white and being Black ... but we surely did learn such lessons and they were inextricably tied to what we learned about being girls and boys. (1988, 100)

The mass media were criticized by feminists for their portrayals of femininity. A discussion paper prepared in 1978 for the Advisory Council on the Status of Women reviewed 'Canadian advertising with respect to the portrayal of men and women.' It reported that women were portrayed in limited and stereotypical roles associated with the home and family and were treated as 'sexual objects' (Courtney and Whipple 1978, 45). Women in this study were considered as a single category. It did not question the ethnicity, race, or class of the women who were portrayed in the advertising. The report noted briefly that 'the absence of older and minority group women from advertising makes them an invisible part of our society' (89), but there was no discussion of the significance of this absence. Similarly, the report did not discuss differences among women based on class. It predicted that, as more women joined the labour force, advertising would change its imagery, but it ignored the experience of the significant percentage of 'immigrant women' who have always had to work to support themselves and their families.

Feminists from Asia, Africa, and the Caribbean have noted that media images of dependent, helpless, frail 'ideal women' do not portray the reality of black women's lives in Canada or of white, working-class women (Brand 1984, 87–92). Feminists from Asia, Africa, and the Caribbean noted that in addition to the gender hierarchy, there were also racial hierarchies in the media's portrayal of women. Black women were portrayed in the most subservient and degrading roles (Carty 1991, 21). When Asian women are portrayed, a different set of negative stereotypes is associated with them; they are depicted as traditional and passive women oppressed by their culture (Agnew 1993a).

But if gender analysis excluded considerations of race, analysis of the representation of minorities in the media excluded gender. 'Visible Minorities in Mass Media Advertising,' a report prepared for the executive of the Canadian Consultative Council on Multiculturalism, presented its findings in a gender-neutral manner. It noted the absence of visible minorities from advertising (except for foreign airlines). Blacks and Asians appeared in advertising for non-profit charitable organizations and were 'invariably portrayed in the role of hungry, needy people receiving hand-outs from whites' (Owaisi and Bangash 1978, 21). Reports that documented racism in Ontario during the 1970s referred to the negative portrayals of racial groups in the media and their role in fostering racism, but the reports dealt primarily with the experience of males (Pitman 1977; Ubale, 1977).

The lack of gender distinction in race analysis and the lack of racial distinction in gender analysis point to the marginality of women from Asia, Africa, and the Caribbean. Black feminists argue that they share certain commonalities with black men and certain others with white women but that they are still considered as 'outsiders.' The status of being 'outsiders' in discussions of race and gender forms the basis of a different epistemology and standpoint. Patricia Collins, a black feminist, argues that 'multiple realities among Black women yield a "multiple consciousness in Black women's politics,"' and an 'oppositional consciousness' (1989, 757).

INCLUDING RACE IN FEMINIST THEORY

In the 1970s feminist theory was criticized for ignoring racism and treating gender as a universal and ahistorical category that encompassed the experiences of all women. Feminist slogans of the 1970s that identified all men as 'the enemy' and all women as suffering 'common oppressions' were initially adopted by women from Asia, Africa, and the Caribbean. But after the initial enthusiasm for articulating the common experiences of gender, some feminists began to critically examine these slogans and their assumption that gender represents the primary source of women's oppression. This re-examination spawned a vigorous and far-ranging critique of feminist theories. Women from Asia, Africa, and the Caribbean used historical data to demonstrate that class and race were as powerful as gender in oppressing and exploiting women (Rollins 1985; Glenn 1986; Carby 1986; Parmar 1986).

In the United States the concept of gender as the universal oppressor of all women was attacked by Angela Davis in *Women, Race, and Class* (1983). Through careful documentation of black slavery, she demonstrated that, contrary to the white feminist view of the family's role in oppressing women, for the female slave the family was meaningful and emotionally supportive. Davis questioned the commitment of white women to black emancipation and portrayed them as racists. The role of the family in oppressing women was probably the concept first identified by feminists from Asia, Africa, and the Caribbean as one that excluded their experiences. White feminists had identified the patriarchal family as the locus of women's subordination and inequality, but women from Asia, Africa, and the Caribbean argued that the family also served as an emotional buffer in a race-biased society and created solidarity between men and women. This contradiction was initially ignored by white, middle-class feminists, who criticized the family on behalf of all women, but eventually white feminists admitted that they had shown ethnocentric bias in describing the experiences of their own class and race as the norm while disregarding the experiences of other women (hooks 1984; Collins 1990; Carby 1986; Barrett and McIntosh 1985; Kline 1989b; Spelman 1988).

In Britain racism in feminism was exposed by Jenny Bourne in *Towards an Anti-racist Feminism* (1984). There were no similar publications in Canada, but Canadian feminists responded to the critiques published elsewhere. These works stimulated a much broader discussion of discrimination and bias within feminist theories and practices. But at the same time they created a crisis of conscience within the feminist community that threatened to undermine feminist positions on male bias, the social construction of women, and the treatment of women as 'objects' in male discourse. Feminists from Asia, Africa, and the Caribbean revealed biases in feminist theories and practices and attacked the assumption of privilege by white feminists in the community of women (hooks 1988; Lorde 1984).

In 1985 Michele Barrett and Mary McIntosh were among the first few

feminists who identified biases in socialist-feminist analysis, which supplemented gender theory with class analysis. Their own previous analyses of forms of household organizations and wage labour, they said, had
'spoken from an unacknowledged but ethnically specific position; its
apparently universal applicability has been specious' (1985, 25). They
further acknowledged that race and ethnicity had effects on working-
class women's wages and their relations within the family that were
quite different from those on white, middle-class women's. Patriarchy,
they admitted, could not explain how white women exercise power,
based on race, over black men.

Barrett and McIntosh tried integrating race, class, and gender within a
Marxist framework, but they could not resolve these problems and concluded by asking:

[S]hould we regard race as easier to incorporate into a classic Marxist analysis
than feminism proved to be? Or should we concentrate on the relations between
race and gender and ignore for the moment the consequences of this for a class
analysis? Or should we back down from these academic debates and adopt a
more pragmatic approach by identifying areas of common and progressive
struggle? Can we argue that racism, like women's oppression, has independent
origins but is now irretrievably embedded in capitalist social relations? (41)

Kum Kum Bhavnani, a South Asian feminist, complained that, by
turning to questions of theory, Barrett and McIntosh were avoiding the
real issue – the differences of power relations between white and black
women and between different classes of white women. She argued that
the real test for the authenticity of white women's commitment to antiracism was whether their analysis generated 'an adequate political practice for women against the complexities of their oppression' (Bhavnani
and Coulson 1986, 85).

Barrett and McIntosh's article generated several other responses that
pointed out additional problems – for example, Barrett and McIntosh
tended to diminish the importance of racism by describing their biases
as ethnocentric rather than racist. Caroline Ramazanoglu, a white feminist, noted: 'The recognition of ethnocentrism in our work does not in
itself render black women's experiences visible. It is only when we try to
take black women's experiences into account that the extremely problematic relationship between general *ideas* of oppression and women's
experiences of oppression becomes [understandable]' (1986, 84).

Some feminists have responded to the charge of racism in mainstream feminism by acknowledging that women are oppressed by race, class, and gender. Women from Asia, Africa, and the Caribbean experience one kind of oppression because of their gender (shared with white women), another because of their race (shared with men from Asia, Africa, and the Caribbean), and a third because of their class (shared with working-class women and men) (Thornhill 1989, 27). But this formulation may suggest that race, class, and gender oppressions are experienced in discrete segments and can be isolated from one another. Women from Asia, Africa, and the Caribbean experience the three oppressions together (Smith 1989, 47; Romany 1991; Amos and Parmar 1984). Emily Woo Yamasaki observes: 'I cannot be an Asian American on Monday, a woman on Tuesday, a lesbian on Wednesday, a worker/ student on Thursday, and a political radical on Friday. I am all these things everyday. We are discriminated against as workers on the economic plane, as racial minorities on the economic and social planes, and as women on all three planes – economic, social, and domestic/family' (quoted in Wong 1991, 293).

Black feminists emphasize the interlocking nature of oppression:

This viewpoint shifts the entire focus of investigation from one aimed at explicating elements of race or gender or class oppression to one whose goal is to determine what the links are among these systems. The first approach typically prioritizes one form of oppression as being primary, then handles remaining types of oppression as variables within what is seen as the most important system. For example, the efforts to insert race and gender into Marxist theory exemplify this effort. In contrast, the more holistic approach implied in Black feminist thought treats the interactions among multiple systems as objects of study. (Collins 1991, 41–2)

Biases emerge in attempts to reformulate Marxist categories to incorporate the experience of race and gender discrimination. An example of this approach is Nancy Hartsock's 'The Feminist Standpoint: Developing the Ground for a Specifically Feminist Historical Materialism.' Hartsock says that women's experience of the 'sexual division of labour' constitutes them as a social group and forms the basis of a feminist standpoint common to all women. Hartsock proposes that feminists lay aside the differences among women across race and class boundaries and instead search for 'central commonalities' (1987, 163–4). She treats gender as a separate category that can be isolated from the experience of race and class, and she does not consider the differences of power between women. Hartsock emphasizes the importance of the individual's material experience; she does not consider the role of white women in subordinating and exploiting women from different classes and races. White, middle-class feminists may theoretically recognize the interconnections of race, class, and gender, but their different location in society makes them less conscious of the privilege of race and thus leads them to emphasize gender. In privileging gender as the basis of a feminist standpoint, Hartsock reproduces familiar biases of the 1970s, which are encoded in concepts of 'sisterhood' and 'women as victims.'

Theoretical proposals by a variety of white feminists about the integrated nature of gender, race, and class analysis have not always displaced the centrality of gender in feminist analysis. Identifying the different sources of women's oppression has not dislodged the hierarchy of race within feminism; it reappears in more subtle and indirect ways. Postmodern literary interpretations of the significance of experience, the provisional nature of 'identity,' the subjectivity of all discourses, and the meanings that can be assigned to the word 'difference' have broadened the categories of oppression. Deconstruction exposes the biases hidden in many categories and definitions, and this has had the effect of depoliticizing the issue of race within feminism (Nicholson 1990; Alcoff 1988; Bulkin, Pratt, and Smith 1985). In addition, these interpretations raise a problem: if discourses reflect political and social structures of gender, race, and class, and these enclose women's identities in specific ways, how can women exercise agency?

Gender, race, and class structure the experience of individuals, and these experiences construct the individual's sense of self and identity. A basic premise of feminist ideology is to use experience as a guide to theory and politics. In the 1970s, consciousness-raising groups (where women recounted their individual experiences) were used as a strategic tool for politicizing and mobilizing women. Feminist theories evolved from the insights gained by analysing the everyday lives of women – their experiences of gender and how these articulate with social organizations of society. But different experiences generate different identities, and these different identities can become barriers that prevent one group of women from understanding and participating in the politics of another group. A difficult question for feminists is how to design a political strategy that is cognizant of these different identities but at the same time is able to generate solidarity around particular issues.

Identities can change. Race, class, and gender are not eternal essences or biological constants; they are socially constructed. The perception of who one is and of one's location vis-à-vis other social groups can change in different contexts. Postmodern feminists view the subject as provisional, located in specific historical situations, and constantly changing. Differences among women are not fixed. A woman's identity as Chinese is different in China, Hong Kong, Malaysia, and Canada. In Canada she becomes Chinese in relation to white, Anglo-Saxon women, that is, on the basis of difference. Difference then becomes a way of establishing 'otherness' and does not dislodge the norm (Minh-ha 1989; Barrett 1987; Parmar 1990). A white woman may experience some race privilege in relation to a Chinese woman, but she may be disadvantaged in relation to another white woman of a different class. The fragmented and provisional nature of subjects highlights the problems of agency, of initiating, mobilizing, and sustaining political struggles over a period of time.

The debate initiated by the discussion of racism in feminism has led to a recognition of different kinds of oppressions: age, sexual orientation, ethnicity, and culture, among others. But this recognition has begun to diffuse the issues of race, power and privilege. bell hooks observes that 'the new cool words of feminism are "hegemony" and "pluralism." Race is out' (1989). Some feminists despair over the fragmentation of the feminist movement through an overemphasis on 'identity politics.' Many feminists are now concerned that the personal will take precedence over the political and undermine the political goals of the movement. Kathryn Harris and Pratibha Parmar, among others, have noted that a consciousness of identity has the advantage of revealing the important ways in which women's experiences differ. But emphasizing the different experiences of women may fragment the movement (Harris 1989; Parmar 1989).

Recognition of the gender and racial identities of the individual does not by itself generate a political consciousness or a common politics among women. June Jordan says that 'much organizational grief could be avoided if people understood that partnership in misery does not necessarily provide for partnership for change: when we get the monsters off our backs all of us may want to run in very different directions' (quoted in Parmar 1989, 62). But Chandra Mohanty notes that a common political commitment to oppose different kinds of domination can generate solidarity among women with diverse identities (1991, 4). Socialist feminists envisage their struggles as taking place within the community and around specific issues. This view enables different groups to come together to oppose and resist domination but does not tie them together on a broad range of issues. The boundaries of these groups and communities are fluid and change over a period of time 'since the operation of power is always fluid and changing' (Mohanty 1991, 4).

A political strategy of coalitions between different feminist organizations is widely supported among white women and women from Asia, Africa, and the Caribbean (Albrecht and Brewer 1990). The recognition of the diversity of feminist organizations, their issues, and political strategies generates support for feminism as a political movement for social change. But it also raises questions about structures of power and relations of domination and subordination within feminism.

The concerns of white feminists continue to dominate feminist theories and practices. Despite discussions of the influence of class, ethnicity, or race, feminist theories still emphasize gender – see, for example, Nancy Chodorow's analysis of motherhood as a common oppressor of all women or Carol Gilligan's distinction between the moral development experiences of males and females (Chodorow 1978; Spelman 1988; Gilligan 1982; Hartsock 1987). Barbara Christian, a black feminist, finds that white, middle-class feminist theorists have made only a half-hearted effort to take into account the different experience of women of other races and classes: 'Often as a way of clearing themselves they do acknowledge that women of colour, for example, do exist, then go on to do what they were going to do anyway, which is to invent a theory that has little relevance for us' (1987, 59–60).

Black women in the United States are now engaged in producing a black feminist theory which attempts to place women's multiple oppressions at the centre of its inquiry (Smith 1989; Christian 1989). White feminists still only rarely challenge the central categories of gender analysis of the unequal power of white women and women from Asia, Africa, and the Caribbean (Kline 1989, 121; Rhode 1991; Romany 1991; Childers and hooks 1990; Open Letters to Catharine MacKinnon 1991; Thornhill 1989; Wong 1991; Russo 1991). Their discourse embodies, even if unconsciously and unintentionally, the race and class biases of the larger society.

In the 1980s a consensus developed that recognized the race and class bias of white feminist theories and practices. But the process of 'inclusion' has further exposed schisms between feminists. The differences in power between women, which are supported and embedded in institutional structures, make it difficult for feminists to come together in support of common theories or practices. The feminist concept of experience as a guide to theory has enabled many groups of women to identify the forms of oppression they suffer. White feminists and feminists from Asia, Africa, and the Caribbean have taken up the challenge to find some 'unity in diversity' in feminist theories and practices. Feminist theory supports local struggles which call upon a network of other feminist organizations for support. But disputes occur and they reflect the power relations among women in these organizations. Challenging one oppression makes women conscious of other oppressions, but the interconnected nature of the oppressions makes them difficult to remove. In the next chapter I examine the difficulties that feminist practice has encountered in staking out a common ground for struggle among women. It shows, within a specific context, how power relations affect feminist struggles.

4

Race, Class, and Feminist Practice

The absence of women from Asia, Africa, and the Caribbean from feminist activity in Canada is the result of the race biases of white feminists. But there has been no detailed account of how race-biased feminist theory articulates with exclusionary feminist practice. The values and norms embedded in the organizational structures and political processes of feminist struggles alienate and exclude some women. But feminist theory asserts that women's organizations can be brought together in coalition politics to represent the interests of all women equally.[1] Such an egalitarian view of social relations presumes that within a feminist context the biases, values, and hierarchies of the larger society do not operate or can be erased.

The exclusion of women from Asia, Africa, and the Caribbean from feminist practice has also been attributed to the differences in priorities of different groups of women. In the 1970s the emphasis on issues of sexuality, reproduction, and abortion did not motivate women from Asia, Africa, and the Caribbean to join white, middle-class women in their struggles. As new immigrants, these women were far more concerned with racism in immigration policy and their lack of access to language-training programs (Agnew 1993b). A number of other issues, such as housing, employment, education, and social services, which cut across lines of race and class, had the potential of bringing women together. But there is little evidence that women from Asia, Africa, and the Caribbean participated in feminist struggles during the 1970s. For example, Nancy Adamson, Linda Briskin, and Margaret McPhail write:

In 1973 a group of Spanish-speaking women in Toronto established the Centre for Spanish Speaking Peoples (CSSP). At the time these women and the CSSP were not seen as a part of the women's movement either by themselves or by feminists ... [W]omen's issues were still narrowly defined in a way that reflected the racial (white) and class (middle) assumptions of its founders. Individual feminists were supportive of such organizing efforts, but the women's movement as a whole did not regard such organizations as an integral part of its struggle ... Although more research needs to be done, it seems that the women of colour actively involved in feminist organizations were few. The reasons are complex: the origins of the women's movement, the definition of 'women's issues,' and racism. (1988, 60–1)

Common issues were not sufficient to bring white, middle-class women and working-class women and women from Asia, Africa, and the Caribbean together in feminist struggles.

The difficulty of incorporating the diversity of women's experiences and identities and yet retaining some focus on gender has created friction among feminists. Catharine MacKinnon argues that women's practice is based on the 'notion of experience 'as a woman' and ... discrimination "based on sex"' (1991, 14). But this was strongly disputed by women of colour:

Writings by women of colour and Third World women acknowledge the existence of gender oppression, but they also maintain that gender oppression never occurs in a racially-neutral or culturally independent context ... Women's experiences which are not shared with white women have been the most difficult to admit into feminist discourse, usually because white feminists classify them as race-based rather than gender-based. We disagree with your notion of an empirical reality which would pervade all experiences 'as a woman' in Third World and in white cultures ... [E]xamples of gender oppression often neglected by white feminists are: the industrial, domestic and supportive services women of colour provide for white women and men in the contexts of colonialism imperialism, and slavery; the exploitation of women of colour which is gender specific but attributed to race; and the subordination of women as defined by Third World cultures, which differs from patriarchy in white culture. (Open Letters to Catharine MacKinnon 1991, 178–9)

A feminist practice involving women of different classes and races needs to identify its goals and objectives in terms that appeal to gender yet distinguish between the different forms of oppression of women.[2] In the 1980s feminists tried to organize struggles at local levels and around specific issues. Alliances and coalitions among a wide spectrum of organizations in support of each other's struggles would empower a large number of women. Not surprisingly, the process of 'inclusion' has been difficult.[3] The diversity and range of feminist organizations create tension between feminists representing different organizations. Their coming together within umbrella organizations creates demands for representation and participation which challenge existing hierarchies and practices. The diversity of membership and issues makes it difficult for umbrella organizations to devise a strategy or political agenda that can satisfy all. Diversity is sometimes viewed as posing a threat to the survival of large umbrella organizations (Vickers 1988).

Conceptualizing the problem as one of integration or inclusion does not focus attention on the social and political contexts in which feminist theories and struggles are conceived and enacted. Race biases of the larger society are reflected in feminist practices – for example, in organizational structures, political processes, priority of issues, leadership, and unequal distribution of power. Consensual politics are difficult to achieve given the larger context, which distinguishes between women on the basis of race, country of origin, and class. The social context in which feminist practices are embedded creates barriers that exclude some women from them. This chapter explores the marginalization of women from Asia, Africa, and the Caribbean in feminist practice by examining the consciousness-raising activities of the 1970s and coalition politics of the 1980s.

RACISM IN ONTARIO, 1970s–1980s

The 1970s was a period marked by overt and explicit racism in Ontario. Race bias was particularly evident in Toronto, where a large proportion of immigrants had settled. From 1961 to 1970 approximately 20 per cent of the new immigrants to Canada came from Asia, Africa, South and Latin America, and the Caribbean, compared to less than 2 per cent in the years between 1951 and 1960 (Samuel 1990, 384). The well-educated, professional, and middle-class newcomers were different from immigrants who arrived before the Second World War, but the racial and cultural differences between the established Canadian population and immigrants from Third World countries were frequently identified by government agencies and the mass media as a cause for social tension and conflict.[4] In the mid-1970s this tension found expression in overt and explicit incidents of racism. Among the new immigrants, South Asians were the prime targets of verbal and physical violence (Pitman 1977, 33).

Pressured by media attention that focused on a few violent acts of racism, government agencies responded by appointing a task force and commissioning reports. In 1977 the government of Ontario appointed a task force chaired by Walter Pitman to investigate racism in Ontario. Wilson Head and Bhausaheb Ubale were commissioned to prepare reports for the Ontario Human Rights Commission on the experiences of blacks and South Asian immigrants, respectively; in addition, Frances Henry began to investigate the attitudes of white Torontonians towards blacks and South Asians (Head 1975; Ubale 1977; Henry 1978).

Henry's study documented that approximately 16 per cent of the population in Toronto tended to be very racist and 35 per cent, somewhat racist; 18 per cent of the population had very liberal views about race and 30 per cent were somewhat liberal. Individuals least likely to be racists were those with high socioeconomic status, particularly those under the age of thirty-nine, employed, and with university education (1–4). Commenting on the widespread nature of racism, Walter Pitman noted: 'there may be more than a very small number of citizens prepared to act out their aggressions by beating up a member of a visible minority on a subway, or whose violence at that level would be tolerated by those who tend to be racist. However, ethnic jokes, harassment, name-calling take place within a context and it is clear that in Toronto there is a body of racist opinion and a broad spectrum of racist attitudes which form the background to these actions, encourage their initiation and give them support' (1977, 28). The reports reveal extensive race biases in employment, housing, education, mass media, and the police. They emphasize attitude and behaviour but also include some discussion of systemic racism, particularly in the police force and in immigration policies. None of the reports refers specifically to the experience of women.

Racism in its more overt and violent forms abated after the mid-1970s, but the problem did not disappear. In 1983 the federal government appointed a task force, called 'Participation of Visible Minorities in Canadian Society,' which sought to recommend models of race relations 'pertaining explicitly to ameliorating relation within Canada between visible minorities and other Canadians.' The task force received 300 briefs, heard from 130 groups of witnesses, and received hundreds of letters. Its report, *Equality Now* (1984), documented racism in employment, public policy, law, media, and education. The report noted that racist attitudes continued to provide 'differential advantages and benefits to people of different races.' In comparison with earlier reports, it documented the prevalence of systemic racism in greater detail and argued that solutions for 'institutional racism' were more significant than those pertaining to 'individual racism' and that programs were needed to create more awareness of racism within the public (Canada, House of Commons, 1984, 6).

Equality Now does not ignore issues of gender but integrates the experiences of 'visible minority women' in its analysis. It notes that '[f]requently, visible minority women are isolated in their homes by the restraints of culture. Because of language and skill deficiencies and discrimination, they may find themselves in exploitative work situation ... Visible minority women have not been actively encouraged to participate in the planning of community services, nor are they participating in major women's organizations' (19). It recommends that 'governments should continue to fund community efforts which assist visible minority and immigrant women to become self-sufficient participants in the economic and social life of the community' (20).

Race imposes a common identity upon women, an identity which imprisons them and whose boundaries are determined by the dominant group (Minh-ha 1989). A black feminist notes: 'I know that my feelings of exaggerated visibility and invisibility are the product of my not being part of the larger cultural picture. I know too that the larger cultural picture is an illusion, albeit a powerful one, concocted from a perceptual consensus to which I am not a party; and that ... these perceptions operate as dictators of truth' (Williams 1991, 56).

Testimonials and oral histories of women from Asia, Africa, and the Caribbean in Ontario in the 1980s testify to the prevalence of racism and its impact on their lives.[5] May Yee, a Chinese-born Canadian woman who conducted extensive interviews for *Voices of Chinese Canadian Women*, notes the alienation experienced by Chinese women as well as their struggle to overcome such feelings:

But how do we individually cope with the pain of knowing ourselves to be 'different'? As we are forever faced with our difference in our contact with the outside world – mouths that ask 'Where do you come from?,' while eyes say 'You don't belong here.' So in certain terms we are forced to 'get used to' this alienation ... [We are] forced to rationalize and accept. Many of the women ... have coped with racism by acting ... [S]ome of us are finally fighting back, with political action, community organizing, expressing our cultural identity, sharing our experiences with each other and the community at large. (1987, 181)

A woman from the Caribbean describes the feelings of vulnerability created by the temporary work permits provided by the Department of Immigration. Employers know that the work permit places restrictions on where a woman can work and how long she can be unemployed, and therefore they may use it to exploit the domestic worker.

She is telling me the other day when I ask her if I could leave early, stop working at five o'clock, that Immigration this and that, always bringing up Immigration when I ask to get off a little early. So I turned to her and I say, 'Immigration say I must work from ten until six and I am here every morning from eight' ... She turned to me and said to me, 'Why don't you go in a factory and work?' She knows I can't do that – she know we can only do domestic work while we are on the work permit ... So she take those things and hold against me, so I keep quiet about the hours I'm suppose to work. (Silvera 1983, 108)

A counsellor at an immigrant women's centre describes how she bridges the gulf between the expectations of 'immigrant women' based on their qualifications and experience in their country of origin and the expectations of some employers based on their ideas of 'proper' immigrant women's work:

I ask them what are their expectations, what do they want to do. They say, I was a secretary, I was a manager, an administrator, a teacher. Then instead of explaining to them what the expectations of the employers are, we just show them the job order that describes them all. Then they go through this, because they speak good English, they understand, they can read and then they say yes, but it needs experience, what can I do for that? Then they start thinking realistically ... You cannot get the experience in the same field but then what to do? ... If you want to survive, if you are very desperate, then you have a short-term goal, and the person ends up taking a menial job. (Interview, 14 July 1989)

A South Asian woman describes racism within feminist practices by identifying how abortion affects women in different ways:

I've taken part in pro-choice demonstrations. I've taken part in and participated in International Women's Day Coalition meetings. I represented an organization. But I guess there are differences in how pro-choice affects immigrant communities. We want choice, but we also want the choice to be able to have children, to be able to bring them up in a certain level of comfort. We may exercise the choice of abortion under very restricted circumstances. The real issue for us is determined by our economic situation. (Quoted in Agnew 1990, 68)

Women from Asia, Africa, and the Caribbean have been brought together in struggles against sexual and racial discrimination. The problems associated with adaptation and settlement (locating housing, employment, schools, and social services) generate certain attitudes and behaviours which may keep the individual from interacting across lines of race or class. And racism of the larger society may encourage the individual to remain within the moral and social confines of an 'ethnic' community.

Racism determined, perhaps indirectly, if, how, and on what basis women from Asia, Africa, and the Caribbean would join white feminists in common struggles against gender oppression. Being immigrants in a race-biased society provided unity to the group and a basis for their political struggles, but at the same time it separated women along lines of race.

WOMEN'S ORGANIZATIONS: PROCESSES AND STRUCTURE

In Ontario during the 1970s a number of new women's organizations emerged and existing women's organizations were revitalized. Health centres appeared, as well as rape crisis centres, abortion referral services, and transition houses for battered women (Black 1988, 84). Umbrella organizations like the National Action Committee on the Status of Women (NAC) were formed to bring these diverse groups together in support of women's struggles. Government departments and agencies responded to the revitalization of the women's movement by creating Status of Women offices or appointing advisers on women's issues (Findlay 1987, 31).

In the 1980s, women from Asia, Africa, and the Caribbean established a number of autonomous organizations that focused on issues of specific concern to themselves: racism, sexism, immigration policy, and access to social services (for example, Women Working with Immigrant Women, the National Organization of Immigrant and Visible-Minority Women, and the Congress of Black Women). At the same time, women from Asia, Africa, and the Caribbean formed umbrella organizations to give coherence, direction, and a higher profile to their issues with state agencies and feminist organizations dominated by white women.[6] Women Working with Immigrant Women was initiated by white social workers and immigrant and visible-minority women. However, the social workers slowly withdrew from its active functioning, which enabled immigrant women to manage their own organization (Women Working with Immigrant Women 1985–6).

State agencies supported women's organizations by allocating grants to them and encouraging the emergence of organizations for women from Asia, Africa, and the Caribbean, such as the Ontario Immigrant and Visible-Minority Women's Organization and the South Asian Women's Group (Ontario Women's Directorate 1987, 1). Support by government grants creates some tension in the politics of women's organizations. They must structure their organizations to conform to the requirements of the state, sometimes changing the character of the organization from a volunteer organization to an agency of the state (Ng 1988a). The dependence on state funds constrains the options available to women's organizations.[7] For example, it may restrain their espousal of militant politics or pressure them to become more inclusive of marginalized groups.

Feminist organizations have attempted to form alliances and coalitions with each other either in support of specific issues, such as abortion, or in support of broadly defined goals and objectives like the 'women's movement' or 'women's struggles.' Criticism by women from Asia, Africa, and the Caribbean pressured organizations dominated by white women to address issues of women from Asia, Africa, and the Caribbean. Some organizations, like the National Action Committee and the International Women's Day Committee, after much dispute and acrimony, instituted changes to their structures to make them more representative of the different groups of women in their membership (Greaves 1991; Vickers 1991; Egan, Gardner, and Persad 1988). An analysis of some of these conflicts indicates the difficulties of forming coalitions across lines of race and class.

The critique of the exercise of power in a male-dominated society has motivated feminists to create structures and initiate processes that enable marginal groups to be heard along with the more privileged and the articulate. In ideal feminist organizational structures, there is no hierarchy: all tasks are rotated, and decisions are arrived at through consensus. They favour small groups, which allow for a 'high degree of comfort and recognition of shared experiences,' and they recognize 'the absolute sovereignty of the individual as central to political decision making' and reject representative democracy in favour of direct or participatory democracy (Vickers 1991, 77). If these structures and practices are instituted in organizations dominated by white women, for example, in the NAC, rape and crisis shelters, and social service collectives, they can help working-class women and women from Asia, Africa, and the Caribbean come together with white, middle-class women. But despite theoretical commitment to non-hierarchical structures and the desire not to allocate privilege and power to individual women, in practice hierarchies and leaders emerge nonetheless (Ristock 1991, 41–55; Albrecht and Brewer 1990).[8]

Research indicates that small groups lead to greater homogeneity, conformity, and the development of an 'us' and 'them' attitude. Sheila Rowbotham notes: 'Sisterhood can become a coercive consensus which makes it emotionally difficult for individual women to say what they feel rather than a source of strength ... Our lack of structure can make it difficult for women outside particular networks to join. It can lead to cliquishness and thus be undemocratic. The stress on personal experience makes it hard to communicate ideas' (quoted in Vickers 1991, 85). Members of small groups sometimes find diversity and difference threatening. A worker at a Canadian feminist collective notes: 'We accommodate superficial differences but what that amounts to is real differences remaining hidden. The accommodation is just to allow women into the fold, to make them become one of "us," but differences in feminist analysis, skill and identity remain unacknowledged' (Ristock 1991, 48).

Lack of well-defined procedures disadvantage those who are not part of informal networks. Trust between people is dependent on the identity of the individuals. A middle-class white male can establish a measure of trust between himself and a stranger by indicating a preference for informal processes. But a black women who has to overcome stereotypical negative images of herself finds that formal procedures help to enhance trust (Williams 1991, 147). Well-defined procedures help 'outsiders' to participate and to be treated fairly within an organization.

Feminist processes and organizational structures assume that women have equal strengths, skills, and expertise. In reality, more privileged or articulate women manipulate the decision-making process to their advantage. Some women are able to manage the agenda of the organizations in subtle and indirect ways (Greaves 1991, 101–16; Ristock 1991). The coordinator of Women Working with Immigrant Women noted that her unfamiliarity with Robert's Rules of Order often placed her at a disadvantage with white women. White women familiar with these rules were able to marginalize the issues of women from Asia, Africa, and the Caribbean in the political agenda of these organizations (Interviews, 5 October 1989, 31 May 1989).

In theory, feminists abhor the exercise of privilege or expertise over groups and individuals. Feminists favour processes that distribute power among the participants. In practice, however, commitment to the theory has sometimes led to a refusal to discuss how power is exercised within these organizations. Power is exercised covertly. Power and leadership in feminist organizations shift from individuals to factions within the organization (Ristock 1991, 51–5). As 'outsiders,' women from Asia, Africa, and the Caribbean find it difficult to become part of 'informal networks' or to join the different factions of white women. They may feel disempowered, suspecting that decisions have been made informally by different factions that excluded them. At other times, the issues of women from Asia, Africa, and the Caribbean may be 'included' in order to consolidate power for a particular 'faction.' One black woman discussed her experience of alienation and marginalization at the Women's Press collective in Toronto: 'The one black person or woman of colour is reduced to a minority voice and in the collective process that means one vote ... one voice. It is difficult for one voice to speak out as loudly as it should ... There is an undermining of self-confidence and you are constantly on the other side of the discussion facing nine or ten people who have an opposing point of view. It is always a minority situation ... I would like to see real involvement not just a token presence' (quoted in Kline 1989b, 59).

In theory, feminist political proposals are attempts to respond to the oppression of all women. However, since not all women are 'victims' in identical ways, feminist practice must establish an agenda of priorities and allocate its limited resources to issues affecting women in different ways. Arriving at these decisions has been occasion for dispute. A basic conflict revolves around defining what is an appropriate feminist struggle. Is racism a feminist issue? Even when common issues are identified, evolving an appropriate non-racist strategy may be difficult. For example, workshops on rape and wife battering may discuss how they affect some groups of women while the rest of the discussion purports to consider 'all women' (Russo 1991, 288–96). A demonstration may indirectly reinforce racist stereotypes, such as when a group protesting rape marches through a black neighbourhood (Bhavnani and Coulson 1986, 84). Or an antiracist agenda may be adopted without initiating any structural change within an organization (Newsletter, International Women's Day Celebrations 1986). Such conflicts are about representation, accountability, responsibility, and equal sharing of power and authority.

Integrating people and their issues into organizations that are embedded in a racially stratified society has led to accusations of tokenism by women from Asia, Africa, and the Caribbean against white feminists and, in the caustic language of Trinh Minh-ha, to feelings of 'being part of somebody's private zoo' (Minh-ha 1989, 82). Being outnumbered in an organization increases feelings of isolation, vulnerability, and power-lessness (Kline 1986b, 59). The issue of inclusion has exposed the racial, class, and ethnic composition of feminist organizations that purport to represent all women.

CONSCIOUSNESS-RAISING GROUPS OF THE 1970s

Consciousness-raising groups reproduced the race stratification of the larger society. They represented the issues, interests, and perspectives of white, middle-class women, which centred on sexuality, family, and socialization. Feminist practice initiated debate on these issues, which were later elaborated in feminist discourse and writings. Identification with this agenda or alienation from it became a means of inclusion and exclusion. It functioned like a code comparable to the behaviour and attitudes that are associated with class positions. Dorothy Smith notes that the feeling of being an 'other' or an 'outsider' can be conveyed in a variety of small, symbolic ways (Smith 1985, 59). For example, clothes are sometimes an expression of political beliefs, and the differentiating signals of dress may elude new immigrants.

Consciousness-raising groups were an organizing tool of the women's liberation movement, and they encouraged participation and mobiliza-tion of women at a grass-roots level. Women met informally in small groups of six or eight and talked about their experiences of being female. Such meetings showed women that their experiences were not limited to themselves but were similar to those of other women. Women's oppres-sion was not individual and isolated but systemic. Growth of conscious-ness created a feeling of solidarity and formed a basis for formulating a theory about the political nature of women's oppression and exploita-tion. This was captured in the slogan 'the personal is political.' Gender thus formed a basis of theory and practice.

For those who participated, consciousness-raising groups created a sense of the commonality of women's experiences, which was later reflected in feminist theory. H. Eisenstein notes:

The individual lives of the women in a consciousness-raising group could vary considerably. Their situation in their family of origin – number of and sex of sib-lings; ... their racial and/or ethnic and religious background, and the customs governing the lives of women in that tradition, their history of work experience and education – all of these were variables that made for great diversity in the details and nuances of each woman's personal experience. Nonetheless, despite the differences, certain common elements could be discerned ... The condition of being female was a defining characteristic, cutting across differences of class, race, and sexual orientation. (1983, 38)

Consciousness-raising groups were informal, non-hierarchical, and egalitarian. The groups tried to create an environment that limited class privilege and encouraged participation by all women. Time was allocated equally, and everyone was allowed to finish statements without interruption. The groups attempted to avoid making comparisons or passing judgment, and they aimed to give everyone's experience equal validity. But some women, usually those who were middle class and well educated, were more articulate and could dominate discussions (Eisenstein 1983, 40).

Consciousness-raising groups could have provided a good opportunity for women from different classes and races to share their experiences. But the potential was never realized because the biases of class and race within the larger society influenced the dynamics of the group interactions. There is no indication that working-class women, women of colour, or black women participated in such groups. One reason for their absence was stated bluntly in 1970 in a position paper of the Leila Khalid Collective: 'Women with little time, little education, with families and jobs, or women who have to fight hard to survive on welfare aren't interested in coming to weekly meetings to talk about sexuality and to read Engels.' The absence of women from Asia, Africa, and the Caribbean from such groups is also explained by the influence of racism on their interaction and communication, their different understandings of the nature of their oppression and its sources, and their cultural and social alienation.

The focus of the consciousness-raising groups was gender, and gender oppression was the basis of solidarity and sisterhood. But this perspective was in itself exclusionary and alienating. Feminists within consciousness-raising groups regarded male supremacy as the most important form of domination, and all other forms of exploitation, such as racism, capitalism, and imperialism, were regarded as extensions of male supremacy (Roszak and Roszak 1969, 273).

The differences in interest and experience were alienating and exclusionary. Feminists of the late 1960s and 1970s were interested in cultural issues, particularly those related to sexuality, family, and socialization. The women shared intimate experiences with other women, such as incest, sexual molestation, rape, or abortion (Adamson, Briskin, and McPhail 1988, 44). Such experiences occurred among women from Asia, Africa, and the Caribbean too, but they did not provide a basis for solidarity between members of dominant and subordinate groups.

Cultural practices and mores also create social distance. For example, discussion of sexuality evokes acute embarrassment in South Asian women because their culture regards it as an intensely private and personal issue.[9] Further, members of a subordinate group who experience oppression on the basis of race are reluctant to discuss it, for this may only serve to confirm the pre-existing stereotypical images and attitudes of the dominant group. To articulate the existence of sexism within South Asian families would be to reinforce stereotypical notions of 'traditional' societies and 'oppressive' cultures. A feminist discussion would not necessarily help overcome deep-seated racist attitudes and assumptions, particularly when raising critical consciousness is perceived as referring to gender only.

Uma Narayan, a South Asian feminist, says:

I often find myself torn between the desire to communicate with honesty the miseries and oppressions that I think my own culture confers on its women and the fear that this communication is going to reinforce, however unconsciously, western prejudices about the 'superiority' of western culture. I have often felt compelled to interrupt my communication, say on the problems of the Indian system of arranged marriages, to remind my western friends that the experience of women under their system of 'romantic love' seems no more enviable. (1990, 259)

Immigrants may also hesitate to criticize their new society, fearing they will provoke their audience to make comparisons with the 'old country.'

The status of women from Asia, Africa, and the Caribbean as immigrants and newcomers meant that they had different interests and experiences. The feminist movement did not address the specific conditions of their lives but focused its rhetoric and politics on the experience of white, middle-class women. For example, white feminists emphasized the oppression experienced by women within the family. They have been criticized by black feminists who argue that, in a racist and classist society, family is a source of emotional support and comfort for them (hooks 1984, 43–65; Parmar 1986). This is not to deny the existence of sexism within the family, but rather to say that women from Asia, Africa, and the Caribbean may be reluctant to identify with a movement perceived to be anti-family. The experience of discrimination by women from Asia, Africa, and the Caribbean increases their dependence on the family and ethnic community. Immigrant women who are confronted by attitudes and behaviours that are racist or classist are reluctant to identify with members of a dominant group on the basis of gender. As newcomers, they value the emotional shelter of the family and the sense of belonging in their ethnic group. They are likely to consider relations outside the family and community as stressful and alienating, while relations within the family and community affirm their dignity and identity as women.

Differences in class are also divisive and alienating.[10] Feminist theory sees all women as victims of discrimination, capitalist patriarchy, or biology. The experiential reality of women from Asia, Africa, and the Caribbean, however, is different from that of white, middle-class women. The labour market not only is segregated by gender but is ethnically stratified as well. Women from Asia, Africa, and the Caribbean may work either in job ghettos for immigrant women or in the lower strata of 'female' jobs. Thus, women from Asia, Africa, and the Caribbean experience oppression not only by men but by women as well. The relations of subordination and domination are best exemplified in the nanny and mistress relationship. Thousands of women from the Caribbean and Asian countries have come to work as domestics in white households since the introduction of the Domestic Scheme in 1955 (Silvera 1983, 13; Daenzer 1991). In this situation it is rare for women from Asia, Africa, and the Caribbean to identify with white women as 'victims' on the basis of gender. White, middle-class women may be oppressed by their gender, but they exercise great power and privilege when compared to women from Asia, Africa, and the Caribbean. Women can be both oppressors and oppressed. This is noted by bell hooks, a black feminist writer: 'Women can and do participate in politics of domination, as perpetrators as well as victims – that we dominate, that we are dominated. If focus on patriarchal domination masks this reality or becomes the means by which women deflect attention from the real conditions and circumstances of our lives, then women cooperate in suppressing and promoting false consciousness, inhibiting our capacity to assume responsibility for transforming ourselves and society' (1988, 20). Women from Asia, Africa, and the Caribbean are more likely to share a common sense of victimization with men of their own class and race than with middle-class, white women.

Language can be a barrier to communication. The inability to speak English obviously keeps working-class women from Asia, Africa, and the Caribbean away from feminist meetings of white, middle-class women. Pauline Terrelonge has argued that accent and unfamiliarity with middle-class uses of language set up barriers between black and white women (1984). But knowledge of the language is not enough. Feminists have developed a complex jargon, with terms such as 'herstory,' 'validation,' and 'knowings,' which may be impenetrable for both working-class women and middle-class women from other cultures and societies.[11] In addition, working-class and middle-class white women may share a colloquial language (e.g., the difference between being 'at lunch' and being 'out to lunch') and a store of familiar allusions (e.g., Harlequin romances and the Literary Guild), which are unfamiliar to immigrant women. And certain words have acquired negative connotations within a feminist setting which may disturb immigrant women (e.g., the use of the word 'middle-class'). To women from Asia, Africa, and the Caribbean who have come to Canada in pursuit of a middle-class lifestyle, the disparagement of their goals by feminists is confusing and alienating.

A feminist practice that emphasized gender and ignored racism, colonialism, and imperialism could not gain much support from women who immigrated from Asia, Africa, and Latin America. The differences in experience and motivation for political activism have been a constant source of tension within feminist practice. This situation was outlined in the 1970 position paper of the Leila Khalid Collective, a group of white, college-going feminists:

In practice and in our ongoing debate. . . we treated women's oppression as special and related to other people's oppression only in a mechanical way. We thus reinforced the same abstract politics that had originally frustrated us ... [W]e see a women's liberation movement in North America attacking symbols (bras and beauty contests) and not the oppressor, concerned with individual liberation while black sisters are beaten and tortured, demanding freedom and equality from a decaying society where no one can be free and equal.

The feminist politics of middle-class women revealed 'ignorance of the lives of other women and of factors beyond gender which determine women's lives' (Segal 1987, 61).

Differences in interests and concerns continue to be divisive and alienating. The political struggles of women from Asia, Africa, and the Caribbean include anti-colonial and anti-imperial struggles in their original countries (Narayan 1990; Chow 1991, xi–xvii). In Canada they have engaged in struggles against discriminatory immigration and settlement policies, and they have committed themselves to struggles against racism. A South Asian female activist says:

Some who have tried to participate have experienced great frustration at the unwillingness of most of the predominantly white, Anglo-Saxon women to recognize our concerns as 'women's' issues. Our concerns have focused on such areas as social movements in our countries of origin, jobs and racism: that is, on issues of social justice. Some feminists have stated that these concerns represent 'an erosion of feminist content,' claiming that to talk about political situations was 'divisive' and that to chant in Spanish was to use 'the language of patriarchy.' (Das Gupta 1986, 44)

The assumption in feminist theory of the 1970s was that gender identity existed in isolation from race and class identity. The 'adding on' of race and class brought into focus the identity of women from Asia, Africa, and the Caribbean, but not the racial and class identity of white, middle-class women (Spelman 1988; Frye 1983; Fisher-Manick 1981, 153; Frankenberg 1993).

Women from Asia, Africa, and the Caribbean stayed away not because they lacked a consciousness of their own oppression, but because the movement did not address the specific conditions of their lives. The lack of mutual understanding and trust reinforced social distance and a sense of alienation. Political solidarity based on gender remained an elusive goal.

Race and class influence the relations between women belonging to the same organization and between women in organizations representing different ethnic and racial groups. However, the concept of sisterhood and the idea that the personal is political, which form the ideological core of the women's movement of the 1970s, ignore this fact. The assumption that women belonging to different classes and races can practise solidarity on the basis of sisterhood assumes that all feminists have equal power in society, that the race dynamics of the larger society do not operate between women, and that all have equal power in defining the terms of the feminist debate and in determining the priorities of its political agenda.

A political analysis of mainstream feminist theory and practice of the 1970s enables us to understand that the absence of women from Asia, Africa, and the Caribbean from mainstream feminist practice results not from their culture and values but from their powerlessness, based on race and class. The issues, interests, and perspectives of white, middle-class women were those of women who could relate to each other. Within such a context, the perspectives of other women were either ignored or marginalized.

COALITION AND ALLIANCES IN THE 1980s

A political strategy of coalitions and alliances among different feminist organizations is widely supported by white feminists and women from Asia, Africa, and the Caribbean. In Canada, the recognition of the need to forge a unity amid diversity strikes a responsive chord. Canada's official policy of multiculturalism is based on a need to recognize the contributions of the many different cultural groups that form part of the Canadian mosaic.

The debates within feminism resonate with questions about the role of 'other Canadians' in Canadian society and about the political necessity of integrating 'other Canadians' to achieve a unified society based on a diversity of cultures. Critics argue that multiculturalism emphasizes the cultural differences between groups rather than their differences of power and privilege. They see multicultural policy as a strategy meant only to reduce conflict between different ethnic groups who desire a greater share of resources, power, and privilege. Multiculturalism offers compensation to the powerless by 'accepting' them but not by giving them power or privilege. In other words, multiculturalism does not challenge the nation's political and social structures; it perpetuates them (Peter 1981). A similar complaint may be directed against feminist theory and practice. Recognizing the different experiential realities of oppression in women's lives does not challenge the differences that give power to some women and withhold it from others, and it may reinforce them.

The difficulties of forming alliances and coalitions across lines of race and class can be explored by examining the struggle of women from Asia, Africa, and the Caribbean to gain representation for themselves and their issues in a large national feminist organization such as the National Action Committee on the Status of Women (NAC) and in the socialist-feminist coalition of the International Women's Day Celebrations (IWDC), which is also referred to as the March 8th coalition.

NAC is a large umbrella organization which originated in 1972 with a mandate to monitor the implementation of the recommendations of the Royal Commission on the Status of Women (National Action Committee 1986, 2). By 1988 its membership had expanded to 570 groups, representing a wide spectrum of organizations from across Canada (Greaves 1991, 102). Autonomous organizations of women from Asia, Africa, and the Caribbean and their umbrella organizations are members of NAC. But until very recently NAC was essentially a white, anglophone network to which 'others' sought entrance (Vickers 1988, 59). The diversity of its membership led to demands that NAC change its structure and enable different groups of women to participate. An editorial in IWDC's newsletter of 1986 notes: 'NAC must look to itself and question why different groupings of women have been inhibited from joining. Perhaps the present structure, political approach to issues [and] method of work discourage the building of a more representative participatory movement. We must be open to change.' At the same time, newer members demanded that NAC's executive members be made more accountable to the general membership.

NAC is regarded as the 'formal women's movement in Canada, the official women's opposition, and the public voice and symbol of feminism in Canada.' It has the responsibility to simultaneously 'lead and mirror the Canadian women's movement' (Greaves 1991, 103–4). An organizational review conducted in 1988 recommended that NAC open itself to 'more diversity and ground itself more thoroughly in the grassroots women's movement.' It recommended that NAC ensure that its structure and internal processes include those whom it purports to represent. But Jill Vickers questions whether NAC 'can incorporate in its processes black feminism, ethnic feminism, disabled women's feminism, lesbian feminism, etc ... It may well be that there is a limit to the number and diversity of groups which can operate under the umbrella structures like NAC' (1991, 91).

NAC's primary role has been to manage conflict within the women's movement, which would encourage coalitions between different women's organizations. The relations between small, local organizations and large, 'mainstream' organizations can be cooperative. Large organizations, like the NAC, provide some coherence and political direction to feminist politics at the national level. They need the support of organizations of women from Asia, Africa, and the Caribbean to dispel the impression that the Canadian women's movement is primarily a white, middle-class movement. NAC has to demonstrate that it represents all

Canadian women regardless of race, ethnicity, and class. It needs to prove its representative character to state agencies whose material support is necessary for the organization to survive. These pragmatic issues of survival have pressured NAC to graft issues of race and class onto existing agendas. Women who were previously excluded can now be included.

Cooperation and participation between women's organizations are mutually beneficial. The presence of small organizations of women from Asia, Africa, and the Caribbean within NAC enables these small groups to introduce issues that are of special interest to themselves and which may otherwise be neglected by NAC. Small organizations often need the resources and organizational expertise of large organizations for lobbying politicians and state agencies. Their issues receive wider publicity at a national level through the media attention attracted by large organizations.[12] But occasionally disputes erupt, particularly over representation, priorities, and leadership.

NAC has introduced some structural changes in an attempt to become more representative and more responsive to the demands of women from Asia, Africa, and the Caribbean. Its lack of well-defined structures disadvantages those groups who are not part of the informal networks among white women. For example, NAC policy and resolutions of the annual general meetings are developed within committees. NAC executive members chair committees in particular areas, and executive members are lobbied before or after election for promises to promote a policy committee. Since resolutions are developed within committees, this activity constitutes an informal priority-setting exercise for NAC agenda (Greaves 1991, 106–8). The absence of a committee from a particular area or of a committee serving a particular constituency results in the marginalization of other members and their issues.

NAC committees do not function under a particular plan or structure, and there are no definite guidelines that determine the process of acquiring a budget. The lack of structure gives particular significance to the skill of the chair of a particular committee, her networks within the organization, and the lobbying of committee members. A NAC executive member notes: 'executive members would compete, posture, bargain and trade at the first executive meeting of the year to establish as much money as possible for their favourite committee. Inexperienced executive members were often less successful at this, not realizing that co-operation and openness were likely to render them "losers" in the budget allocation process' (Greaves 1991, 106).

In 1984, as a result of lobbying by women from Asia, Africa, and the Caribbean, an Immigrant and Visible-Minority Women's Committee was added to NAC's other committees. Until this committee was created, the issues of women from Asia, Africa, and the Caribbean were virtually unrepresented. A South Asian feminist who was active in the process of initiating the committee notes: 'Before that [1984], NAC put forward two resolutions relevant to the immigrant women's network – five years apart, in a seven-year period. Just two proposals.' The new committee's 'purpose was not to ghettoize our issues, but it was to get our issues on the floor, get them integrated, and then disband the committee at the proper time' (Interview, 14 August 1989). During the 1991 meeting, the Immigrant and Visible-Minority Women's Committee refused to discuss racism in a separate forum, demanding instead that it be integrated into the themes of the constitution and reproductive technologies that the meeting was highlighting (statement circulated by the Immigrant and Visible-Minority Women's Committee, Annual General Meeting, 1991).

Women from Asia, Africa, and the Caribbean have formed the Women of Colour Caucus within NAC to develop strategies for making their issues an integral part of NAC's agenda. But achieving this goal could be difficult. Since NAC is a national organization, different groups are brought together primarily during its annual meetings. Women from Asia, Africa, and the Caribbean coming to the annual meeting as delegates may represent organizations that focus on women from Asia, Africa, and the Caribbean, or on women's shelters, health cooperatives, or support services. But there is no continuity of delegates from one year to the next. Only those members of the executive or regional representatives of NAC can have some impact on NAC's policies (Women of Colour Caucus, Annual General Meeting, 1991). A change in NAC's structures to make them more inclusive and representative of different groups of women thus takes on added significance.

Under strong pressure from activist women from Asia, Africa, and the Caribbean, NAC instituted an affirmative action policy for its executive. During the 1991 annual general meeting, a Filipina and a South Asian woman stood for election for an executive position. There were already three women from Asia, Africa, and the Caribbean on the executive. However, an amendment from the Women of Colour Caucus asked that four additional members-at-large be designated as affirmative action positions for aboriginal women, women of colour, immigrant women of colour, and women with disability (Women of Colour Caucus, Amendment to Resolution #7, Section 2c, Annual General Meeting, 1991). And they asked that one vice-president be a woman of colour or an aboriginal woman. The implementation of these 'affirmative actions' was resisted by the Lesbian Women's Caucus, whose members believed that their issues were marginalized within NAC as well (statement issued by the Lesbian Caucus, Annual General Meeting, 1991).

During the 1991 annual general meeting, anglophone, francophone, 'immigrant,' and lesbian women were consistently represented at all plenary sessions.[13] But despite its symbolic significance, this representation does not by itself indicate that power is being equally shared among these different constituencies. Which group of women exercises power and authority within the organization remains a difficult and contentious issue.

NAC's mandate to represent the women's movement in Canada means that it must find a balance among the different issues and priorities of women. These issues and priorities have different impacts upon women and these differences must be reconciled as well. But it may be difficult for NAC to satisfy the many groups that it represents.

NAC is responding to the pressure and changing its structures and processes to accommodate new constituencies. Although the changes may be small and achieved with difficulty, they indicate that the relations between white feminists and feminists from Asia, Africa, and the Caribbean are being addressed. A black feminist active within NAC notes: 'It takes a lot of fighting on our part and a lot of challenging to get NAC to listen to what we are saying. From 1986 we have had to push and challenge and insist and get angry and yell and call people racist, but at least when people come out they don't only see white faces on the stage, which is also very important' (Interview, 14 August 1991).

INTERNATIONAL WOMEN'S DAY CELEBRATIONS, 1986–91

Racism divides women from Asia, Africa, and the Caribbean and white feminists both within the feminist movement and in society at large. Women from Asia, Africa, and the Caribbean have argued that white feminist practices ignore or marginalize racism or replicate the racist practices of the larger society within feminist struggles. Although white, middle-class feminists of the 1980s have recognized the different oppressions experienced by women from Asia, Africa, and the Caribbean, developing an antiracist agenda and an antiracist movement can be difficult. It gives rise to several issues: how to introduce an antiracist perspective into the organizational agenda; how to initiate antiracist action; and who is to exercise authority and leadership in the struggle (Bunch 1990; Anzaldúa 1990). The white feminists' assumption of leadership in forming policy and implementing projects for 'their' movement is interpreted by women from Asia, Africa, and the Caribbean as racist. This situation makes alliances across lines of class and race difficult.

The struggle by women from Asia, Africa, and the Caribbean to integrate the issues of gender, race, and class oppression into white feminist practices has been contentious and divisive. But some feminists argue that the differences among women do not have to be a source of misunderstanding and separation but can be used to devise more inclusive feminist theories and practices. Audre Lorde notes: 'We have been raised to view any difference other than sex as a reason for destruction, and for Black women and white women to face each other's angers without denial or immobility or silence or guilt is in itself a heretical and generative idea. It implies peers meeting upon a common basis to examine difference, and to alter those distortions which history has created around our difference. For it is those distortions which separate us' (quoted in Russo 1991, 309). In practice, however, the coming together of individuals or groups in a common understanding has not been easy. Differences of perspective and power continue to divide women.

Different perspectives on what constitutes an antiracist practice can be illustrated by analysing the conflicts and tensions generated during the 1986 International Women's Day Celebration in Toronto. A single theme, 'Women Say No to Racism from Toronto to South Africa,' was chosen for the celebrations in March 1986 to indicate the importance feminists attach to the issue of race and their concern for building an antiracist women's movement.

The International Women's Day Committee (IWDC) of Toronto is a socialist-feminist organization committed to organizing mass actions. One aim guiding its politics is to create coalitions of oppressed groups such as women, immigrants, people of colour, lesbians and gays, and workers (Egan, Gardner, and Persad 1988, 113). Since its inception, the organization has included race as one of the issues that it was particularly concerned with. In 1986 it decided after some debate to focus on racism as its primary theme. The alliance between organizations representing black women and the IWDC had hoped to overcome divisions based on race, but this goal proved difficult. Black women were wary of their white counterparts and conscious of the history of the 'expediency of white women,' which exploited the racial issue to serve the interests of white feminists. The sentiments of black women were expressed in a statement addressed to the IWDC by the Black Women's Collective: 'Our historical memory does not allow us to forget our political, economic and social relationship with white people, particularly since it is a relationship which extends to this day – the relationship of oppressor and oppressed, the exploiter and exploited, privileged and underclass.' Doubts were raised about the attitude of white, middle-class feminists and their commitment to antiracism. Black women argued that racism was their issue. Their experience provided them with insights which were very different from those of white women. The reluctance of white women to allow black women to exercise leadership or authority led to misunderstandings and accusations. The statement by black women concluded bitterly:

This coalition, in our point of view, has organized white women over the last ten years. In selecting this theme perhaps it was not fully aware of the step that it was taking. Simply, it was seeking to organize black women! Did the coalition consider how it would have to change in order to do so? What matters it would of necessity discuss and how that would change the very face of the women's movement?

The conflict generated by the 1986 International Women's Day Celebration led to greater consciousness and sensitivity about how assumptions based on everyday racism can be replicated unintentionally within a feminist organization. In the IWDC's newsletter Carolyn Egan, a white feminist, asked:

The question is, where do we go from here? Socialist-feminists have to ask why a systematic analysis of racism has not been incorporated into our politics. White women, no matter if they are products of a colonized background, come from working-class families, suffer oppression as lesbians and women, gain a certain privilege in a racist society. Neither guilt nor defensiveness [is] helpful, but we must develop a recognition that an anti-racist analysis is often overlooked because of this. We have taken up issues, but we haven't put the same energy into educating ourselves and developing an analytical understanding of racism, as we have with sexism and class oppression.

The IWDC proposed and implemented two kinds of change. White women organized a workshop in which they attempted to examine their own attitudes and to 'unlearn' racism. They accepted the contention of women from Asia, Africa, and the Caribbean that racism could not be isolated in the agenda of the IWDC but had to be integrated in all the debates and discussions of the organization. Its pamphlets published from 1987 to 1989 contained this statement:

It is not enough to simply add racism as one more item to a list of feminist issues. An anti-racist perspective must be integrated into our feminist organizing. We do not believe that racism is merely a misunderstanding among people, a question of interpersonal relations, or an unchanging part of human nature. It, like sexism, is an integral part of the political and economic system under which we live. This system uses racism and sexism to divide us.

The confrontation between women in 1986 led the IWDC to initiate some procedural changes as well. In preparation for its 1987 celebrations, it called a meeting to discuss 'leadership, decision-making process, committees, and caucuses.' The IWDC included women's organizations representing women from Asia, Africa, and the Caribbean in its planning process. It was cautiously optimistic that a shared commitment to bring about social change would help feminists overcome the divisions among themselves and engage in common political action. The IWDC promised to continue to make racism a major focus of its movement. It acknowledged the role of women from Asia, Africa, and the Caribbean who were participating and 'providing organizational and political leadership in an atmosphere which demands dialogue and accountability.' Following is a comment from an editorial in its newspaper, *Rebel Girls Rag* (April 1987), entitled 'Fighting Racism and Sexism Together,' which was the theme for the celebrations in 1987:

The women of colour who have chosen to work in the coalition have made a political decision to develop a stronger anti-racist consciousness in the broader women's movement. They expect white women to deal with the economic and political structures which maintain racism in our society, but also to deal with the personal and organizational ways in which racism has become institutionalized in our lives and our politics. Recognizing existing antagonisms and contradictions is crucial if we are to break down barriers, and build the necessary unity to overcome the racist, capitalist system which maintains our oppressions.

However, race and racism could not simply be wished away by an expression of good intentions. In 1991, during the IWDC's annual celebrations, an article in *The Globe and Mail* questioned why the organization emphasized racism instead of focusing on 'women's issues' such as day care and abortion:

In Canada recently, some black women have argued unequivocally that the women's movement is guilty of false consciousness since it has failed to focus most of its energy on racism and class struggle ... To suggest that women fighting for equality and equal power to realize their personal aspirations should first take up the gauntlet against classism, capitalism and racism is to suggest once again that women should satisfy the hunger of others (and secure others' rights and happiness) before they come to the table to eat. (18 June 1991)

Women from Asia, Africa, and the Caribbean viewed the article as a challenge to the inclusion of antiracist issues and struggles in the 'women's movement.' The article generated further conflicts over who ought to reply to it and revived old issues of appropriation, authority, and leadership among white feminists and feminists from Asia, Africa, and the Caribbean. Four women from the IWDC coalition responded by reiterating old arguments:[14]

To this day, white feminists cling to the false assumption that the women's movement is a homogeneous group, experiencing the same forms and degree of oppression. With this assumption, white feminists have not only monopolized the movement with their interests and privileges, but have also carried their equality struggle, in the name of gender, at the expense of aboriginal women, black women and women of colour. (*Globe and Mail*, 18 June 1991)

Problems in feminist practice raise the issue of how, and on what basis, do individuals overcome gender, race, and class biases and participate in 'common' struggles? Feminist theory has not sufficiently explored how differences in experience can be overcome to create a common understanding. These differences pose the threat of relativism, which 'implies that a person could have knowledge of only the sorts of things she had experienced personally and that she would be totally unable to communicate any of the contents of her knowledge to someone who did not have the same sorts of experiences' (Narayan 1990, 264). Can white feminists understand the oppressions of another group? Or does understanding come only from lived experience of oppressions?

Feminists argue that experience of oppression gives one insights into a particular oppression that is not shared by others. Even those sympathetic to the oppressions of a particular group may be unaware of the various nuances of how that oppression is experienced. Uma Narayan notes: 'The view that we can understand much about the perspective of those whose oppression we do not share allows us the space to criticize dominant groups for their blindness to the facts of oppression. The view that such an understanding, despite great effort and interest, is likely to be incomplete or limited, provides us with the ground for denying total parity to members of a dominant groups in their ability to understand our situation' (1990, 265).

Newly empowered groups may be wary of forming alliances with members of the dominant group. They have experienced white domination and the suppression of the experience, culture, individuality, and dignity of the colonized. Women from Asia, Africa, and the Caribbean, conscious of the biases of feminist theory and practice in the 1970s, may question the motives behind white feminists' interest in their struggles. They fear that white women who are sympathetic to their cause may use that as a pretext to speak on their behalf, thereby suppressing their 'voice' once again. The alliance of women from Asia, Africa, and the Caribbean and white feminists is motivated by a common commitment to struggle against a male-dominated society. But women from Asia, Africa, and the Caribbean experience race, class, and gender oppression simultaneously, and this experience puts them at odds with white feminists and makes a working relationship between them problematic.

The exercise of privilege and domination in feminist practice has expressed itself in different ways over a period of time. The biases of feminist theory of the 1970s meant that feminist practices were ethnocentric. In the 1980s the emphasis on the different identities of women in feminist theory made feminists more sensitive to the different experiences and issues of women from Asia, Africa, and the Caribbean. Feminist practices are embedded in institutional structures that assign power and privilege unequally on the basis of gender, race, and class. Problems arise when white feminists act on assumptions that their experiences categorize as 'normal,' 'natural,' or merely 'routine'. Their activities are experienced by the subordinate group as oppressive. Inequalities based on race and class are articulated within feminist practices through the constant struggle and tension between women representing diverse identities and perspectives.

The process of challenging white feminist practices has empowered women from Asia, Africa, and the Caribbean. Hilary Lips identifies the ability to doubt, question, and resist the status quo as a power that subjugated groups can exercise. 'The challenge, coming as it does from a new confidence in one's own meanings and metaphors, may be more transformative and ultimately disturbing to the established system than would any change coming from within the hierarchical framework' (1991, 9). Women from Asia, Africa, and the Caribbean have had some success in challenging the status quo of race relations in small and in large diversified feminist organizations. They have successfully exercised the 'power to' name their oppressions and to define the conditions of their participation in feminist struggles dominated by white women. However, the liberating and energizing power of discovering their own strength and the collective capacity to act are balanced by the power relations in feminist organizations.

5

The Politics of Discourse

Women from Asia, Africa, and the Caribbean in Canada have been absent from Canadian literature on ethnic groups and women's history until the last two decades. Recent work by oppressed groups to document their experiences from their own perspectives is part of their struggle against the domination of the British- and French-Canadian male elite. Oppressed groups have argued that their absence from the literature is symbolic of their general invisibility in Canadian social, political, and economic life. Women from Asia, Africa, and the Caribbean who confront the multiple oppressions of race, class, and gender find that their experiences are absent even from the writings of progressive movements and groups.

Feminist epistemologists have noted that, despite male assertions about the value of objectivity and neutrality, researchers' biases nevertheless infect their analyses. The male researcher writes from his own point of view and assigns importance to some kinds of information and not to others. The decision on what 'facts' are to count as significant structures the argument in a particular way (Smith 1990, 61–82). A white, male perspective dominates some disciplines where it is viewed not as one among many different perspectives, but as the only correct one. This singular perspective forms a standard against which all other analyses are measured (Said 1979; Mudimbe 1988; Miller 1990). For example, in the past, immigrants were evaluated for their contributions to Canada's economic development, in other words, by their paid work. The contributions of women were unacknowledged or only partially represented in the literature about immigrants, since their work included work within the home and in the community (Iacovetta 1992, 288–96). Work in the home and community is critical in integrating newcomers to their environment, but it was until recently invisible in the writings of male scholars of immigration and ethnicity.

Feminist theoreticians have noted that the exclusion of a subjugated group from a body of knowledge or 'discourse' is a technique by which those in power consolidate and perpetuate their domination. The exercise of this power may not be conscious or intentional, but its effect is to oppress or repress the marginalized and excluded groups.[1] Foucault explains that knowledge is power not just in the sense that knowledge enables people to acquire power, but also in the sense that those in power determine what is to count as knowledge: '[K]nowledge is not gained prior to and independently of the use to which it will be put in order to achieve power (whether over nature or over other people) but is already a function of human interests and power relations' (Hoy 1986, 129). People in power also control the diffusion of knowledge. Knowledge produced in one discipline is adopted by others, and its appearance in a variety of disciplines lends it greater credibility. Knowledge produced by the dominant group thus comes to construct the reality and experience of the subjugated groups (Said 1979; Mudimbe 1988). In the last two decades, ethnic scholars have documented the experiences of their own groups, but women remain absent from their accounts.[2]

The discourses of ethnic historians tend to subsume women's experiences under the category of 'the family,' which renders women invisible (Juteau-Lee and Roberts 1981, 6–7). Frances Iaconetta writes: 'The family itself is depicted as an indistinguishable unit, as a nongendered and reified collectivity that acts in a self-interested manner. At the same time, however, this lack of a gendered perspective has not precluded most scholars from in fact highlighting, and thus prioritizing, the experiences of men' (1992, 265). Danielle Juteau-Lee and Barbara Roberts make this point by showing how accounts of 'the immigrant experience' focus on the work that men did on the railroads, on farms, and in the mines. The settlement of land in western Canada was an integral aspect of immigration policies. Male immigrants could get homesteads, but the law prohibited women from doing so. This gender discrimination is explained by Juteau-Lee and Roberts as an attempt by the state to ensure that homesteaders had a supply of women for wives. The unpaid labour of wives was essential to making the homestead viable, and the restriction on the rights of women ensured their dependence on marriage. Yet in ethnic histories, 'women and children are presented as adjuncts, as part of the baggage brought along, to support what is presumed to be a male experience' (1981, 5–6).

Chinese, Japanese, and South Asian communities prior to 1960 were predominantly male societies, whose primary function from the perspective of white Canadians was to provide a pool of cheap labour. Women's contribution to the survival of the family and community is marginalized in the literature (Con et al. 1982; Chan 1983; Chadney 1984; Adachi 1976).

An analysis of the literature on women from Asia, Africa, and the Caribbean reveals how 'facts' about them reflect the biases of those in power. The exclusions, marginalizations, and biased representations of the lives and experiences of women from Asia, Africa, and the Caribbean have been exposed by middle-class women from Asia, Africa, and the Caribbean. This exposure is part of their struggle to overthrow the domination of race and gender and to empower women from their own ethnic and racial groups.

A historical perspective on the politics that generated interest in the study of ethnic and racial groups reveals the many layers of oppression encountered by women from Asia, Africa, and the Caribbean. But it sometimes presents an image of the women as passive victims who are acted upon rather than as active agents. Much less visible have been their struggles to empower themselves.

INCLUDING ETHNIC GROUPS IN CANADIAN HISTORY

Canadian history has generally been limited to the history of the English and French in Canada. Jean Burnet notes:

Professional Canadian historians have in the past emphasized political and economic history, and since the country's economic and political institutions have been controlled largely by people of British and French origin, the role of those of other origins in the development of Canada has been neglected. Also, Canadian historians in the past have been almost exclusively of British and French origin and have lacked the interest and the linguistic skills necessary to explore the history of other ethnic groups. (1988, vii)

Efforts to include the perspectives of other ethnic groups can be traced to the politics of multiculturalism in the 1960s and 1970s.

In the 1960s, oppressed groups in North America questioned existing hierarchies and organized themselves to struggle against social injustices of race, ethnicity, and gender. In Canada this was reflected in the discontent voiced by the French over their subordinate political, cultural, economic, and social status. Nationalist sentiments in Quebec led to demands for a separate Quebec. In 1963, the government responded to the threat of separation by establishing the Royal Commission on Bilingualism and Biculturalism. During this period also the First Nations and other groups questioned the political and social dominance of the Anglo élite and the national preoccupation with French and English relations (Burnet 1988, 223–8).

The Royal Commission on Bilingualism and Biculturalism was charged with the responsibility to 'recommend what steps should be taken to develop the Canadian confederation on the basis of equal partnership between the two founding races, taking into account the contribution made by the other ethnic groups to the cultural enrichment of Canada' (Fleras and Elliott 1992, 72). The commission provided a forum for groups that were not English or French to challenge the emphasis on French-English relations and to argue for greater political integration and representation in society and government (Fleras and Elliott 1992, 72–4). These groups attacked the hierarchy implicit in the terms under which the commission was established, which marginalized the contributions made by 'other' ethnic groups. They resented the restriction of the debate about Canadian culture, social composition, and future prospects to a discussion of the dissatisfactions of the French with their subordinate social, cultural, economic, and political status.[3]

The 'other' ethnic groups challenged the assumption of a Canada divided between the French and the English. The political skills of these groups were demonstrated by their success in putting their concerns on the government's agenda. They noted their own contributions to Canadian development and aggressively lobbied the government for an equal voice in Canadian society. They argued that together they constituted one-third of the population and that as a 'third force' they could play a mediating role between the French and the English (Burnet 1988, 223–8; Kallen 1988).

The seminal study of Canadian society by John Porter, *The Vertical Mosaic* (1965), demonstrated the unequal ranking of various ethnic groups in Canadian occupational and income hierarchies. The non-English and non-French groups used his research data to demonstrate the dominance of the British and the exclusion of all others. They noted the failure of past policies that had emphasized assimilation and lobbied for governmental support to maintain ethnic and cultural differences, arguing that only in this way could equality be achieved (Burnet 1988, 224).

The policy of multiculturalism within a bilingual framework, announced in 1971, was an attempt to respond to the enhanced status of ethnic and racial groups (Elliott and Fleras 1990, 64). But the policy sent conflicting messages. Multiculturalism attempted to accommodate the growing political strength of the 'other' ethnic groups and made some important overtures towards formally conceding equality to them, but bilingualism reasserted the privileged position of the 'two founding races.' Some critics questioned the motives of the policy makers and argued that multiculturalism was an attempt at appeasement, designed to 'contain' discontent rather than to promote equality among all ethnic groups (Peter 1981).

The policy of multiculturalism within a bilingual framework replaced the ideology of conformity and assimilation which had characterized Canadian institutions and popular attitudes in the past. Policy makers had expected that over time the different cultures of ethnic and racial groups would become part of a homogeneous, unified Canadian culture.[4] But assimilation was a continuing source of friction between generations within immigrant families. They frequently experienced the two goals of maintaining elements of their cultural identity and aspiring to social mobility as incompatible, which forced them to choose one goal over the other. Those who wanted to assimilate, to distance themselves from their cultures, were discouraged when they encountered exclusion and rejection socially and professionally.[5] Others, particularly racialized groups, were stigmatized for forming ghettos and secluding themselves with members of their own groups.[6]

Multiculturalism treated the different cultures of Canadians as resources rather than as barriers or obstacles. This change encouraged research and writing on the histories of ethnic and racial groups. Initial support for the documentation of ethnic histories is found in the work of the Royal Commission on Bilingualism and Biculturalism; the fourth volume of its report was devoted to 'other' ethnic groups. In addition to prescribing measures for the maintenance and preservation of cultural diversity, the policy of multiculturalism encouraged the federal government to commission 'histories specifically directed to the background, contributions and problems of various cultural groups in Canada' (Burnet 1988, vi). The series 'Generations: A History of Canada's Peoples' has begun the process of documenting the contributions of the many ethnic and racial groups to Canada's diverse heritage. It is the most visible current project aimed at including ethnic groups that are not English or French in Canadian history.

However, the authors of histories of Chinese and South Asian immigrants in the series are, with one exception, male. In *Continuous Journey: A Social History of South Asians in Canada*, women are more or less absent from the 250 pages; they are discussed only with reference to community and social organizations. The authors are a white male and a female of South Asian origin from Fiji, who received help from a South Asian associate author (Buchignani and Indra 1985). The authors of *From China to Canada: A History of the Chinese Communities in Canada*, a 369-page volume, are all Chinese males. Their account aims to present a 'Chinese perspective, talking about themes of interest to the Chinese communities and using viewpoints derived from Chinese sources' (2), but women are mentioned only in passing in discussions of the demographic make-up of Chinese communities prior to 1960. Only a couple of paragraphs are devoted to women's organization and their volunteer work during the Second World War (Con et al. 1982).

Multiculturalism is widely supported by Canadians, and it has encouraged social scientists to focus on studies of pluralism and ethnicity (Henry 1986, 2–7). State agencies, such as the Secretary of State and Multiculturalism Directorate, support research on multiculturalism through a variety of programs. Consequently, the literature on ethnicity has grown enormously since the 1970s (Henry 1986; Buchignani 1984; Burnet 1988). However, there has been greater emphasis on research on ethnicity than on research on race, and the literature sometimes reveals gender biases.

The literature about ethnic and racial groups reflects hierarchies and stratifications in the society at large. White ethnic groups that are well represented in Canadian institutional structures (e.g., Jewish Canadians) have written about their groups, but research and writing about racial groups that are marginally represented in such structures remain more limited. Further, the literature by white ethnic groups has emphasized culture, language, and ethnic identity – issues relating to the maintenance of cultural identity. The literature produced by non-white groups shows a preoccupation with discrimination in employment and housing – issues relating to equality (Henry 1986, 7; Ubale 1977; Head 1975).

The emphasis on ethnicity rather than on race, particularly in the 1970s, also reflects disagreements among scholars about how to conceptualize race and ethnicity. In Canadian literature on ethnicity and immigration, 'ethnic' is frequently used to describe all groups except those of British and French origins. The word 'ethnic' is derived from the Greek root *ethnikos*, meaning 'national' – 'gentile' or 'foreign.' It can apply to any large group of people who share racial, national, tribal, religious, linguistic, or cultural origins or backgrounds. On this definition all Canadians are ethnic, including the French and the British, but the word usually implies a contrast to such historically dominant populations. In Canada the term 'charter groups' is used to distinguish French and English Canadians from all others. These distinctions imply a hierarchy and perpetuate existing power relationships. In everyday speech, the word 'ethnic' implies a lower status for the groups it is applied to. Linda Hutcheon notes that 'whether in its earlier associations with "pagan" and "heathen" or in its more recent ones with "foreign," the word "ethnic" always has to do with the social positioning of the "other" and is thus never free of relations of power and value' (Hutcheon and Richmond 1990, 2).

Some sociologists claim that race is just one aspect of ethnicity – that is, culture. Race can be defined by reference to phenotypical or genotypical traits (negroid, mongoloid, or caucasian). However, 'race' has also been applied to groups that share certain cultural characteristics, such as 'the French race' or 'the Jewish race.' Although races are typically defined on the basis of physical traits, the use of the term is not fixed by 'innate and immutable physical characteristics.' Physical appearance can be changed through surgery, and perception of physical differences is affected by cultural assumptions (Ujimoto 1990, 214). The difficulty in differentiating between definitions based on physical criteria and definitions based on cultural criteria further blurs the distinction between race and ethnicity.

Marxists have generally subordinated race to class, identifying class as the primary oppressor. Recently, however, they have begun to see racial oppression as an autonomous phenomenon rather than as an epiphenomenon of class (Stasiulis 1990, 270–81). But differences among scholars about how to conceptualize or theorize about race, added to the limited presence of members of diverse racial groups in Canadian academe, result in limited data about how race contributes to divisions in Canadian society (Henry 1986, 6–7).

Some racial groups have been more thoroughly studied than others because of the presence of scholars from those groups. Gordon Hirabayashi, a Japanese Canadian, has been writing on issues of Japanese Canadians in North America since the 1940s (Buchignani 1984, 5). Peter Li has written extensively on Chinese Canadians.[7] A lack of scholars from a particular group may lead to its relative neglect. Blacks are perhaps the least well represented group within academe. They have some visibility as subjects in studies of race relations and racism and in literary works, such as those of Austin Clarke.

There may be differences within a particular group as well. For example, within the Asian group, Chinese, Japanese, and South Asian immigrants have been more thoroughly studied than more recent arrivals like Koreans, Malaysians, and Vietnamese. Filipinas have gained some visibility in Canadian literature on ethnicity through the research of Anita Beltran Chen, herself a Filipina.[8]

An increase in literature on a particular group sometimes results from the exigencies of political circumstances. The sudden Indochinese migration of approximately 60,000 refugees in 1978–81 was identified as a public issue, and a great deal of literature on their settlement and adaptation emerged. But the interest may be short-lived. Buchignani notes: 'Academics, social service personnel, and government approached Indochinese settlement in a "problem mode" from the first and a considerable social problems literature on these groups arose very quickly ... Indochinese refugees are no longer "news" even though the present recession has made many of their social problems far worse than they were earlier; research activity on Indochinese social problems and social issues has similarly declined' (1984, 13).

Although scholars from ethnic and racial groups are frequently drawn to research about their own groups, not all of them are comfortable with writing about ethnicity (Mistry 1990, 259; Ondaatje 1990, 202; Padolsky 1990). They may prefer to identify more closely with the community of scholars and artists in their disciplines rather than being pigeonholed as 'ethnics' (Bissoondath 1992). Neil Bissoondath and Michael Ondaatje resist the label of 'ethnic writer' and the stereotyping that it implies. Such writers fear becoming marginalized or ghettoized and falling prey to tokenism.

DISCOURSE ABOUT WOMEN FROM ASIA, AFRICA, AND THE CARIBBEAN, POST-1970s

Canadian discourse about women from Asia, Africa, and the Caribbean has evolved through several stages. Prior to the 1970s, studies on immigration emphasized the experiences of males. The power to include males and to exclude females belonged in the first instance to males and, with developments in the Canadian women's movement, extended to middle-class, white women. Women were discussed in studies of the family and community in different racial groups. But the studies often overlooked the significant contributions made by women to the physical and material survival of the family. In the post-1970s, the paid work of southern European women and women from Third World countries has been studied, particularly in the garment industry and domestic work.[9] The literature about women from Asia, Africa, and the Caribbean has emphasized their vulnerabilities and characterized them as 'victims.'[10] Now women from Asia, Africa, and the Caribbean have begun documenting their own histories, sometimes disputing the analyses of other researchers. Their work represents their desire to become active, participating subjects of their own history.

Gender is excluded from studies of the early history of Asians and blacks in Canada. These histories emphasize the racial oppression that they experienced in Canada. They document both institutional or systemic racism, such as that of Canadian immigration policies, and individual acts of racism at work or in a variety of social settings. There are several accounts of the racism experienced by the Asians in British Columbia in the early 1900s as well as specific accounts of the experiences of the Chinese, Japanese, and South Asians in various parts of Canada throughout this century (Adachi 1976; Johnston 1979; Con et al. 1982; Chan 1983; Roy 1989a, 1989b; Ward 1989). Women do not feature prominently in these accounts partly because racism prevented their entry in any significant numbers into Canada prior to the 1960s. (Males were stereotyped as cheap labour, which allowed them to enter Canada.) The experiences of blacks have been documented by Robin Winks (1971), but his 500-page *The Blacks in Canada* has only scattered references to the experiences of women, and Frances Henry's *Forgotten Canadians: The Blacks of Nova Scotia* (1973) discusses racial discrimination, but there is no reference to gender.

In the literature on racial groups, women are frequently stereotyped in the traditional female roles of maintaining the family and preserving the cultural traditions of the group. This view is particularly evident in master's and doctoral dissertations on South Asian women written prior to the 1970s. Similar biases show up in later works as well. For example, Norman Buchignani's 1987 survey of research on South Asians in Canada discusses women under headings 'Social Psychological and Individual Level Adaptation' and 'Family Organization and Family Level Adaptation.' Women are absent from discussions of community organizations, immigration, and migration, all of which are discussed in a gender-neutral terms. Such absences perpetuate stereotypical images of women from Asia, Africa, and the Caribbean as dependants who passively follow male immigrants to Canada and, once there, are confined to the home, family, and ethnic community. Women are not perceived as significant actors in the migration process or in the family's survival.

Women from Asia, Africa, and the Caribbean gained some recognition as subjects of research and analysis with the growing awareness among scholars of gender, race, and class biases in knowledge emanating from different disciplines. Awareness of gender as a significant analytical concept has resulted in women's experiences being included in accounts of ethnic and racial groups (Li 1988a, 1990; Oiwa 1991; Yee 1988). The integrated nature of gender, race, and class oppression created a need to document specific accounts of women from Asia, Africa, and the Caribbean. Consequently, more literature has emerged on women from Asia, Africa, and the Caribbean.

A large proportion of this literature exhibits a liberal perspective. It has been sponsored by a variety of government and social service agencies which require information about women from Asia, Africa, and the Caribbean in order to identify problems, eliminate biases, and develop public policy (Estable 1986; Seward and McDade 1988; Boyd 1989; Chan 1989; Go 1987; A. Papp 1990). Such writings document the particular circumstances of groups of women and argue for the need for culturally specific services or organizations.[11]

A much smaller part of the literature on women from Asia, Africa, and the Caribbean is socialist-feminist. It is also supported by state agencies but, since the mandate of academic research funding agencies is different, it can pursue a broader range of issues and take a more critical stance on the oppressiveness of race, class, and gender in Canadian society. This literature has followed developments in feminist theory. For example, South Asian women initially identified gender as oppressive and later showed how race intensified and aggravated their problems (Naidoo 1980; Ghosh 1981). They now see race, class, and gender as experienced together (Bannerji 1987; Naidoo 1990; Agnew 1991; Dhruvarajan 1991; Sheth and Handa 1991). Women from the Caribbean have documented how race and gender construct their identity and how they have been stereotyped as only domestic workers (Silvera 1983). Women of Chinese and Japanese origin have described their experiences in terms of isolation, exclusion, and racial oppression (Kogawa 1981; Sunahara 1981; Nipp 1983; Yee 1987).

The literature on women from Asia, Africa, and the Caribbean often treats them as victims rather than as active agents struggling to change the conditions of their lives. The initial aim of this literature was to compare the experiences of women from Asia, Africa, and the Caribbean to those of white Canadian women. Women from Asia, Africa, and the Caribbean documented the discrimination they experienced by collecting testimonials about the conditions of their lives (Khosla 1983; Brand and Bhaggiyadatta 1986). For example, Makeda Silvera's *Silenced* (1983) collected stories about the experiences of domestic workers from the Caribbean who were exploited by their white female employers. Other studies have documented the exploitative conditions of Third World and southern European women working in the garment industry.

There is little literature on women from Asia, Africa, and the Caribbean who came to Canada as refugees (Spencer-Nimmons and Wong 1989). Women from Vietnam, particularly those referred to as 'boat people,' are sometimes described as being victims of sexual abuse and rape (Grant 1979). Women from Somalia are described as victims of rape and torture.[12]

The literature on women from Asia, Africa, and the Caribbean documents the constraints they experience in the labour force: limited marketable skills, lack of proficiency in English, and devaluation of their work experience or educational qualifications from their countries of origin (Estable 1986; Seward and McDade 1988; Boyd 1986, 1989). Gender-related issues such as lack of day care and the relegation of family responsibilities to women are also discussed. Invariably, there is some mention of the ways in which culture-specific gender norms may create additional difficulties for these groups of women (Chan 1989; South East Asian Services 1992; A. Papp 1990; Paredes 1987). The aim of most of this literature is to make a case for allocating resources to English-language classes, training in job-related skills, ethno-specific social services, and women's shelters. Sometimes it argues for allocating funds to organize women politically, as in the case of the National Organization of Immigrant and Visible-Minority Women. The attempt to initiate social policies requires documentation of the oppressiveness of race, class, and gender for the most disadvantaged among the group, such as those who have limited job-related skills and knowledge of the English language. Thus, only a particular segment of the entire group gains some visibility in this literature. All women from Asia, Africa, and the Caribbean are stereotyped on the basis of problems encountered by some of them.

The invisibility of middle-class women in accounts of women from Asia, Africa, and the Caribbean reinforces the stereotype of these women as victims. But middle-class women from Asia, Africa, and the Caribbean have made the transition from their country of origin to Canada without help from social service agencies, and they tend to be the most vocal critics of the race and gender biases embedded in institutional structures. As counsellors, social workers, community activists, and volunteers within a variety of organizations, they are viewed as representatives of their racial groups. They are thus drawn into a common struggle against racism and sexism on behalf of themselves and their working-class sisters.

Documentation of the experiences of women from Asia, Africa, and the Caribbean has played a valuable role in eliminating many of the biases against them. For example, documentation of sexist biases led to the elimination of discriminatory immigration policies that reinforced the dependent status of women. Revelations of the 'double-day' gave the lie to the assumption that women were confined to the home, family, and ethnic community, and led to changes in regulations governing access to English-language training and skill-upgrading programs. Similarly, documenting the experience of women from Asia, Africa, and the Caribbean in the labour force created an awareness of their exploitation and led to the creation of community groups and organizations to provide employment counselling and other services. Revelation of cultural and language barriers in shelters for victims of violence led to a separate shelter for women from Third World and southern European countries.[13]

THE STRUGGLE TO NAME AND DEFINE WOMEN

Feminist theory is now moving slowly away from emphasizing the victimization of women to focusing on their self-empowerment. Black feminists in the United States are particularly wary of being portrayed as victims, and their scholarship now indicates how women have used their exploitative and oppressive situations to achieve some dignity and self-esteem (Dill 1988; Rollins 1985). In Canada, women from Asia, Africa, and the Caribbean are engaged in many struggles to overthrow domination by males and white, middle-class women. These struggles have not been widely documented.

The struggles of women from Asia, Africa, and the Caribbean give priority to racial politics over gender politics. In formal and informal meetings, women from Asia, Africa, and the Caribbean are more inclined to discuss racism than sexism. Racial stereotypes are the butt of their jokes, which reveal the underlying tensions and resentments shared by the women. Women from the Caribbean and the Philippines are sensitive to the stereotype that characterizes all of them as domestics. Asian women resent the stereotype of passivity and references to their culture that imply that it victimizes them. The camaraderie and self-awareness that their meetings generate have enabled these women to come together and engage in common struggles. But there are differences among them in defining and naming their oppressions and in determining strategies to overcome them.

One of the issues concerning women from Asia, Africa, and the Caribbean involves the category itself. Its significance was brought out at conferences where I presented papers on various aspects of the experiences of women from Asia, Africa, and the Caribbean. Invariably, regardless of the issues addressed in my papers, discussion centred on definitions. There was heated debate on how these women were to be defined and by whom. Did these women share common characteristics that would justify grouping them together? Did the category include both whites and non-whites, middle-class and working-class women? Did it apply only to immigrants or to their Canadian-born offspring as well? No consensus over the appropriateness of any term has yet emerged. The underlying issue was the oppressiveness of race and class. But women who proposed and debated alternative definitions, names, or labels were asserting their prerogative in assigning significance to differences that they considered important aspects of their identity and politics.

Albert Memmi has argued that at various points society categorizes some people as different by highlighting specific characteristics. Audre Lorde has noted that it is the social significance attached to these differences, rather than the differences themselves, that forms the basis of exclusion and separation; it is historically created social differences that divide women and distort the relations between them (Rothenberg 1990, 42, 54). Women from Asia, Africa, and the Caribbean have attempted to describe themselves in their own terms and to redefine the differences between themselves and 'Canadian women' as part of their struggle to be subjects in their own history. They have documented how race, class, and gender oppress them and how they have struggled to overcome their victimization in a race-, class- and gender-biased society. Through such representations, women from Asia, Africa, and the Caribbean have attempted to transform their image from passive victims to individuals who exercise agency. They have disputed their location as the 'other' or 'at the margins' of feminist discourse by questioning what constitutes the centre. Such debates reveal the power structures of society and social hierarchies of race and culture. Challenging these categories enables women from Asia, Africa, and the Caribbean to assert the totality of their experience, which includes both domination and resistance to it.

Power relations are embedded in terminology, and terminology reflects social and political realities, influences perception, and determines the material and social reality of individuals and groups. Women who are not part of the dominant white society are described as 'visible-minority women,' 'women of colour,' 'black women,' 'racial minority women,' 'non-white women,' 'immigrant women,' and 'Third World women.' All these terms refer to women who come from Asia, Africa, and the Caribbean, or to women who trace their origins to Asia, Africa, and the Caribbean (second or third generations). Most of these terms are found in Canadian sociological and feminist literature in the postwar period. Some have been in use for a long time; others are new. 'Visible-minority women' has been replaced by 'immigrant women,' which has been challenged in turn. Some of the terms may obscure the race and class of the women to which they are applied, but all imply the separation of these women from the white, middle-class norm. The debate on terminology has several themes: authorship, specific history, struggle, otherness, marginality, and difference. What constitutes difference and who decides what is different?

Women are concerned about their identity and wish to name themselves. 'Our subjectivity and our identity are intimately linked – they do not exist outside of or prior to language and representation but are actually brought into play by discursive strategies and representational practices' (Martin 1988, 9). However, it is not just the identity imposed by these terms that is being challenged but also the political or social relationships that such terms encode and attempt to obfuscate. Analysing these terms exposes the power relations embedded in them and suggests strategies for resistance and struggle.

The term 'visible-minority women' is criticized because the criteria of visibility are vague and ill-defined. 'Visible-minority women' refers to perceptible qualities that are taken to indicate race. As Himani Bannerji notes, the category marks people as 'not only being different, but also inferior or inadequate' (1986, 27–9). Glenda Simms objects to the word 'minority' in this phrase because it implies a disadvantaged status. Disadvantages can be socioeconomic, political, or psychological, and all human beings have some disadvantages. It is invidious to try to differentiate among women on the basis of judgments about who is more disadvantaged (47–8). Linda Carty and Dionne Brand argue that 'visible-minority women' is a state-imposed category. They reject the categorization as apolitical and ahistorical, 'devoid of any recognition ... of class struggle or struggle against racism' (1989, 39).

The term 'women of colour' has gained wide popularity among feminists. It was intended to include both 'black women,' in recognition of their history as slaves, and other women of colour who share a common history of colonialism and imperialism. The term implies a unity among non-white women and can therefore be interpreted politically as a reaction to white supremacy and racism (Kline 1989b, 50). However, this term categorizes under one label people with varied histories, traditions, and struggles, and it appears to some to deny their identity and uniqueness. In Britain, the term 'black women' is used politically to symbolize the solidarity of all non-white people. But women from Asia resist this term when it is applied to themselves because of the more negative connotations associated with the term 'black.'

Most of these terms posit white women as the norm and the rest as 'other.' The concept of the 'other' is part of a binary opposition that not only makes one different but places one lower in a hierarchy. Yet 'non-white' is preferred by some precisely because it highlights race as a principle of social organization.

The term 'Third World women' imposes a homogeneity among women who are separated from each other by different geographical locations, different histories of colonialism and imperialism, and different class memberships, religions, political affiliations, and attitudes towards feminism. Some have migrated, permanently or for brief periods, to Europe and North America. There can be no common identity with such a wide range of differences. The expression 'Third World' encodes the poverty and 'underdevelopment' of certain countries, with only a faint suggestion of the 'First World' sources of these conditions. Chandra Mohanty notes that the use of the term 'oppressed Third World women' by white feminists codifies their paternalistic attitudes towards Third World women. Such attitudes produce an image of Third World women as 'religious (read "not progressive"), family-oriented (read "traditional"), legal minors (read "they-are-still-not-conscious-of-their-rights"), illiterate (read "ignorant"), domestic (read "backward") and sometimes revolutionary' (Mohanty 1989, 65).

Some terms have more subtle implications. For example, 'racial-minority women' suggests inferiority in much the same way as the condescending term 'disadvantaged,' a euphemism for 'poor.' The term 'women from Asia, Africa, and the Caribbean' can be criticized for similar reasons but it is used here to focus on the women's racial identities and the common location that gives their struggles some coherence and unity.

A CASE STUDY OF THE TERM 'IMMIGRANT WOMEN'

The term 'immigrant women' has recently gained popularity for its supposed neutrality and objectivity. However, the term 'immigrant' has a history that is embedded in the power relations of society. It has been used selectively to refer to some immigrants and not to others. The racial or ethnic identity of the groups so labelled has varied at different periods of time, but it has usually been a pejorative term.

Technically, the word 'immigrant' refers to a person who was born outside the country and lives in Canada as a permanent resident. The word is most commonly used in this way in statistical data produced by governmental agencies such as the Department of Immigration or Statistics Canada. But the word 'immigrant' was used in the late nineteenth century and the early part of the twentieth century to refer specifically to European ('Continental') immigrants. It was seldom applied to newcomers from Britain. 'Immigrant' was not the only term used in this way. In Ontario in the early 1900s the words 'foreigner,' 'newcomer,' and 'non–Anglo-Saxon' were commonly used derogatorily to refer to groups of people such as Jews from eastern Europe, Catholic Italians, and orthodox Macedonians (Harney 1981, 3). Suffragettes adopted the word 'immigrant' to contrast 'untutored' and 'unlettered' European males to 'Canadian' women in an attempt to use fear of the erosion of race and class privilege in order to win support for white women's suffrage (Valverde 1991a).

Class and race privilege gave certain white women the status of 'Canadian women.' In Sylvia Van Kirk's *Many Tender Ties,* women who immigrated from Europe or Britain to western Canada are called 'white women' or 'British women,' and aboriginal women are called 'native women.' The book is one of the early accounts of Canadian women's history and attempts to document the role of women in the early fur trade. It examines changing racial attitudes in western Canada in the late eighteenth and nineteenth centuries. When white women settled in this society, aboriginal women – who had previously been accepted by white men – were disdained, and mixed-blood women were treated as outcasts from 'civilized society': 'A direct relationship can be traced between the growth of racial prejudice and the arrival of white women on the scene ... White women showed little inclination to approach their native sisters in terms of equality or friendship. In addition to feeling racially and morally superior to native women, British women expressed an active hostility toward "squaws" because they feared competition for white husbands' (Van Kirk 1980, 201). This fear resulted from the women's complete dependence on marriage and motherhood. Over a period of time, distinctions increased between British women and aboriginal women. Women of mixed blood who were the wives or daughters of the male British élite attempted to assimilate British norms and attempted to 'pass' by hiding their mixed ancestry (Van Kirk 1980, 201–42, esp. 234–7). The designation 'Canadian women' did not apply to the aboriginal women even if they were wives or daughters of men of the emerging ruling class in Canada. Marriage 'à la façon du pays' was regarded as legal and binding by the courts in 1867, but that status was overturned in a case in 1886 (240–1).

British women in Canada were the norm against whom all others were measured. It did not matter whether the women came to Canada for brief periods of time or became permanent residents. For example, the upper-class, British-born women in Marian Fowler's *The Embroidered Tent: Five Gentlewomen in Early Canada* (1982) are described as 'Canada's most representative ancestors' and as 'leading 19th century women who made Canada their own.' But Catharine Parr Traill, Susanna Moodie, Anna Jameson, Elizabeth Simcoe, and Lady Dufferin were certainly not representative of French-Canadian, aboriginal, Ukrainian, or working-class Canadian women.

Single British women who came to Canada in the early 1900s to work as domestics were identified by scholars and government officials as immigrant women, but 'immigrant' was not used to designate them as inferior (Barber 1985). Women from Britain were helped by organizations of upper-class Canadian women (referred to as 'ladies') who wanted to 'participate in the work of nation building' (Roberts 1990). Domestic workers who immigrated from the Caribbean and the Philippines in the 1970s and 1980s were not described as engaged in nation building (Calliste 1989).

Roxana Ng notes that 'immigrant women' is a socially constructed category. And her research shows that their locations in the job market are determined by the process of documentation – the process through which women from Asia or Latin America register at a community-based, non-profit employment agency, receive counselling, and find work. Counsellors describe women from Asia and Latin America in terms required by potential employers, which become the categories on the registration form. The process first transforms 'women from Asia and Latin America' into 'immigrant women.' Then it assigns them to a particular stratum of the labour force. Roxana Ng compares this process to the production of a commodity (Ng 1986, 1988a).

The term 'immigrant women' is now commonly used to refer to women from southern European and Third World countries. It is used to label women who do not speak English fluently and who are employed in jobs that require limited skills, such as assembly-line factory work, janitorial services, home-based sewing work, and domestic employment. However, the term 'immigrant' does not apply to second- and third-generation women from Third World countries, so some service agencies and women's organizations also use the term 'visible minority.' These agencies and organizations represent working-class women, but middle-class women assume the organizational and administrative roles. They are the members of the boards, the spokeswomen, and the community workers and counsellors.

The struggle of women from Asia, Africa, and the Caribbean to name and define themselves is revealed by the controversy surrounding the publication of a report in 1988 on 'immigrant women,' which had been commissioned by the Canadian Advisory Council on the Status of Women and written by Shirley Seward and Kathryn McDade of the Institute for Research on Public Policy. The report used a legal (literal) definition of an 'immigrant woman' and interpreted Canadian census data from that perspective. Using the category of 'foreign-born' from the census, they concluded that, 'as a group, immigrant women are doing relatively well. They are, for example, somewhat better represented in managerial and professional occupations than Canadian-born women. And, on average, immigrant women have higher incomes and lower unemployment rates than Canadian-born women.' The report warned, however, that its averages were 'very misleading, given the great heterogeneity which characterizes the female immigrant population.'

'Immigrant women's' groups were enraged by the conclusions of the report, despite its qualifying sentence. Carmencita Hernandez, Ontario vice-president of the National Organization of Immigrant and Visible-Minority Women, complained about 'sweeping generalizations and interpretations of statistics' in the report. She noted that the report failed to: 'highlight that since 1975 most immigrants came from Asia and other Third World countries. Immigrant women were all lumped into one category, ignoring the fact that real life experiences of an immigrant woman from Asia or the Caribbean are different from those of an immigrant woman from the United States or United Kingdom' (1988).

Despite the importance of racism for immigrant women, the report did not specifically deal with this topic. At a press conference (8 Feb. 1988), community groups of women from Asia, Africa, and the Caribbean stated: 'For us, systemic racism is an integral part of every barrier we encounter – be it language-training programs, credential evaluations, in education or health care and social service delivery. An analysis of barriers immigrant and visible-minority women face, out of the context of racial discrimination in this society, is analogous to an analysis of Charter-related issues without examining the Charter.' The organizations representing women from Asia, Africa, and the Caribbean particularly feared the impact of the report on public policy and programs affecting their members. Some noted that the report was a 'dangerous tool' which the government might use in setting policies, while others argued that the report would provide a perfect excuse for the government not to initiate any policies to improve the employment of immigrant women or to take action on employment equity.

The failure of the authors of the report or members of the advisory committee to consult with 'immigrant and visible-minority women's groups' was widely interpreted as an insult. These groups were invited for consultation on the day the report was to be publicly released, but 2,000 copies had already been distributed (*Toronto Star*, 9 Feb. 1988). A number of organizations representing immigrant and visible-minority women then came together to denounce the report. These groups included the National Organization of Immigrant and Visible-Minority Women, the Congress of Black Women, the United Council of Filipino Associations of Canada, the Women's Committee of the Canadian Ethno-Cultural Council, the Chinese Canadian National Council, Women Working with Immigrant Women, and Intercede. The controversy provided a forum for voicing resentments and airing grievances. By demanding their right to be consulted and challenging the conclusions of the report, spokeswomen for these organizations served notice that they wished to participate fully in any discussions and would not allow others – males or middle-class, white females – to make decisions about them. Although the organizations were not able to have the report withdrawn, the federal government appointed a black woman, Glenda Simms, as president of the Canadian Advisory Council on the Status of Women.

Knowledge about women from Asia, Africa, and the Caribbean is embedded in the power relations of society. In the 1970s, ethnic and racial groups noted their exclusion from, or marginalization in, research on Canadian history. The Royal Commission on Bilingualism and Biculturalism provided racial and ethnic groups with an opportunity to assert their stake in the debates about Canada's future social, economic, and political goals. The recognition of ethnic groups as a 'third force' in Canadian society enabled them to document their histories from their own perspectives. However, women remained invisible in most of this literature.

Discourse on women from Asia, Africa, and the Caribbean has been informed by the politics of gender and race. A large proportion of this literature is intended to give information to state agencies and make a case for the allocation of resources to these women; consequently, it emphasizes their victimization. Disputes over this literature indicate how women from Asia, Africa, and the Caribbean are increasingly challenging and questioning the categories used by males or by middle-class, white females to describe them. Such discussion reveals not only that women are oppressed by race, class, and gender but also that they are struggling to resist these oppressions.

6

Systemic Racism

During the 1960s, following changes in Canadian immigration policies, women from Asia, Africa, and the Caribbean were among the large numbers of immigrants from Third World countries who began arriving in Canada. Their arrival coincided with the re-emergence of the women's movement as a major political force, when women's organizations began demanding legal reforms and social changes to ensure more justice and equality for women. In the late 1970s and early 1980s, these women from Asia, Africa, and the Caribbean would join second-generation women from Third World countries in criticizing the biases of feminist theories and practices.

Ironically, new immigration policies in 1962, which aimed at removing racial biases that had plagued earlier immigration policies, applied 'universal,' or 'objective' standards to all potential immigrants regardless of nationality and country of origin, while the women's movement focused on gender as the source of women's oppression and largely ignored class and race biases.

An analysis of the report of the Royal Commission on the Status of Women (1970) and the research studies it initiated reveals the prevalent attitudes towards racialized populations. The appearance of 'everyday racism' in progressive discourses like these reveals the difficulties of overcoming the racial biases of society. Deeply entrenched racist notions often prevent us from seeing that state-initiated programs for the settlement and adaptation of new immigrants fail to reach certain women or fail to meet their needs. Some people argue that the culture of immigrant women creates 'problems' and overlook the systemic biases of society that are the obstacles to their integration and settlement.

This chapter analyses the race and class biases of past immigration policies and the values and norms of white Canadian society that are revealed in the report of the Royal Commission.

IMMIGRATION POLICIES: RACE AND CLASS BIASES

Canadian immigration policies throughout this century have always reflected a conflict between desires to increase the population and fears of 'the impact of immigration on Canadian ways and on the ethnocultural and racial composition of the country' (Harney 1988, 52). The state consults with a number of interested groups, such as businesses, trade unions, and advocacy groups, each with priorities of its own. It responds to public sentiments, often garnered through the media, on 'questions of ethnic and linguistic change, the impact of immigrants on jobs, [and] national humanitarian obligations' (Simmons and Keohane 1992, 444). In attempting to strike a balance between the different contending forces, however, immigration policy leaves some groups dissatisfied and exposes itself to continuing criticism for class, race, and gender biases.

The racial biases of immigration policies prior to 1962 have been widely documented in the literature on immigrants (Roy 1989a; Ward 1978, 1989; Li 1988a; Bolaria and Li 1988; Harney 1988). After 1962, Canadian immigration policy was informed by a desire to reunite families and by humanitarianism, particularly towards people who were fleeing persecution, and thus explicit racist biases disappeared from legislation governing immigration. The elimination of racism was morally right, but it was also motivated by a concern to provide skilled and professional labour for the Canadian economy.[1] Special programs, such as the entrepreneur and investor programs that attracted many immigrants from Hong Kong, showed a desire to bring international capital to Canada. Robert Harney argues that, despite the changes, immigration policy still assumes that 'immigrants should not only fit into the economy but also into the ethnic and racial needs of the country' (1988, 58).

Immigration regulations and their implementation showed some gender biases as well, such as the practice of designating the male as the head of the household. Such practices categorized females as 'dependent spouses,' and thus denied them access to language-training programs, exposed them to threat of deportation (along with the deported spouse), and sometimes denied them welfare (Boyd 1986, 49–50; Ng 1988b, 185–9). The Domestic Movement Program, and programs which preceded it, attracted a large proportion of women from the Caribbean and the Philippines. But these programs showed class and race biases (Daenzer 1991).

Prior to the Second World War, immigration policies had demonstrated racial biases by categorizing some countries as 'preferred nations' and 'traditional sources' and by describing their nationals as coming from the 'right stock.' The regulations explicitly denied entry to immigrants from Asia and Africa (Elliott and Fleras 1990; Harney 1988). Officials argued that immigrants from vastly different cultures had difficulty in assimilating to Canadian norms or in adapting to the Canadian climate (Baureiss 1987, 17–19).

Racial biases against immigrants from Third World countries were reiterated in 1947 by Prime Minister Mackenzie King in his well-known statement on immigration. In it he reaffirmed his government's commitment to ensuring the growth of Canada's population through increased immigration, but he also said that immigration to Canada was not a 'fundamental right' of outsiders but a 'privilege' that Canadians could selectively extend to others of their own choosing. He added:

The people of Canada do not wish to make a fundamental alteration in the character of their population through mass immigration. The government is therefore opposed to 'large-scale immigration from the Orient,' which would certainly give rise to social and economic problems, which might lead to serious international difficulties. The government has no intention of changing the regulations governing Asiatic immigration 'unless and until alternative measures of effective control have been worked out.' (Quoted in Hawkins 1988, 92–3)

The newly independent nations of Asia and Africa were sensitive about their status in the recently created Commonwealth of Nations and had to be appeased. The Canadian government reached agreements with some countries to establish a small quota for their immigrants. In 1951 a quota of 150 immigrants annually was established for India, and was increased to 300 in 1957. In 1952 similar arrangements were made with Pakistan and Ceylon (now Sri Lanka), which allowed each country a quota of fifty immigrants annually (Green 1976, 31). However, these quotas were not always filled (Richmond 1967, 11). In 1951 the government allowed a small number of immigrants from the Caribbean to be admitted either because of 'exceptional merit (i.e., professional and skilled)' or 'on humanitarian grounds and by executive direction.' And in 1955 the Domestic Scheme enabled some women from Jamaica and

Barbados to enter Canada as well (Calliste 1989, 140–41; Richmond 1967, 13). After the repeal of the Chinese Immigration Act in 1947, spouses of Chinese immigrants in Canada and unmarried children under the age of twenty-one were admitted (Li 1988a, 90).

Racism was articulated in the Immigration Act of 1953 by coded references to racial preferences. Some groups were limited or prohibited on the following grounds:

(i) nationality, citizenship, ethnic group, occupation, class or geographical area of origin;
(ii) peculiar customs, habits, modes of life or methods of holding property;
(iii) unsuitability, having regard to the climatic, economic, social, industrial, educational, labour, health or other conditions or requirements existing temporarily or otherwise, in Canada or in the area or country from or through which such persons come to Canada; or
(iv) probable inability to become readily assimilated or to assume the duties and responsibilities of Canadian citizenship within a reasonable time after their admission. (Quoted in Hawkins 1988, 102–5)

The act avoided terms like the 'suitability of stock' which would offend the United Nations Charter (Harney 1988, 60), but the act was declared invalid in 1956 by the Supreme Court of Canada for 'giving imprecise powers to junior officials.' The amended act in 1956 enumerated the countries from which people would be allowed into Canada (Richmond 1967, 11–12; Hawkins 1988, 103–5). Asian, Caribbean, and African countries (with the exception of Egypt) were not included.

During the 1960s, immigration policy aimed to meet two different sets of objectives. On the one hand, there was the demand of the labour market for 'professional, skilled, and service workers,' who could be 'absorbed in almost unlimited numbers' by the Canadian economy (Green 1976, 35). On the other hand, there was the demand by immigrants already in Canada (e.g., Italians, Ukrainians, and Jewish groups) to be reunited with their relatives by sponsoring them for admission. But many of these sponsored relatives had limited skills and education, and 'there was a decreasing demand for unskilled persons' (Green 1976, 34–42; Hawkins, 1988 139–60).

The immigration regulations introduced in 1962 were guided by other considerations as well. The massive 'reconstruction of Europe and Asia, major political realignments and new regional conflicts, large-scale population displacements and growing numbers of refugees made it increasingly apparent that Canada's traditional selective immigration policies, based on ethnic/racial and cultural suitability criteria, were too outmoded and morally indefensible for Canada to retain' (Kalbach 1990, 25).

Freda Hawkins argues that the motivation to introduce a non-racist policy came from within the Department of Immigration itself; it was 'primarily based on the enlightened vision of senior immigration ministry bureaucrats' and was not the 'result of Parliamentary or popular demand' (quoted in K.W. Taylor 1991, 4). But others have argued that the Canadian government was hard-pressed to meet the demands for a professional and skilled workforce from 'traditional sources' when prosperity was keeping the European population at home (Simmons 1990, 147). Ethnic and racial groups lobbied hard for the introduction of new legislation, and pressure from international agencies, such as the United Nations and the International Labour Organization, forced Canada to remove racist criteria from its selection policies (K.W. Taylor 1991, 4).

The immigration regulations introduced in 1962 by the Conservative government proposed to treat all immigrants alike by removing references to race and nationality. The regulations emphasized education, training, and skills as the main conditions for entry into Canada. The 'new regulations meant that any suitably qualified person, from any part of the world, could be considered for immigration to Canada entirely on ... merit, without regard to ... race, colour, national origin, or the country from which [the person] came' (Richmond 1967, 17). In 1967 these regulations were legislated into the point system which established objective assessment criteria for the admission of immigrants. Points were assigned for education and training, occupational demand, skill, age, knowledge of English or French, arranged employment, employment opportunities in the area of destination, and relatives in Canada. But some points were to be assigned 'on the basis of the immigration officer's assessment of the applicant's adaptability, motivation, initiative and other similar qualities' (Green 1976, 41).

The 1967 regulations created three groups of immigrants: family, independent (selected workers), and refugees (Green 1976, 41–2). The 1962 regulations had treated immigrants from Asia and Africa (excluding Egypt) differently by limiting their rights to sponsor relatives, but the 1967 regulations eliminated this remaining bias as well (Richmond 1967, 14–17; Hawkins 1988, 121–6). Immigration regulations of 1962 and 1967 were incorporated into the Immigration Act of 1976.

The act of 1976 reaffirmed that the purpose of immigration was to 'foster the development of a strong and viable economy and the prosperity of all regions in Canada' (Cannon 1989, 42). For the first time, the principles underlying immigration policy were explicitly noted: 'non-discrimination, family reunification, humanitarian concern for refugees, and the promotion of Canada's social, economic, demographic, and cultural goals.'[2] The act provided for annual forecasts of the number of immigrants to be admitted and linked immigration flows more directly to labour-market requirements. It expanded the family class and the independent worker category to include business immigrants, such as investors and entrepreneurs (Canada, Employment and Immigration, 1989, 3–13).

The policy encouraged the immigration of skilled and professional people to Canada and led to allegations of a 'brain drain.' B. Singh Bolaria and Peter Li argue that after the Second World War Canada was transformed into an advanced industrial country and needed a highly skilled labour force for capitalist expansion and accumulation. To meet this demand, throughout the 1960s and 1970s Canada allowed for the entry of professionals, particularly in the fields of education and medicine. They argue further that the brain drain enabled advanced capitalist countries like Canada to tap the global reserve of professional labour at the expense of Third World countries (1988, 207).

Opinion is divided on whether racism was eliminated from immigration policies by the regulations of 1962 and 1967. Freda Hawkins and Alan Green claim that the new legislation wiped away racist discrimination, and the white-Canada policy was virtually dead. But, while the explicit racist criteria were eliminated, racism persisted in the discretion exercised by immigration officers. The fifteen points allocated at the discretion of the immigration officer could be withheld because of racial or gender biases, thereby denying entry to some applicants.[3]

Hawkins visited several overseas offices in 1966 and found that immigration officers showed some preference for British immigrants because of their 'greater familiarity with British norms.' They preferred northern Europeans because of their higher education and 'verifiable skills or professional training.' Immigration officers were handicapped in their assessment of individuals from southern European countries, particularly Italy, because of the applicants' lower education and their limited facility with the English language (Hawkins 1988, 280–1).

Administrative measures, such as the allocation of officers and the size of the office overseas, can affect the flow of immigration. In 1964 the Department of Citizenship had thirty-two offices in twenty-one countries. Seventeen offices were in Europe (six in Britain). There was no permanent office in Central or South America, and only one in Delhi serving the entire Indian subcontinent. In 1966 the White Paper on Immigration noted that 'new offices have been opened in countries which traditionally have contributed large numbers of immigrants to Canada and also in some not previously served directly' (quoted in Richmond 1967, 18–20). K.W. Taylor argues that by 1973 the percentage of immigrants from European and non-European countries corresponded exactly with the 'proportion of immigration officers working in European cities' (1991, 10). Based on these facts, he concludes that the 'immigration bureaucracy now operate[s] as an egalitarian admission agency selecting applicants from all origins on the same occupational and educational criteria' (1991, 1; see also Canada, House of Commons, 1984, 59).

Taylor's tabulation compares the numbers of applicants that are processed in different parts of the world but does not compare the total numbers of applications made in each office or the time required between application and decision, which indirectly controls the flow of immigration. While the number of applications is the same in India and the United States, there is only one office in India (versus twelve in the United States), and it takes 150 days to process an application in New York (versus 286 days in New Delhi) (Malarek 1987, 253–4).

Gunter Baureiss observes that, although 'today's immigration policies are not outright discriminatory, they are selective with regard to the "fit" of the immigrant into the social and/or economic structure' (1987, 20). Despite changes in immigration policies, biases persist. Robert Harney observes:

Over time, the use of language has become circumspect. 'Founding nations' replaces 'founding races' as a label for the French and British. Immigrants are categorized by their assimilability or place within a multicultural mosaic rather than in terms of their 'stock.' Interethnic and interracial antagonisms are given the pseudodistance of social science. Immigrants from certain groups are not undesirable because of their distance from the racial and cultural core but because of the impact they may have on those already in Canada, those 'somewhat nervous about rapid ethnic change.' (1988, 55)

Immigration policies have changed the source countries of immigrants from Europe to the Third World. But the overall impact on Canadian population is not very significant. In 1986 visible minorities (i.e.,

'people who are identifiably non-white and/or non-Caucasian') num-
bered 1.4 million, or 5.6 per cent, of the total population (Samuel 1990,
385). The trend towards increased migration from Third World countries could continue if Canada follows its traditional policy of supple-
menting its population growth through immigration. Although increasing population continues to make good sense, public opinion does
not always support it (Samuel 1990, 389; see also DuCharme 1986;
Malarek 1987). The Economic Council of Canada noted that increased
immigration would stimulate the Canadian economy but recommended
against it: 'Canadians must be aware that even if tolerance continues to
grow and the economy remains reasonably buoyant, the incidence of
ethnic friction may nevertheless increase. That is because, with more visible minority members in a given area, the opportunities for expression
of prejudice grow even if the average level of prejudice is declining'
(quoted in Foster 1991, 11–12). Discussions about how many immigrants
Canada needs and from where sometimes mask racist concerns (Harney
1988, 92). But a spokesman for one group put it plainly: 'we [European
descendants] must decide whether we want the Canada of the future to
be made up of our children or those of others' (Foster 1991, 12).

ADDITIONAL PROGRAMS FOR IMMIGRATION

Women from Asia, Africa, and the Caribbean have entered Canada as
independent immigrants or as spouses or children of independent
immigrants.[4] Some have come under special programs for domestic
workers, refugees, and entrepreneurs. The refugee program and the
entrepreneur and investor programs bring to Canada people with
diverse financial and personal resources. While the refugee program is
motivated by compassionate and humanitarian objectives, the entrepreneur and investor programs are designed to attract capital and create
jobs in Canada. In addition, the government has sometimes given
amnesty to illegal immigrants in Canada, enabling them to become permanent residents (landed immigrants). The immigrants who gain entry
through these different programs add to the diversity of women from
Asia, Africa, and the Caribbean.

    Canada has shown humanitarianism in accepting a number of refu-
gees, particularly when compared to some European countries (Malarek
1987, 81–99). Section 3(g) of the 1976 Immigration Act recognizes the
need to 'fulfil Canada's international obligations with respect to refugees and to uphold its humanitarian tradition with respect to the dis-

placed and the persecuted (quoted in Malarek 1987, 105–6). The act recognized refugees as a distinct category that is subject to a different set of evaluative criteria (Canada, Employment and Immigration, 1989, 10). The Canadian definition is based on the United Nations definition of a Convention Refugee, and states that a 'refugee' is a person who: 'by reason of a well-founded fear of persecution for reasons of race, religion, nationality, membership in a particular group or political opinion ... is outside the country of his nationality and is unable or, by reason of that fear, is unwilling to avail himself of the protection of that country, or (ii) not having a country of nationality, is outside the country of his former habitual residence and is unable or, by reason of that fear, is unwilling to return to that country, and (b) has not ceased to be a Convention Refugee by reasons such as voluntary repatriation (Canada, Employment and Immigration, 1989, 24–5).'[5]

In addition to Convention Refugees, individuals from 'refugee-like' situations could be granted entry for humanitarian reasons as designated classes (Canada, Employment and Immigration 1989, 10). Gender was not such a category, and some refugee boards refused to recognize the claims made by women based on gender persecution and violence. But some women successfully argued that their claims could be included under 'social group' and were granted refugee status on that basis. Other women were allowed to stay, on humanitarian grounds, after the intervention of human rights activists and at the discretion of the minister in charge of immigration (York 1993; Oziewicz 1993).[6] However, protests by women's groups led to new guidelines being issued to refugee boards in March 1993 to 'grant refugee status to women because they are women. In other words, gender may be used as a basis for defining persecution' (Valpy 1993).

Female refugees have come to Canada from several Third World countries; for example, South Asians came from Uganda in the 1970s, Vietnamese came in the mid-1970s, and Cantonese-speaking Chinese came from Indochina in 1979–80 (Malarek 1987, 101; Li 1988a, 91–2). Although 75 to 80 per cent of the world refugee population are females, more males than females apply and gain entry to Canada (National Action Committee 1987, 1).[7] In 1987, 11,564 males and 8,165 females entered as refugees. Of these, 9,017 males gained entry as heads of household, compared to 2,660 females (Spencer-Nimmons and Wong 1989, 45). These figures suggest that 'a series of systematic discriminatory practices occur in Canada's refugee determination system' (National Action Committee 1987, 2).

Refugees are assessed 'often but not always on social adaptability criteria identical to those for immigrants' (Simmons and Keohane 1992, 431). The Department of Immigration observes that its criterion is whether refugees 'can fit into a life here, whether they can adjust. And obviously that is going to be easier for someone who's educated, who can speak English, and has some sort of training, than for an illiterate rice-farmer.' As Monica Boyd (1989) points out in her discussion of female immigrants, since males generally have better educational qualifications and more job training, individuals may voluntarily choose to have the male act as principal applicant. But the point system, which favours educated and skilled individuals, automatically excludes female heads of families, who predominate in refugee camps.[8] Such biases have generated criticism that Canada's refugee selection method is driven by labour market considerations and Canadians are alleged to have 'skim[med] the cream from refugee camps' (Grant 1979, 175; also Malarek 1987; Whitaker 1987).

Regulations have been based on the assumption that refugees would be selected in camps abroad and that Canada would not be a 'point of first entry' or 'country of first asylum.' But since the early 1980s some people have been claiming refugee status after their arrival in Canada; the number of these claims increased from 1,600 in 1980 to 18,280 in 1986. Claimants have come from Sri Lanka, Ghana, Ethiopia, Somalia, and India (Malarek 1987, 105). Public support for these refugees has wavered, and media stories about bogus refugee claims, organized refugee scams, and alleged misuse of the refugee determination process by 'economic refugees' have inflamed racist sentiments (Simmons and Keohane 1992, 435). 'The state is very mindful of widespread anti-immigration sentiment and incipient ethnocentrism, even racism, in large segments of the Canadian public' (Simmons and Keohane 1992, 438), and such negative public opinion creates a disincentive for the state to move swiftly in solving the backlog of refugee cases that have clogged the system in recent years (Malarek 1987, 100–49).

Women who come to Canada under the entrepreneur program may, like refugees, wish to find a safe asylum, but their conditions of entry are vastly different. Recent accounts portray them as educated and successful businesswomen confidently managing their family businesses or pursuing middle-class careers (Cannon 1989; Man 1991). In 1988, 4,294 Chinese women immigrated as principal applicants, versus 6,059 males (Man 1991, 6). Some Chinese men either have been unable to transfer their businesses to Canada quickly or are afraid of giving up their 'high status and lucrative professional jobs in Hong Kong to face possible unemployment in Canada.' They have chosen instead to live in Hong Kong while their wives and children reside in Canada. Becoming single parents in Canada has meant loneliness and isolation for some women, but others have enjoyed their 'new-found independence' (Man 1991, 11–12).

New programs to attract wealthy immigrants were informed by the need to stimulate Canada's industrial and economic development. The Department of Immigration explains that 'there is a strong consensus in Canada that the recruitment and selection of business immigrants should be fostered, because these newcomers provide significant economic benefits to Canada through increased capital formation and job creation' (quoted in Malarek 1987, 217). The category of independent immigrants now includes entrepreneurs, investors, and the self-employed. Under the investor program, an individual must have a successful record in business, have accumulated a personal net worth of $500,000, and should be willing to invest in a 'project which is of significant economic benefit to the province in which it is located, and which will contribute to the creation or continuation of employment opportunities for Canadian citizens or permanent residents' (Canada, Employment and Immigration, 1989, 11). In the self-employed category, individuals must create jobs for themselves, but the entrepreneur and investor categories require the creation of additional jobs for Canadians as well.

These business programs have attracted approximately 3,000 immigrants from Hong Kong each year. In 1985, 51 per cent of the 2,176 visas issued to business immigrants went to Hong Kong (Malarek 1987, 216–17). The investor program has attracted the smallest number of people; by 1986, seventeen had been approved and they brought in $27 million. Between 1979 and 1986, 6,258 entrepreneurs created an estimated 21,099 full- and part-time jobs (Cannon 1989, 224). The obvious class bias of these programs has led some critics to describe them as programs in which citizenship and visas are for sale (Malarek 1987, 215). Margaret Cannon argues that these programs are a new form of 'head tax' imposed upon the Chinese (Cannon 1989, 222; also K.W. Taylor 1991, 11).

But the wealth of these newcomers has not shielded them from racism. The stereotypes change over time but biases persist. One Chinese man who was looking to rent space for a bookstore remarked: 'The owner assumed that I was planning to open a restaurant. That's one stereotype. When he found out I was originally from Hong Kong, he offered to sell me the building. That's the new stereotype' (Cannon 1989, 15).

Peter Li, Gunter Baureiss, and Cecil Foster argue that racism has created a group of exploited individuals who live in Canada as illegal immigrants (Li 1988a, 90; Baureiss 1987; Foster 1991). Their exact number is not known. Foster describes the life of illegal immigrants trying to 'stay one step ahead of deportation officers'. He writes: 'They endure the indignity of low-paying, back-breaking jobs few Canadians want, unable with any surety to plan their lives, marry and raise kids or visit doctors when sick, to complain to authorities when exploited, to have an apartment listed in their name or to have letters sent from home addressed to them. If these people felt they had a real chance of making it through the front door, they would never choose this life' (1991, 13).

Before 1960 some Chinese entered illegally from Hong Kong by misrepresenting themselves as spouses of immigrants already in Canada, and some who gained entry as children did not accurately report their ages. In 1960 an amnesty was granted to Chinese people who had entered Canada illegally before 1 July 1960, and 'who were of good moral character and had not been systematically engaged in illegal immigration' (Hawkins 1988, 132–3). Some women from Jamaica, Guyana, and other Caribbean countries, who had originally come to Canada to work as domestics, continued to live here without valid authorization. Between 1983 and 1985 the government gave amnesty under the Long-Term Illegal Migrant Program to women who had been living illegally in Canada for five years and allowed them to apply for landed immigrant status (Boyd 1989, 7). But others have now taken their place: in 1993 some immigration lawyers estimated that there were as many as 25,000 to 30,000 illegal domestic workers in Toronto (Mitchell 1993).

IMMIGRATION POLICIES: IMPLICATIONS FOR WOMEN

Changes in immigration policy and new programs for immigrants have led to a dramatic shift in source countries – from Europe and the United States to Third World countries (Kalbach 1990, 24–7; Simmons 1990, 148–50). In 1968, 65 per cent of the immigrants to Canada were from Europe; in 1984, the figure was down to 24 per cent. Immigration from Asian countries rose from 12 to 50 per cent (Harney 1988, 92). The proportion of immigrants from Africa is 'small but constant' – 3.8 to 6.1 per cent of arrivals in any year (Simmons 1990, 150). In 1976, six of the top ten source countries, led by Britain and the United States, were non-European. In 1984, seven of the ten source countries were non-European; Vietnam and Hong Kong were numbers one and two, while Britain dropped to fifth place and the United States to seventh (Driedger 1989, 79). Most of these immigrants, including females, have settled in Ontario, British Columbia, and Quebec, with the largest settlements in Toronto, Montreal, and Vancouver (Samuel 1990, 386; Boyd 1989, 10).

Since the Second World War, 50 per cent of immigrants have been females. In the years prior to 1945, the top ten countries of birthplace for female immigrants were the United States and European countries, but in the period between 1970 and 1977 the top ten were the United Kingdom, the United States, Portugal, India, Jamaica, the Philippines, Hong Kong, Italy, Guyana, Trinidad and Tobago. Between 1978 and 1981, all the top ten source countries – except for the United Kingdom and the United States – were Third World countries: Vietnam, India, the Philippines, the People's Republic of China, Hong Kong, Jamaica, Haiti, and Guyana (Boyd 1989, 42). Immigration from Africa is 'disproportionately composed of well-educated young-adult males,' and few women come. In contrast, the migration from the Caribbean is led by women (domestic workers, nurses, and office workers) who later sponsor their children, spouses, and mothers. There is almost an equal number of male and female immigrants from Asia, and this population is characterized by 'extremely high' educational levels (Simmons 1990, 148–54).

Women from Asia, Africa, and the Caribbean form a heterogeneous group whose educational levels, ages, skills, and marital statuses vary. The 1981 census shows large differences in knowledge of English and French among foreign-born women. While 45.7 per cent of women from the People's Republic of China could not converse in English or French, only 7.6 per cent from Hong Kong and 2.8 per cent from Guyana could not speak English or French (Boyd 1989, 47).

Women from Asia, Africa, and the Caribbean are found in a variety of different occupations and at both ends of the labour market. There is no distinct pattern that characterizes the location of immigrant women in the labour market, and there is no one occupation in which they are employed (Giles and Preston 1991). Their employment depends on their skill, educational level, and knowledge of English or French. Women who do not speak English and French are the most disadvantaged. They find employment in ghettos with women from their own ethnic groups who work at low-skilled, menial, and low-paid jobs. But women from Asia, Africa, and the Caribbean may also be found in professional, managerial, technical, clerical, sales, and service jobs and in nursing (Basa-varajappa and Verma 1990, 298))

All women from Asia, Africa, and the Caribbean face discrimination, both overt and indirect (Abella 1984, 47).[9] Racism may be experienced during job interviews or it may be systemic, as in the requirement of 'Canadian experience' and in the devaluation or non-recognition of educational and work experience acquired outside the country (Abella 1984, 46–51; Canada, House of Commons, 1984, 40–1).[10] Their experiences were summed up in this way in a report from the Urban Alliance on Race Relations and the Ontario Women's Directorate:

Visible minority women are burdened by both gender and race stereotypes. Studies show that in the workplace visible minority women are often treated differently. As a result, they can feel intimidated, isolated, and alienated. The women who were interviewed for this project reported feelings of 'being constantly watched' on the job; of not being made to feel welcome or given a sense of belonging; of having constantly to 'prove' themselves, or to work twice as hard as their fellow workers in order to keep their jobs. (1)

According to the 1981 census data, within Toronto '16 percent of the visible-minority population have post-secondary degrees, diplomas or certificates compared to only 12 percent of the general population. However, they earn less and they are less likely to be employed in their chosen field.'

The experience of discrimination encountered by the women may vary by class and at different times. Monica Boyd explains:

For some groups, higher education may offset or prevent discriminatory behaviour associated with gender, immigrant status or visible-minority status. This especially could occur under conditions of high demand for skilled or well-educated labour. Conversely, even when income-generating characteristics are similar, experiences can be shaped by gender, or being a member of a given ethnic or visible-minority group. Such shaping can reflect overt discrimination and systemic barriers, in which recruitment and promotion practices over the years and organizational structures either intentionally or inadvertently exclude some groups and not others. (1991, 22)

Sometimes statistics show no discrepancy between the earnings of women from Asia, Africa, and the Caribbean and those of 'Canadian-born' women, but these figures can be misleading. Boyd argues that, when educational qualifications and settlement in large metropolitan centres or 'wealthier provinces' (which usually mean higher earnings) are tabulated along with other factors, a verifiable picture emerges of disadvantage based on gender, visible-minority status, and country of origin. These women earn the 'lowest wages and salaries compared to Canadian-born women and foreign-born women who are not members of visible minorities' (Boyd 1991, 19).

The problem of racial discrimination in the workplace is recognized by state policies, such as Employment Equity, which seek to remedy the situation. Judge Rosalie Abella argues that 'it is a waste of human resources that these people are consistently underemployed for reasons that have less to do with their professional qualifications or qualifiability and more to do with the insularity of some professional organizations. Having been selected as immigrants to Canada, many on the strength of these very qualifications, it is unfair to put insurmountable impediments in the way of their practising the professions they may be qualified to practise' (1984, 50).

There is widespread expression of good will, and manuals constantly exhort employers to hire members of racialized groups. For example, the Urban Alliance on Race Relations and the Ontario Women's Directorate advise employers to 'get ahead of the game!': 'Visible minority women can be an asset to your company. They bring to the workplace a wealth of ideas, new approaches and perspectives, talents, skills and abilities. Survival in today's competitive world requires effective management of all human resources. Unused human resources are wasted potential.'

But programs to eliminate the barriers encountered by women from Asia, Africa, and the Caribbean are painfully slow. In 1987 the government of Ontario appointed the Task Force on Access to Professions and Trades. It submitted its report in 1989, and in 1993 a department was set up to implement its primary recommendation to establish the Prior Learning Assessment Network. It will take some time to hire staff and establish a data base before any assessment can take place (Cumming 1993).

THE ROYAL COMMISSION ON THE STATUS OF WOMEN

The establishment of the Royal Commission on the Status of Women is frequently used to mark the beginning of the second-wave women's movement (Bégin 1992). The commission was appointed in 1967 after vigorous lobbying by women's organizations (such as the Committee on

Equality for Women), by various professional and service groups, and by such feminists as Doris Anderson and Laura Sabia (Black 1988, 85–9).

The commissioners were to 'inquire into and report upon the status of women in Canada, and to recommend what steps might be taken by the Federal Government to ensure for women equal opportunities with men.' The commission did not have 'an explicit conceptual framework or a shared philosophy, other than its commitment to the "equal rights" approach, which coexisted with general notions of the value of a specifically "female culture" ' (Bégin 1992, 29). At that time, there was little feminist literature available, but the report starkly reveals the feminist bias of its time: women are discriminated against on the basis of their gender alone. There is no suggestion that race might also be a barrier to women in attaining the three goals the commission set out to investigate: 'equal opportunity with men,' 'an adequate standard of living,' and 'freedom to choose a career.' The analysis made racism invisible and marginalized the concerns of women from Asia, Africa, and the Caribbean.

Three years after the commission was set up it submitted its report, which 'became the blueprint of mainstream feminist activism in the 1970s' (Vickers 1988, 35). The National Action Committee on the Status of Women was formed to monitor the implementation of the report's recommendations, which formed the nucleus of many government programs and policies and led to the establishment of departments, directorates, and Status of Women offices throughout government agencies. The recommendations about immigrant women dominated the agendas of immigrant women's organizations and programs and policies of governmental agencies such as the Ontario Women's Directorate throughout the 1970s and 1980s.

The report discussed women as one category, although it paid some attention to women who live in poverty or in remote communities. In discussing poverty, it focused on three groups: 'sole support mothers,' elderly women, and 'Indian, Metis, and Eskimo women.' Immigrant women were notably absent from the sections entitled 'Women and the Canadian Economy' and 'Women and the Family.' Although one chapter was devoted to immigration and citizenship, it comprised only eight pages, and immigrant women were discussed on only four. The other four pages discussed the issue of Canadian women losing their citizenship after marrying an alien. The report was 488 pages long.

The report identified gender as the only source of oppression for immigrant women, and it located their 'problems' in the culture of their ethnic and racial groups. In discussing women who do not speak English or French, the report argued that 'the social customs of some immigrant communities may not permit the housewife to leave home in the evening to attend the language classes and other courses that she badly needs' (361). But it conspicuously failed to question the scheduling of these classes, who was eligible to attend them, where they were held, or their curricula. And there was no discussion of the child-care responsibilities and the necessity to contribute to the material survival of the family that might make it impossible for women to attend language-instruction classes.

The report showed little understanding and no sympathy for immigrant women. At one point it quoted a brief presented to the commission as summing up 'the problem very well':

Having little to say in the discussions prior to their coming to Canada, the wives are frequently quite ignorant of the difficulties they will have to encounter in adapting themselves. Often, they speak neither English nor French and, being unable to relate to their environment, they become prey to a psychological solitude which not only crushes their spirit but is also harmful to their children ... In short, women immigrants would be far better off on arrival in Canada if the government took family and social factors, and the fact that they are women, into consideration, along with the economic factors which must of necessity govern immigration policies. (361)

The commission requested two studies on immigrant women, Edith Ferguson's 'Immigrant Women in Canada' and Freda Hawkins's 'Women Immigrants in Canada.' (Aboriginal women were classified separately and were the subjects of two additional studies.) These studies, which were not published in the final report, represented an attempt by the commission to include all women. Since its premise was gender discrimination, the studies reproduced several biases of class, ethnicity, and race. They described immigrant women in ways that subordinated them to 'Canadian women' and ascribed a second-class status to them.

Ferguson's report discussed the problems of settlement and adaptation for professional and women with limited job skills. (Women from southern Europe formed the basis of her research.) Hawkins found no race or gender biases in immigration policy. Her report adopted an optimistic tone:

Women now travel freely alone. They are seeking and experimenting with new economic opportunities and environments. They form a significant part of the brain drain. They are not only moving from one developed country to another, they are also leaving developing countries in increasing numbers. Armies of nurses, secretaries and other professional and skilled women are booking passages on airlines and, very frequently, working their way around the world. (1970, 1)

Ferguson identified several issues that remain problems for immigrant women. She noted that qualifications obtained outside Canada might be rejected and an individual be required to recertify, which was problematic for women with domestic responsibilities. Like male immigrants, women might fail to receive credit for experience gained outside Canada. In addition, women might encounter prejudice 'against people of other races and nationality,' or 'simply because they are women.' West Indian nurses had no difficulty in finding employment; they were well qualified by Canadian standards, and 'nurses are scarce.' But generally in all helping professions, immigrant women faced discrimination and differential treatment because of different cultural norms. Ferguson argued that immigrants need to conform to white, Anglo-Saxon norms (1970, 7–13).

Hawkins argued that immigrant women will always be outsiders:

[A]ny woman who has come to Canada after the age of 25 (and earlier for some) will always have a double personality, however close her attachment to Canada may be. And with the strong economic and achievement drive, which is characteristic of many immigrants of all income groups, will go a persistent tendency to look at Canadian society as an outside observer. It is therefore congenial for many women to lead working lives which are Canadian and social lives which are not. (1970, 22)

But the private and public spheres are interrelated. Biases and prejudices that make immigrant women social outsiders do not disappear at the workplace.

Hawkins never specifically discussed the issue of race or class. Ferguson acknowledged the existence of race bias in employment for some categories of workers but denied it in housing, particularly in Toronto (1970, 8–16). The studies compared Canadian women to immigrant women in a superficial way and found no substantive differences. Ferguson noted:

Semi-professional women, or those with a fair education, but no training, usually fit into the Canadian labour market in somewhat the same manner as Canadian women. A secretary, typist or clerical worker, once her language facility is adequate, can find work without much trouble. But no matter how good her performance, or how high her qualifications, a woman typist remains a typist and rarely moves into an executive's chair. Banks are eager to hire young women who can speak the language of their customers, but they very infrequently get beyond the teller's wicket ... Immigrants in these occupations received somewhat similar treatment in their own countries and do not expect anything more ... If a woman wishes more opportunity to use her ability, she can probably use it by going into business for herself. (15)

The language of the report was condescending and patronizing. Women were treated as objects – as passive rather than active participants in defining themselves or identifying their problems. They were portrayed as dependent on the good will of Canadian women. Hawkins conducted a survey of fifty women's organizations to inquire whether 'Canadian women help immigrant women in the difficult process of adjustment to Canadian life.' Her report concluded with the following observation:

In the author's view, women immigrants are unlikely to make dramatic changes in the status of women in Canada. Rather we have to think of raising the status of many women immigrants to more acceptable levels. We have to think of ways in which the adjustment of many women immigrants to Canadian life can take place with greater speed and ease. We have to be particularly vigilant that women immigrants with little education are not exploited in employment, particularly within their own communities ... [W]e must now make real efforts to help women immigrants from developing countries both at home and in employment. (1970, 37)

Race and class differences were treated in the report as added-on characteristics of some women rather than as integral components of race, class, and gender oppression. Gender oppression remained primary. Race and class were considered special, additional problems, just for immigrant women:

[We talk about] the racial and class identity of Black women, or of poor women, but not about the racial and class identity of white, middle-class women. Talking about racism and classism thus ends up being talk about something experienced by some women rather than something perpetuated by others: racism and classism are about what women of colour and poor women experience, not about what white, middle-class women may help to keep afloat. (Spelman 1988, 167)

The recommendations of the report identified language training and the acquisition of working skills as the most significant issues for immigrant women. These two recommendations were widely adopted by 'immigrant women's organizations' and by state agencies. Consequently, the term 'immigrant women' came to be used to refer to those women who lacked an adequate command of the English language and had limited job-related skills. Middle-class immigrant women who spoke English or did not need skills upgrading became invisible.

By describing the 'problems' of 'immigrant women' in terms of settlement and adaptation, the report attributed the problems to the women themselves rather than to gender, race, or class biases. Power and powerlessness based on gender, race, and class were made invisible.

The commission made 167 recommendations. Immigrant women were the subject of three of them. It recommended a review of language-training programs; the removal of sexist bias in immigration policy, which categorized women as dependants and automatically assumed the male to be the 'head of a family'; and the protection of the right of wives to apply for immigration as independent immigrants and to be so informed by immigration officials (407, 415–16).

The provision of language-training programs and the removal of sexist bias in immigration policy were the focus of political activity and lobbying efforts by women's organizations in the 1970s and 1980s. Soon afterward, job training, skills development, and violence against women were added to the agenda. Throughout this period, conferences and workshops were held at the provincial and federal level on 'immigrant and visible-minority women,' which identified difficulties with language training and skills development. Women's departments within the state bureaucracy, such as the Advisory Council on the Status of Women, documented the problems associated with these issues and the need to address them (Estable 1986; Seward and McDade 1988).

Language-training and skills-development programs are the major focus of the services offered by immigrant women's organizations and form the subject of their political lobbying. The solutions proposed by immigrant women's voluntary and community-based organizations and state agencies are the same. However, there are disagreements about the source of their oppression and about political priorities. While acknowledging sexism and problems associated with culture, immigrant women's organizations emphasize racism. State agencies are reluctant to adopt such a perspective, and without denying sexism or racism, they emphasize the culture of the women. Women from Asia, Africa, and the Caribbean have begun to redefine the problem on their own terms, that is, in the context of race.

The report of the royal commission reveals how different ideologies influence how we think and what we think about groups of people. Insights of white feminists based on everyday experience are constrained by political, institutional, and ideological structures. Feminist theory that emphasizes gender cannot adequately explain the different situation of women from Asia, Africa, and the Caribbean.

The report of the royal commission informed public policy for the next two decades. It lent support to the lobbying efforts of women's groups to eliminate the discriminatory aspects of legislation and to introduce new and creative programs for ensuring equality for women. But its emphasis on gender discrimination and its silence on racism were oppressive. The recognition of gender oppression in public policy provided opportunities for women from Asia, Africa, and the Caribbean to articulate their own oppression based on gender, race, and class. How they have organized themselves in movements for social change and their struggles against race, class, and gender oppression are the subjects of the next three chapters.

7

Women's Community Organizations

Immigrants invariably established volunteer organizations whenever large numbers of them settled in Canada, and these organizations played a crucial role in developing a sense of community among them. Women volunteers directed various activities in these organizations to serve the social and recreational needs of the members, but women's groups were usually ancillary bodies associated with churches, temples, or ethnic organizations. The women who participated in these organizations were motivated by a sense of 'noblesse oblige' to help women less fortunate than themselves (Simmons 1986; Roberts 1990).

In the mid-1970s, women from Asia, Africa, and the Caribbean began to establish autonomous groups whose activities were quite different from the charitable, social, or volunteer work performed by upper-class women. They too began as volunteers helping the settlement of new immigrants, but their ideology encompassed other goals. They aimed at securing equality and social justice for their constituents by asserting their right to social services from the state. Their political agenda was premised on the belief that race and gender biases of mainstream institutions excluded and marginalized them.

The emergence of ethno-specific women's groups in the 1970s can be traced to dissatisfaction with the politics of settlement organizations and of the women's movement. Minority organizations subordinated the specific interests of women to the collective rights of entire ethnic groups. The women's movement advocated change on behalf of all women but specifically addressed only the concerns of middle-class, white women. Minority women wanted groups that would address their concerns. One woman noted:

We felt we should be developing our own organizations. We experience racial discrimination, inequality in employment, and [lack of access to] language training. These are some of the issues that affect us directly. They have a priority for us. These are issues that [white women] are not going to organize around because they don't affect them. Not that other issues don't affect us equally – [for example,] pay equity. I support the issue, but it doesn't affect the people I work with. It doesn't affect me. How are we going to benefit from that? We need to have jobs first. (Interview, 5 Oct. 1989)

Middle-class women from Asia, Africa, and the Caribbean now provide services in community organizations to women from their own ethnic groups. The services offered through community groups are conceived as bridging programs, as temporary arrangements (e.g., shelters). Individuals can move on to use social services provided through mainstream agencies to all Canadians.

But work with community groups raises difficult dilemmas for the service providers. Community work provides employment opportunities for middle-class women from Asia, Africa, and the Caribbean, but wages and benefits are not on a par with mainstream social service agencies. These unequal conditions reproduce the racial stratification of society in 'women's work,' demonstrating the difficulties of overcoming the structural barriers of race and class. Women from Asia, Africa, and the Caribbean find work with community groups to be personally rewarding, and it brings them greater job satisfaction than working elsewhere. But some of them fear becoming ghettoized in groups serving women from their own communities and being diverted from their long-term career goals. Similarly, when women from Asia, Africa, and the Caribbean are hired by mainstream agencies to serve women from their own groups or to provide 'multicultural services,' they suspect that their ability counts for less than their gender and race.

DOING FEMINIST RESEARCH WITH COMMUNITY ORGANIZATIONS

My research investigates the role of immigrant women's organizations in empowering immigrant women, and documents the ways in which racism impedes their struggle against sexism, both in society at large and in the mainstream feminist organizations from which they have been excluded or in which they have been marginalized. Feminist research has evolved from the stage of adding women to an existing knowledge base to using feminist methodologies that create a new and different understanding of women's experiences (Millman and Kanter 1987). Dorothy Smith argues that feminist research must locate the subject in women's everyday experiences. The everyday nature of women's experiences gives them the appearance of being normal and natural, and this impression of normality renders invisible the power relations that structure and mould these experiences. Research from the 'standpoint of women' attempts to see through the appearances of immediate experience to the social reality (Smith 1987, 122–40).

My research attempts to give a voice to women from Asia, Africa, and the Caribbean who are politically active in immigrant women's organizations, work in shelters, or serve as social workers in mainstream service agencies. Feminists have used the metaphor of moving from silence to speech to describe the process of struggling against their oppressions and their resolve to become self-determining. For bell hooks, 'speaking becomes a way to engage in active self-transformation and a rite of passage where one moves from being object to being subject' (1988, 12). Mariana Romo-Carmona writes:

Each time a woman begins to speak, a liberating process begins, one that is unavoidable and has powerful political implications ... The stages of increasing awareness become clear when we begin to recount the story of our lives to someone else, someone who has experienced the same changes. When we write or speak about these changes we establish our experiences as valid and real, we begin to analyze, and that analysis gives us the necessary perspective to place our lives in a context where we know what to do next. (Quoted in hooks, 1988, 12–13)

My research with community organizations in Toronto began in 1988. With the help of some well-known immigrant women's organizations, I met with several volunteer activists to discuss their concerns. I interviewed about twenty-five women, and on the basis of these discussions I planned the present study of immigrant women's organizations. Two students, one of Caribbean descent and the other of South Asian descent, assisted in collecting data and interviewing women. In 1991 I began my fieldwork by interviewing activist women in grass-roots organizations of women from Asia, Africa, and the Caribbean in Toronto. During this part of the research, a South Asian and a white Canadian student assisted with fieldwork and interviews.

The criterion for selecting women for interviews was their present or past affiliation with community organizations of women. They included founding members of women's organizations, board members, executive directors, settlement workers, counsellors, and English-language teachers. After each interview I requested three names of potential interviewees and contacted them by phone. In all, I have interviewed approximately 100 women. I did not interview any women who were using community organizations to gain access to services, but some of the service providers I interviewed were former clients. My research findings are presented from the perspective of middle-class service providers and political activists from Asia, Africa, and the Caribbean.

My research was intended to be collaborative. Interviews were usually taped at the workplace of the respondents. The interviews lasted for ninety minutes or two hours and were sometimes followed by more informal discussion over lunch or coffee. (A few respondents asked that our interviews not be taped. My discussion of them is based on notes I made immediately after our meetings.) The format of the interviews was unstructured and open-ended, but I used an interview protocol to guide them. All the interviews were conducted in English.

I did not wish to impose a research agenda on my subjects that would ask them to fit their experiences into my categories. Joyce Ladner has argued that research questions that discard Eurocentric conceptual categories and are derived from the experience of the subject can provide us with new and different ways of seeing the oppressed. Such questions can take us past looking at the 'problems' that are often attributed to the oppressed and direct our attention instead to the racism that structures their experiences (Ladner 1987). I saw the women's experiences, particularly their struggles, as a resource to generate a set of questions that could expose the race, class, and gender biases which oppressed them (Harding 1987, 181).

I developed the interview protocol in the course of some initial research with immigrant women's organizations in 1989–90. After conducting a few interviews in 1991, I added new questions, which emerged from my discussions with women from Asia, Africa, and the Caribbean. I often tested ideas suggested by previous interviewees by asking new respondents about similar situations or issues. Some assumptions had to be discarded after a few interviews, and new issues were identified. For example, I had thought that legislation covering violence against women would empower South Asian women. This was not the experience of South Asian women who were survivors of abuse.

In interviews I did not ask respondents to answer all my questions;

rather, I attempted to engage them in a dialogue. Questions were used 'as openings, as pathways into relationships' with the women, and the interview followed directions 'in which they would feel free and able to speak their thoughts and their feelings' (Brown and Gilligan 1992, 19). Setting aside the protocol to allow respondents to talk about their own areas of expertise, or to discuss issues of particular interest to them, enabled them to relate events as they experienced them and to describe the connections they perceived between racism and sexism. They identified what they experienced as oppressive and described their own struggles to empower themselves and other women.

Between 1988 and 1992 I attended many workshops, conferences, and seminars presented by community organizations, and I read their brochures, leaflets, reports, and newsletters. In the summer of 1992 and 1993, I attended a three-day conference in Orillia conducted by the Ontario Council of Agencies Serving Immigrants, and I became a volunteer board member (a two-year term) of the South Asian Family Support Services. In 1992 I also started attending meetings of the Multicultural Alliance for Women against Wife Assault, a group representing service providers in ethno-specific agencies. I have also contacted organizations with broader bases, such as Women Working with Immigrant Women, the Cross-Cultural Communication Centre, the Coalition of Visible Minority Women, and the Peel Multicultural Association. (A complete list of organizations appears in the Appendix.) At these meetings, I had informal discussions with many women about my research and I requested their responses to my tentative conclusions.

Between 1988 and 1992 there was some shift in the activities of community-based organizations. In 1988–9 the primary focus of women's organizations was employment and English-language training, but in 1991–2 they adopted programs to serve victims of wife abuse. My decision to include a chapter on wife abuse reflects my interactions with community organizations that focus a great deal of their attention on this issue. In the summer of 1992, I attended four conferences on wife assault organized by South Asian service providers affiliated with various agencies and community groups.

Traditional fieldworkers have often adopted the stance of independent observers doing 'research on' a particular group of people. If the researcher was an outsider to the society being studied, his or her research was considered to be neutral (a positive value) and an objective reporting of facts. Objectivity and neutrality have been widely critiqued

by feminists to show the unacknowledged biases of androcentric knowledge (Nicholson 1990; Harding 1990). Lorraine Code argues:

Theories and research methodologies in the social sciences 'objectify' the human
subjects they study. Experiments are designed to predict human behavior and to
analyze it quantitatively, for only behavior amenable to statistical analysis is
judged worthy of scientific study. The methodology produces explanations of
personality and of social structures that take into account neither the consciousness of the subjects studied nor the meanings and interpretations of their experiences for these subjects. (1991, 34)

Feminists have been critical of the value system that underlies such
research techniques and have argued for the use of methodologies for
doing 'research with' the subject. In contrast to male paradigms, they
argue that researchers are not impartial or dispassionate but have
feelings, emotions, and values that form a necessary part of their
understanding of the phenomenon being studied (Jaggar 1983, 377–
89). The location of the researchers, their historical contexts, and their
goals shape and guide their inquiries. Research that consciously
acknowledges and follows these principles has the potential of transforming the consciousness of both researchers and subjects (Code
1991, 27–56).

Feminists contend that in conventional methodology the researcher
exercises control, authority, and ownership. The research belongs to the
researcher, who appropriates the experiences of others to prove theories
and exploits the objects of the research to serve personal goals. Such
research reduces the subject to an object and makes the researcher the
expert. Feminist research does not objectify the research subjects but
gives them the role of active participants in the inquiry (hooks 1988,
42–5).

Feminist research methodology, in contrast to conventional research
methodologies, engages the subject of the inquiry in the research process, acknowledges the expertise of the subject, and provides a forum in
which suppressed and subordinated voices can be heard (Oakley 1981).
Subjects of the inquiry collaborate with the researcher in determining
the questions that guide the study. Questions arise from the grass-roots
level and develop through interaction between the subject and the
researcher. The research serves the needs, goals, and objectives of the
subject as well as those of the researcher. Equal participation transforms

the power relations between the subject and the researcher and makes the research non-exploitative (Reinharz 1992; Pennell, 1992).

Feminist research methodology requires the subject to be engaged in all aspects of the research. For example, if an interview is conducted, the subject must have an opportunity to read the transcript of the interview and to modify, delete, or add to any of his or her statements. These rules eliminate misrepresentations and inaccuracies and allow the subject to exercise control and authority (Geiger 1990). Research that follows these rules empowers its subjects.

My research with immigrant women's organizations and South Asian women confirms these doubts about traditional research methods. Many groups believe that they have been 'researched to death,' or that research is often used by those in power as a substitute for solving problems. But they are also sceptical of the value of the new methodologies. Their different experiences of race, class, and gender oppression give them a very different view of research and of the need to document their lives in feminist writings. The women from Asia, Africa, and the Caribbean who are the subjects of my research are not as interested in doing 'research with' me as feminist theoreticians might expect. Rather, they wish to engage in activities that they perceive as contributing more directly and concretely to reducing biases of race, class, and gender. One must not simply assume that, when research is participatory, non-exploitative, and empowering, the subject shares the researcher's belief in its efficacy as a strategy for transforming the unequal power relations of society. The subject may not regard knowledge production as an integral part of the process of changing or transforming the inequitable social relations of society.

Research on women from Asia, Africa, and the Caribbean does form part of the work that community organizations engage in, and it is crucial for presenting their claims for services from state agencies. The organizations see themselves as initiating and conducting research for assessing needs and documenting bias in the delivery of services. But despite their commitment to this type of research and despite my being a 'visible-minority woman,' community organizations are apprehensive about my motives. For example, at the meetings of the Coalition of Visible Minority Women, I am considered an outsider and am treated with some wariness. The coordinator of the coalition is a black woman from the Caribbean; its most active members are black, and most of the women who attend the meetings are black, working-class women. The coalition's board is ethnically diverse, and I have interviewed two middle-class Chinese women and one middle-class South Asian woman on the board. But my identity as a middle-class South Asian woman and the academic nature of my research were obstacles to gaining the trust and cooperation of members of the coalition. They were familiar with research sponsored by state agencies, with research that had issue-specific goals and was action-oriented. They were much less enthusiastic about academic research, and they were sceptical of my arguments for constructing a theory of race and gender oppression or building a knowledge base that could influence public policy. They asked: Why was I doing this research? Who was it being done for? Who would benefit from it?

Black women were reluctant to be interviewed – 'again.' While all racially identified groups experience racism, blacks are more frequent targets of racism, and they have been the subjects of extensive research in the past – research that has not often produced satisfactory results. An inquiry into women's organizations conducted for Ontario's Multiculturalism Directorate noted that, while 'analysis' and 'need assessment' of immigrant women have been done many times, a mechanism was required that would create the political will to ensure that the needs of women from Asia, Africa, and the Caribbean are met (Seydegart and Spears 1985, 26). Stephen Lewis, reporting as the race relations adviser to Ontario Premier Bob Rae, noted in a letter: 'We both shied away from a formal Inquiry because it was hard to imagine that visible minority communities would have the slightest patience for it. There have been so many inquiries and reports, with so many recommendations repeated ad nauseam, that another tortured examination of the obvious wouldn't wash' (9 June 1992). Women from Africa and the Caribbean were most doubtful of the value of my research.

My communication with South Asian women's organizations raised different issues. Past and present coordinators of South Asian women's organizations, board members of immigrant women's organizations, politically active women, and a variety of professionals agreed to meet with me. But they often assumed a broader range of shared values and beliefs than really exists among South Asian women.

There were many commonalities between me and the South Asian women I interviewed, and these made our differences invisible at first. Similar physical appearance created comfort and quickly led to engaging conversations. My respondents were usually first-generation immigrant women, like me, and by our professions we could all be categorized as middle-class. We dressed in Western clothes. Our interviews were conducted in English because we did not always share another common language or dialect and felt more comfortable expressing ourselves in English. My South Asian respondents usually assumed that I shared their views about the racial biases of white Canadians, about South Asian family norms, and about the needs of South Asians in Canada. For example, my respondents frequently said that there was a need for what state agencies call 'linguistically appropriate and culturally sensitive services' for South Asians and other ethnic groups. But when I asked them what these 'culturally sensitive services' would include, my question was often met with surprise. This situation led to discussions that revealed significant differences between South Asian women.

My research provides an opportunity for South Asian women to express their views and to be heard. But my respondents did not always perceive themselves as co-researchers. They met with me either to oblige a friend who referred me to them or from a desire to demonstrate ethnic solidarity. They were supportive, and they enjoyed guiding a woman from their own ethnic group. Although at the beginning and end of each interview, I invited them to read the transcript of their interviews and to modify it as they chose, no one took up my offer. Rather, they expressed confidence in me and suggested that I use my discretion in selecting the information from the interviews. Often they were circumspect in their remarks, refraining from saying much that could be interpreted as 'politically incorrect' or that could jeopardize their position in any way. And once the tape recorder was shut off, more critical and pointed comments were frequently made. As my South Asian respondents perceive it, the research is my project, and they do not think it has practical consequences for them. I suspect they do not consider academic research as a likely way to initiate change.

Equal participation in this research could lead to difficult problems. The South Asian women I interviewed are all engaged in feminist work, in shelters, providing services to women, or initiating programs for 'immigrant women.' However, their consciousness of feminism varies. Some are radical feminists, while others are traditional South Asian women comfortable with the gender roles prescribed by Hinduism or Islam. Many are strongly committed to mediating conflicts within the family. Some reject the concepts of empowerment and individualism as alien to South Asian values and norms. Not all of their diverse views can receive equal representation in my research and writing.

Feminist methodology raises more general questions. How should

feminists working with subjects with differing views of feminism interact with them? Do feminist researchers have a responsibility to inculcate
a consciousness of gender oppression among all women? South Asian
women who go to shelters for women may be satisfied with traditional
gender roles and family relations but want to escape violent behaviour
occurring in their own homes. Should feminist South Asian workers at
the shelters attempt to raise the consciousness of gender oppression
among these women, which may lead to a breakup of the violent family,
or should they work on seeking a reconciliation? South Asian feminists
are aware of the racial biases of the larger society and the difficulties that
a divorced South Asian woman, for instance, confronts among some
segments of the South Asian community. They always insist that the
choice lies ultimately with the individual woman. But the difficulty
remains of deciding how much of the feminist agenda to follow in situations marked by structural inequalities of race, class, and gender.

Although academic feminists are committed to grass-roots struggle,
there is some (mostly unacknowledged) divergence between the goals
and struggles of academic feminists and those of community-based
activist feminists. Academic feminists are engaged in discussing theoretical issues, revealing biases of existing knowledge, and debating feminist theory. Such discussions have had significant impact on the
understanding and treatment of women by society at large. But the
struggles of community-based feminists are rooted in the here-and-now
and in practical everyday struggles against gender, race, and class
oppression. Thus, goals set by middle-class academic feminists may not
be embraced by women outside academia. My research with community-based organizations of women from Asia, Africa, and the Caribbean reveals that the oppressed and the victimized do not generally
consider academic feminist discourse as a forum in which to assert
equality. Knowledge and experience inform one another. But knowledge production is at most a long-term goal for the oppressed, who aim
at overcoming race, class, and gender oppression in everyday living.

Feminist methodology provides opportunities for understanding the
world from the standpoint of the oppressed. Those voices that have been
suppressed can be heard in feminist writings. But power relationships
also exist among women. White, middle-class feminists have spoken on
behalf of all women, and women from Asia, Africa, and the Caribbean
have critiqued the biases inherent in such assumptions. Middle-class
women from Asia, Africa, and the Caribbean now face the challenge of
avoiding the reproduction of class relations in their academic and

community-based work, and they need to build a framework for discussion which speaks to their own experience and the experiences of their working-class sisters.

SOCIOPOLITICAL CONTEXT OF THE EMERGENCE OF IMMIGRANT WOMEN'S ORGANIZATIONS

Evelyn Kallen notes that ethnic protest develops when social conditions change and new alternatives become available to minorities. The increased immigration of middle-class families from Third World countries in the late 1960s and early 1970s changed the social composition of Metropolitan Toronto and altered the positions of different ethnic groups within the overall hierarchy (1982, 183).

The protests by women from Asia, Africa, and the Caribbean against race, class, and gender discrimination and their demands to ensure equal access to social services for women from their ethnic and racial groups are premised on three interlinked rights: first, the right to maintain their cultural distinctiveness; second, the right to equal treatment under the law; and third, the right to special programs (a form of affirmative action) designed to eliminate and compensate for the historical disadvantages resulting from race, class, and gender oppression.

The ethnic and racial diversity of the Canadian population was recognized by the policy of multiculturalism in 1971. Multiculturalism has served as a guideline for government policy at both the federal and the provincial levels, by providing a framework for national discourse on the reconstruction of Canadian society (Elliott and Fleras 1990, 62). The 1988 Multiculturalism Act gave formal sanction to initiatives 'which sought to promote cultures, reduce discrimination, and accelerate institutional change to reflect Canada's multicultural character.'

Section 27 of the Canadian Charter of Rights and Freedoms (1982) requires that the Charter 'be interpreted in a manner consistent with the preservation and enhancement of the multicultural heritage of Canadians' (Eberts 1985, 55). Multicultural rights might appear to conflict with 'the right to equal protection and equal benefit of the law without discrimination' (section 15), but subsection (1) of section 15 notes that it does not preclude 'any law, program, or activity that has as its object the amelioration of condition of disadvantaged individuals or groups, including those that are disadvantaged because of race, national or ethnic origin, colour, religion, sex, age or mental or physical disability' (Eberts 1985, 53). The Charter provides for a balance between the rights of individuals and those of groups. Multiculturalism has been described as reaffirming two fundamental human rights in Canadian society – the right to be different (preserving culture) and the right to remain the same (receiving equal treatment) (Elliott and Fleras 1990, 65).

Community-based groups have used the principle of multiculturalism to gain some leverage for themselves with state agencies. Their *raison d'être* is the need to provide services to the many ethnic and racial groups in Canada. They appeal to multiculturalism to promote practical goals, such as economic (job) opportunities for members of their own groups, to protest against policies and programs which do not recognize their cultural distinctiveness, and to advocate antiracist policies. State agencies and mainstream institutions have attempted over a period of time to incorporate culturally plural paradigms for their policies and programs. However, community groups frequently characterize these initiatives as inadequate responses to the changing demographic make-up of Canada.

Women from Asia, Africa, and the Caribbean have argued that women from their groups are discriminated against by the biases of race, class, and gender in the programs and policies of mainstream social service agencies and that there are systemic barriers that deny them equal access to social services. And they have asserted that the special circumstances of the women from their groups require the introduction of new programs and policies to address their needs, such as language training in the workplace. But only in isolated cases have community groups made explicit appeals to the rights guaranteed by the Charter. In one case, community groups formed an alliance on behalf of immigrant women to challenge legislation on language training that gave allowances to men for attending language classes, but not to women. The groups argued that immigrant women were being denied equal rights guaranteed by the Charter. Such challenges require long struggles, and oppressed groups suffer from lack of organizations and resources.

Provincial and federal legislative initiatives reflect some commitment by successive governments to address the concerns and grievances of oppressed groups. But, while the guarantees of equal opportunity or of equality of rights may ensure that procedural laws apply equally to everyone, they do little to change the existing social inequalities of race, class, and gender. In the 1980s the task force reviewing the Ontario Human Rights Code recognized the barriers encountered by oppressed groups to attain equality and acknowledged that 'discrimination is not only a matter of intentional incidents against individuals, but also of unintentional, systemic patterns of discrimination against groups of people.'

Judge Rosalie Abella's report on the Royal Commission on Equality in Employment noted that 'sometimes equality means treating people the same, despite their differences, and sometimes it means treating them as equals by accommodating their differences':

We now know that to treat everyone the same may be to offend the notion of equality. Ignoring differences may mean ignoring legitimate needs. It is not fair to use the differences between people as an excuse to exclude them arbitrarily from equitable participation. Equality means nothing if it does not mean that we are of equal worth regardless of differences in gender, race, ethnicity, or disability ... Ignoring differences and refusing to accommodate them is a denial of equal access and opportunity. It is discrimination. (1984, 3)

Judge Abella's report named four groups that ought to receive special treatment as compensation for historical disadvantages and to accommodate their different circumstances: women, visible minorities, native people, and disabled persons. Women from Asia, Africa, and the Caribbean claim that equity programs for women benefit primarily white women and that programs for visible minorities help men from Asia, Africa, and the Caribbean. Projects, such as handbooks on how to introduce employment equity programs for visible-minority women (as published by the Urban Alliance on Race Relations and the Ontario Women's Directorate), indicate that the problem is receiving some attention.

The recommendations of Judge Abella's report had been preceded by other recommendations, such as those made by the Royal Commission on the Status of Women in Canadian Society (1970). Similarly, the House of Commons Special Committee on Participation of Visible Minorities in Canadian Society (1984), which had been established to identify means of promoting 'harmonious relations' and 'racial tolerance,' made wide-ranging recommendations which touched on almost every concern of people from Asia, Africa, and the Caribbean. Some recommendations, such as those related to the funding criteria of state agencies and the introduction of new language-training policies, had significance for women's community groups (vi, 135–41)

Task forces and royal commissions may set out programs of far-reaching changes, but their recommendations may only be partially and selectively implemented by politicians. Members of oppressed groups continue to express reservations about the weakness or ineffectiveness of laws meant to address their concerns. Royal commissions, reports, and laws provide some formal recognition by the state of the diverse needs of different groups, but they are not by themselves solutions to the problems of discrimination and inequality in Canadian institutions and policies.

The ethos of the 1970s and 1980s lent legitimacy to the complaints of women from Asia, Africa, and the Caribbean that they were being denied equality and social justice by the race and gender biases of society. The state acknowledged the oppression of women from Asia, Africa, and the Caribbean in 1981 when the Multiculturalism Directorate sponsored the first National Conference on Immigrant Women, which was held in Toronto. The conference attempted to bring together immigrant women, community organizations, and decision makers from various government departments that served immigrant women. Only a few grass-roots immigrant women's organizations attended.

The conference report, *The Immigrant Woman in Canada: A Right to Recognition*, noted that, despite government support for multiculturalism, Canadian society as a whole showed scant regard for the 'cultural traditions and rich heritage and life-styles' of different racial and ethnic groups, and particularly of women from these groups. The report went on to note:

Institutions, particularly, are hampered in their efforts to serve immigrant women as well as their families, because of the dominance of Anglo/French-Canadian values and attitudes which are reflected in their personnel and program designs. Further, although various government and institutional programs have been designed to assist newcomers to adjust and integrate, many of these programs have developed in isolation from the groups they are intended to serve. Conference participants believe it is crucial that immigrant women be included both in the design and implementation of these programs. (3)

Participants asked that funds be made available 'for regular innovative programs run by local community agencies, which respond to the needs of immigrant women,' and also for establishing a coalition of grass-roots organizations of immigrant and visible-minority women (3–5).

The need to encourage the formation of such organizations was reiterated by the House of Commons Special Committee on the Participation of Visible Minorities in Canadian Society, which noted that 'immigrant women have not been actively encouraged to participate in the planning of community services, nor are they participating in major women's organizations.' It recommended that governments fund 'community efforts which assist visible minority and immigrant women to become self-sufficient participants in the economic and social life of the community' (19–20; see also Seydegart and Spears 1985).

Racial discrimination inhibits the participation of women in mainstream organizations, even when such organizations form part of the state bureaucracy – for example, the Ontario Women's Directorate (Hernandez 1988b, 166–89). However, there are additional barriers to women from Asia, Africa, and the Caribbean: inability to speak English; high registration fees; no interpreting services; and lack of outreach to include immigrant and visible-minority women. Household and child-care responsibilities are added deterrents (Ontario Women's Directorate 1983, 69).

Although the need for immigrant women's organizations is acknowledged in principle, it is difficult for white women to give up entrenched patterns of speaking on behalf of women from Asia, Africa, and the Caribbean and taking leadership roles. The problem is illustrated by the conflict that arose during the first conference on immigrant and visible-minority women. In 1983 the Ontario Human Rights Commission's Race Relations Directorate and the Ontario Women's Directorate sponsored 'The Visible-Minority Woman: A Conference on Racism, Sexism, and Work.' During the planning of the conference, a struggle developed between the organizers – primarily white women – and women from Asia, Africa, and the Caribbean over the question of who speaks for, and on behalf of, immigrant and visible-minority women.

The conference was attended by approximately 500 visible-minority women. An advisory committee of visible-minority women had been formed to help with the planning of the conference, but its members had been selected by the organizers rather than nominated by community groups. Middle-class women from Asia, Africa, and the Caribbean were critical of the token role that was assigned to them by the organizers. Carmencita Hernandez noted bitterly that 'the enthusiasm about our participation centred on cultural events and the entrees we were planning to serve' (1988b, 159). A representative of the South Asian Women's Group complained: 'Again and again the committee members were not given serious consideration when we raised our concerns or made constructive suggestions. For instance, a proposed panel of prominent visible-minority women speakers ... was conveniently eliminated' (Ontario Women's Directorate 1983, 69).

After much acrimony and conflict, immigrant and visible-minority participants were able to have one of their participants included in the list of speakers. The protest was viewed by the women as a signal to the organizers that 'we visible-minority women were no longer going to be relegated to entertainment, exotica, and food, that we want a voice in our future' (Hernandez 1988b, 161). The conflict between the organizers and immigrant and visible-minority women provided an impetus for the establishment of the Coalition of Visible Minority Women before the end of the conference.

The conference highlighted the differences in power and privilege among women who belong to different racial and ethnic groups. Women from Asia, Africa, and the Caribbean wanted to organize to promote the interests of women from their communities and to challenge the presumed right of middle-class, white women to speak for them. During the 1980s, organizations such as Women Working with Immigrant Women began with the help of white service providers, who eventually left to allow women to speak on their own behalf. The pressure of women from Asia, Africa, and the Caribbean has forced state organizations to give their groups specific representation in meetings, conferences, and task forces, apart from that given to women's organizations or to groups representing ethnic and racial groups.

Although some organizations appeared in the 1970s, many more emerged in the 1980s to address the concerns of working-class women from Asia, Africa, and the Caribbean (Seydegart and Spears 1985, 27). By providing services to working-class women, middle-class women from Asia, Africa, and the Caribbean attempted to mobilize women from their own ethnic and racial groups to gain state recognition of the integrated oppressions of race, class, and gender. The claim of these women to equal opportunity initially took the form of starting service-oriented organizations which provided working-class women with English-language training and help in locating employment. In addition, several umbrella organizations came into existence in Ontario and other parts of the country. Service organizations form the political base through which women from Asia, Africa, and the Caribbean have exerted some political pressure on the state and have claimed a share of the resources of society.

IMMIGRANT WOMEN'S ORGANIZATIONS

At the present time there are numerous organizations representing women from Asia, Africa, and the Caribbean. These groups usually originate with a small group of dedicated volunteers who help women from their own ethnic communities obtain social services that they are unable to get on their own. Typically, they start in the basement of someone's house or in a room in a church. The demand for help leads them to organize formally so that they can ask federal, provincial, municipal, or private agencies to support their counselling work, research projects, need-assessment studies, conferences, or workshops. They organize formally by incorporating themselves, adopting a constitution, and electing a board of directors. Once a community group has some funds, it can obtain an office and hire staff.

Women from Asia, Africa, and the Caribbean have also organized in response to being marginalized in women's organizations dominated by white, middle-class women. They are motivated by their need to have a separate voice and to become a force to be reckoned with. A Chinese activist in immigrant women's organizations notes that the desire to organize came from a 'need to be heard, to find a way that we could best be heard, and be listened to.' (Interview, 12 May 1992). A Filipina woman explains the rationale for organizing the Coalition of Visible Minority Women: 'We decided to take common action, educate ourselves about what the issues were and how to do things together. As a group we also wanted to create a support system in our struggle against racism and sexism in immigration, housing, health, social services and [the] justice system' (Interview, 24 March 1992). Glenda Simms, past president of the Congress of Black Women, notes that in the early 1980s black women felt the need to organize nationally 'so that they could have a strong voice to advocate on their behalf' (Nonqaba n.d., 39). As stated in its brochure, the Congress of Black Women seeks 'to provide a network of solidarity for Black women in Canada, and to be a united voice in the defence and extension of human rights and liberties for Black women in Canada.'

Women's community-based organizations may represent a particular ethnic group, local or national (e.g., the Afghan Women's Support Organization, the Korean-Canadian Women's Association). Or they may have a broader constituency (e.g., the Coalition of Visible Minority Women, the Congress of Black Women). Despite a broad label, an organization may represent just one or two groups. The Coalition of Visible Minority Women was originally started by women from Asia, Africa, and the Caribbean and continues to have on its board women from different racial and ethnic backgrounds. However, its executive director is a woman from the Caribbean and, at its monthly meetings, I saw primarily black women from the Caribbean and Somalia.

The ethnicity and especially the spoken language of the staff may encourage women from a particular ethnic or racial group to use the services of a community-based organization. The ethnic or racial identity of the membership or the clients of the organization sometimes shift over a period of time with changes in the neighbourhood or in the staff. For example, the Riverdale Immigrant Women's Centre primarily serves women from South Asia and Vietnam, the two communities most strongly represented in their neighbourhood.

A community-based organization can provide services specifically to a particular ethnic group. For example, the Filipino Community Centre provides programs specifically directed to the needs of domestic workers seeking to qualify for landed immigrant status (Interview, 30 Jan. 1992). The Somalian Women's Group helps women who are victims of torture or abuse in refugee camps trying to obtain refugee status in Canada (Interview, 20 Jan. 1992). Some groups, such as the Immigrant Women's Health Centre or the Immigrant Women's Job Placement Centre, may direct their services to a larger population. The fact that state and private agencies favour organizations that serve more than one ethnic group encourages community groups to define themselves in broad terms. (Toronto is sometimes an exception to this general principle because of its large and diverse immigrant population.)

Some organizations focus on advocacy, such as Women Working with Immigrant Women and Intercede (the Toronto Organization for Domestic Workers' Rights). Advocacy may take the form of making representations to state agencies when changes are being proposed, in the delivery of job-training programs, for example, or in English- or French-language programs, or in immigration policy. The process of initiating a group or making proposals to various state agencies for resources to provide services is also a form of advocacy. An organization that originates as an advocacy group may eventually expand into providing services. For example, Intercede began by advocating changes in immigration policy on behalf of foreign domestic workers seeking work permits in Canada, but it now provides information about immigration and labour legislation to its members. Similarly, the Coalition of Visible Minority Women originated as an advocacy group but now performs a variety of other services.

Community-based organizations most frequently aim to provide working-class, non–English-speaking women with language training and help in finding employment. They provide information to women from Asia, Africa, and the Caribbean about services and resources available to them in mainstream social service agencies; escort them to the courts or to social service agencies; give referrals; and provide linguistic and cultural interpretation. Middle-class women from Asia, Africa, and the Caribbean have established health clinics which provide medical and social services to women in a variety of different languages (e.g., the Immigrant Women's Health Centre). And they have conducted research studies to assess needs in particular areas of service, such as wife abuse (Chan 1989; A. Papp 1990; Paredes 1992). Community groups also organize workshops and seminars on antiracist practices, cross-cultural counselling, homophobia, and wife abuse for service providers from other community groups or from mainstream agencies.

The services provided by community-based groups do not replace those offered by mainstream agencies such as Welcome House in Toronto, employment centres of the Department of Employment and Immigration, the Children's Aid Society, or hospitals. Rather, these community-based service organizations supplement services available elsewhere. They are oriented to serve women who have difficulty in obtaining services from mainstream organizations because of their lack of fluency in English, their unfamiliarity with the concept of social services, or their experience of cultural alienation or racism in Canadian institutions. The clients are working-class women and the service providers are middle-class women from Asia, Africa, and the Caribbean. Middle-class women who speak English are able to gain access to services from mainstream agencies and can obtain services from private family counsellors, lawyers, and others. However, they too may experience alienation and discrimination in Canadian institutions. The common experience of discrimination and alienation brings working-class and middle-class women from Asia, Africa, and the Caribbean together in community groups.

Women are the primary users of the services offered through community groups, and they are the main service providers. At the 1992 professional development conference of the Ontario Council of Agencies Serving Immigrants (OCASI), attended by 280 service providers, only about twenty-five were men. In Ontario, community groups associated with OCASI provide services to as many as 300,000 immigrant and refugee clients. Some community groups serve all immigrants, while others serve only women. Community groups that serve immigrants have also introduced special programs for women.

Women are the target group for 63 per cent of all services offered through community groups that serve immigrants, while the figure for men is only 16 per cent. However, there is no distinction by gender in the types of services that are used by men and women. For example, 31 per cent of services available to women and 27 per cent of services available to men relate to employment. The figures for social support services are 20 per cent for women and 21 per cent for men; for settlement services, 18 per cent for women and 19 per cent for men. Similarly, there is no substantial difference in legal services or language training available to women and men. Services relating to community participation show a marked difference: 15 per cent for women and 8 per cent for men. And women have access to more diverse services, such as crisis intervention programs, child-care services, support groups, and specialized counselling and recreation activities (OCASI 1990, 8).

Community-based women's organizations are engaged in feminist work. They place women at the centre of their programs and attempt to view their 'problems' from women's perspectives. Community groups initiate programs to enable women to compete for paid employment, organize support groups for women who are isolated at home, escort them to places that seem intimidating, give information on legislation, and provide referral to professional services. They are committed to equal rights and opportunities for all women regardless of race, ethnicity, or class. Community groups advocate the elimination of racism and sexism from all legislation and are critical of the racist and sexist biases of society at large. But not all community groups articulate feminist principles in their constitutions or in their promotional literature. Further, a community group started by feminists with well-articulated and defined feminist principles may, with changes on its staff and board, begin to identify itself with a more conservative and traditional philosophy; this has been the case with the South Asian Family Support Services, for example.

Only a small proportion of women who work at these community groups identify themselves as feminists, and their feminism is usually articulated in terms of equal rights and opportunities. A Chinese woman said: 'I guess, for me, being a feminist is recognizing a vision of equality and justice, and recognizing the strength of women collectively. I sort of see the need to link being a feminist and being an antiracist, a human activist – it is part of the same thing' (Interview, 12 May 1992). A South Asian woman said: 'I may not fall into one of those categories of white feminists, but I am a feminist ... I don't subscribe to patriarchy. I'm a socialist ... I believe in universal health care. I believe in more equality, pay equity, and equal opportunity' (Interview, 8 May 1992). A Filipina explained: 'I think feminism means that you want to better yourself, have better opportunities for immigrant women, make sure that the barriers are eliminated ... Racism and sexism are linked ... but I think, in terms of political activism, immigrant and visible-minority women emphasize racism because we have to survive and have to overcome racism' (Interview, 24 Mar. 1992).

Service providers in community groups use feminist language and institute some feminist practices within their organizations. For example, the most common rationale given for services for immigrant women is the need for empowerment. A leaflet of one community group, ACCES for New Canadians, notes: 'Through participation in the workforce, [immigrants and refugees] are empowered to participate in Canadian society and integrate into the community.' The wide institution of support groups for women is reminiscent of the consciousness-raising sessions of white, middle-class women in the 1970s. The support groups differ in being formally organized and having a facilitator but they serve similar functions. In these support groups, women share their experiences of being isolated at home, surviving wife abuse, being a lesbian in a heterosexual society, or being a new immigrant.

Service providers in community groups attempt, not to view their clients as 'deficient' individuals or as objects of their services, but to 'give them a voice' and include them in planning and delivering programs. Programs are sometimes designed by community groups after consulting with the women who are likely to use them. But community groups often rely on the experiences of paid staff to guide them. For some service providers, there is conflict between their desire to include their clients and the expectations of funding agencies. They perceive this conflict as a challenge to find creative and ingenious ways of meeting both demands. For example, a protest meeting in support of claims by First Nations people during the Oka crisis of 1991 was labelled as assertiveness training for immigrant women.

INTEGRATING FEMINIST IDEALS INTO HIERARCHICAL
STRUCTURES

Women's groups aim to empower the oppressed and to increase their involvement in programs and policies that affect them. Some women's community-based organizations emphasize open decision making and consultation with women, but state agencies do not favour allocating resources to non-hierarchical or collectively organized groups (Das Gupta 1986, 37). Hierarchical structures contradict feminist principles, but lack of funds threatens the survival of open groups. Community groups try to strike a balance between these different modes of operations but conflicts often result.

To receive state funds, community groups must be incorporated. Each group must appoint a board of directors which represents the community and is responsible for the organization's activities. The board has a formal structure, with a president, treasurer, and secretary. All staff members are hired by the board and are accountable to them. The executive director of the community group is the primary administrator and is responsible for writing proposals, estimating budgets, supervising staff, and administering its programs. Counsellors, settlement workers, language-training teachers, and secretarial staff are hired for the duration of specific programs. Power is exercised by the board over the staff (Ng 1988a).

Community workers distinguish between the formal division of power or authority and everyday practice. They note that the division of authority and responsibility between the board and paid staff depends on the temperament of the executive director and members of the board. A strong executive director may control the board or the chair of the board may exercise authority. There may be conflict between the board and the hired staff. A South Asian founding member of a women's organization noted: 'It is what they call dynamic tension – sometimes the board is very strong, and other times the board is very new and the staff has been there a long time. It is a situation that is rife with conflict even though everyone is there for the same reason. The roles are never very clear and the lines of communication are weak. The staff feel they are overworked and under-appreciated. [The staff and board members] need to come together, but as the agency gets bigger it becomes more and more difficult' (Interview, 22 May 1992). Some disputes between board and staff can be resolved by mediators appointed by state agencies or through organizational reviews suggested by them. Private agencies, such as the United Way, offer seminars on board and staff relations. When organizations volunteer to undergo such training, their applications for future grants may be viewed more favourably.

Disagreements arise over the role of board members, the kind of leadership they provide, and the degree of autonomy exercised by the staff. These issues become the sites of struggle between the board and staff.

Conflicts may occur because the board and the staff lack a sense of shared values. For example, a community group may have a hierarchical organization, but the values of its staff may be oriented towards a collective mode of operation and decision making. Feelings of hostility and ill-will may arise when the board attempts to exercise power over the staff. In other situations, disagreements may surface over the ways in which power is exercised by the board. The community that the group serves is usually a silent partner in the daily workings of the group, but it may be mobilized by a staff or a board seeking greater power for itself.

Disputes sometimes erupt when a board exercises its power to hire and fire staff. The board's ability to terminate a staff member may be challenged on procedural grounds. The staff may raise questions about the purpose of evaluations. Are the evaluations intended to improve the performance of the staff, to establish a need for training, to measure the effectiveness of programs, or to grade the performance of the staff? The staff may assert its right to see these evaluations and to respond to them (see, for example, the letter of Barbara Isaac to the senior policy analyst, Ontario Community Health Branch, 24 Oct. 1991). Establishing evaluation procedures, even in unionized workplaces, usually requires intense negotiation between union and management, and their final form takes shape over years of negotiation. It may be impossible for a fledgling organization to establish procedures quickly, and the lack of procedures may lead to a struggle for power between staff and the board.

Conflicts between board members and paid staff may be exacerbated by suspicions of racial biases, particularly in the hiring of staff. Sometimes women from Asia, Africa, and the Caribbean have denounced well-known white, middle-class feminists on the boards of social-service agencies for being unwilling to share power (Rose 1992). The charge of racial discrimination has class connotations as well. Frequently only well-established white feminists have the power and resources to raise funds privately, to submit elaborate proposals to state agencies, and to tap into a network to get substantial funds allocated to their projects. These women may dominate boards and choose their own nominees for appointments to community groups. While they seek to be inclusive, it is they who exercise the power to include women from Asia, Africa, and the Caribbean.

The struggle for power between board and staff is well illustrated in the case of Women's Health in Women's Hands, a community group in Toronto which was established by women who had been active in supporting Henry Morgentaler's right to offer abortion services. The group was led by June Callwood, and included several other prominent white feminists. As members of the Centre for Women's Health Steering Committee, they consulted with hospital administrators, women's organizations, and government staff before submitting their proposal to establish a clinic that offered a 'holistic range of health services' to women. The committee's proposal noted: 'Programs of the Centre [will be] based on an approach which includes the consumer in her health decisions, ensures sensitivity to the social context of women's health and reinforces the individual woman's knowledge, skills, and confidence.'

The proposal outlined the group's philosophy and goals, its structure, staff positions, a timetable for phasing in new appointments, and health programs. The target populations were immigrant women, disabled women, teenaged women, and older women. The proposal noted that the needs of immigrant women for health services were not being met because of 'language and cultural barriers, racism, lack of information,' and their low income. It added that 'ill-trained health and social service personnel are insensitive to cultural issues,' and 'few of the boards of community-based organizations have ethnocultural representation.' The proposal was accepted by the Ontario Ministry of Health, which gave approximately $1.5 million to the project in December 1989.

The centre's board consisted of twenty-one women, and they were predominantly white. Conflict developed almost immediately between the board and the staff. The board hired a white woman as executive director, a black woman as health promotion coordinator, and two black women as community health workers. However, this racial mix disturbed some white board members, and racial tensions immediately surfaced between the predominantly black staff and the predominantly white board (Interview, 22 July 1992). Both sides appealed to the provincial Ministry of Health for support. The ministry suggested an organizational review by an outside agency to resolve the dispute.

The review by consultants further exacerbated the conflict. The reviewers allegedly did not consult with the staff or with other community health clinics (Palmer 1991, 8). They recommended firing (with a severance package) the white executive director and offering the three black women either secondments to other agencies or termination with severance packages (Letter of Carol Cayenne to staff, 28 Oct. 1991). One of the board members, commenting upon the reviewers' report, charged that 'the entire process is flawed.' She disagreed with the recommendations of the review and, in an open letter addressed to the staff, the minister's office, and the board, she asked the board to resign:

There has been a consistent lack of support [for the staff], combined with a consistent lack of direction from the board. I have felt that this lack of support and leadership has meant that staff have had to take their own initiative, establish priorities and basically implement programs independent of board input. I have also felt that the board has continuously neglected to read information (i.e., staff reports, etc.) sent from staff and have thereby failed to make sound decisions and carry out the mandate of an effective board. (Letter of Jacqueline Daley, 1 Nov. 1991)

There was clear polarization on the basis of race between the board and staff. However, the board, anticipating allegations of racism as the conflict developed, replaced its white president with a black woman. The new president attempted to appease both the white women who had appointed her and the black staff with whom she had some racial solidarity. She leaked the recommendations of the reviewers to the staff.

The black staff members refused to accept the decision of the board, and the board in turn locked them out of the office. Later they were allowed into the office to collect their personal belongings. At this point they decided to stage a sit-in. The sit-in went on for three days, with board-appointed security personnel watching over the situation (Interview, 22 July 1992). The three black staff members had mobilized support from immigrant and black women's groups, whose members joined them in the sit-in. Both sides lobbied the Ministry of Health through letters and press releases. The government appointed a mediator – the president of the National Action Committee on the Status of Women – but she failed to resolve the dispute. After further negotiations, the sit-in ended and the staff accepted mediation by St Stephen's Community House (Sarick 1991). No one was fired.

In thanking immigrant women for their support, the black staff wrote: 'We feel that ... the community has a right to know what goes on in organizations such as ours, whose mandate is to provide holistic services for women. It is important to communicate the types of problems that will occur even in women-run organizations. As a women's community we need to have a dialogue about women working with women, in order to devise better ways of working together and working through issues' (Women's Health in Women's Hands 1992, 4).

The crisis faced by the board and staff of Women's Health in Women's Hands reveals the difficulty of integrating hierarchical structures and feminist ideals and of rejecting the exercise of power in favour of 'empowering' disadvantaged women. Boards and staffs of women's groups have difficulty working out cooperative relationships, even if all the women belong to the same ethnic or racial group. These conflicts are intensified when the women are further divided by race and class. The public acrimony between board and staff of Women's Health in Women's Hands is not the norm for community organizations, but conflicts occur regularly in community groups. Such disputes reflect poorly on the women's movement and are perceived by state agencies as signs of instability, which reduce the group's chances of future funding.

WOMEN'S WORK WITH WOMEN

Work within community groups provides opportunities for employment where an individual's race and ethnicity are advantages. However, work that values racial and ethnic identity can become another way of channelling women into low-paid and insecure employment.

Working with women from their own ethnic and racial groups or with other immigrants is the preferred choice of many service providers. The assumption that the service provider and the client share an understanding of the difficulties experienced by immigrants creates a comfortable feeling between them and facilitates communication. Service providers often express their satisfaction in being able to help women from their own communities; their work acquires a meaningfulness which may be lacking in other kinds of employment. A Chinese woman explains: 'I wanted to be part of a community. From 1968 to 1975 I drifted from one job to another. Finally I got a job at Settlement House in the heart of Chinatown. It felt right. This was my community and this was where my roots were. This [my work] was much more meaningful. I'm doing something for my own community rather than having to fit into a white institution. There was also the fear of getting into a white institution and getting lost' (Interview, 12 May 1992). A South Asian woman who is a member of the board of a community group notes: 'When I came to Canada I had to establish my roots. I had this identity crisis where I asked myself, who are you? There was that need inside me which made me want to become part of a community ... develop a sense of belonging. Somebody said to me, "Would you like to be involved [in setting up

Riverdale Immigrant Women's Centre]?" I was ready to get involved, I felt the need for it. Then for the next seven years that's all I did' (Interview, 22 May 1992).

Sensitivity to diverse cultural practices provides women from racial and ethnic groups with advantages in finding employment with community groups. They are well-suited to be service providers in community groups that serve immigrant women. In community groups that provide services that are 'culturally sensitive and linguistically appropriate,' the ethnicity of the service provider is a resource and an asset. A Filipina explains: 'We have culturally sensitive services in the language of [the client]. We are aware of some of the cultural biases they may have, and they feel comfortable with us ... [Filipinas] like to call on us to help them, have someone to listen to them. They call us because they really don't know where else to go ... The women [prefer that] we advocate for them with mainstream agencies and request we call [on their behalf]' (Interview, 30 Jan. 1992). The Korean-Canadian Women's Association explained: 'Some Korean women had difficulty in seeking help because of their social and family upbringing ... We became their speakers and listeners. There were also times when we became friends to many lonely, frightened, and despairing women by offering our time and conversation' (1989, 4).

Founding members and executive directors of community-based organizations are dynamic, enterprising, and enthusiastic women. They have organizational skills and leadership potential and are willing to take a chance. They start with no resources other than their own ideas and hopes for themselves and for women from their own group. Transforming these ideas into realizable goals requires skill, commitment, and ingenuity. Their goals – helping integrate immigrant women into Canadian society, improving their chances of finding a job, challenging sexism or racism – have to be presented to funding agencies 'in a language [agencies] can understand' and that will meet with their approval. When the group is first established, it is usually middle-class women who write proposals, identify needs, and organize services for women from their own communities. In the process, they create jobs for themselves and for women from their own communities as English-language teachers, counsellors, program coordinators, settlement workers, administrators, or office staff. Together these women become the mediators and negotiators with state agencies for the more disadvantaged women from their own communities.

Since familiarity with the culture and the social norms of ethnic and racial groups is the prime consideration, women with a variety of educational qualifications may work with community groups. Community groups usually do not have stringent educational requirements but value practical experience instead. For example, a counsellor or settlement worker does not necessarily need an undergraduate or graduate degree in social work, either from a Canadian institution or from her country of origin. Many service providers in community groups have post-secondary degrees from their countries of origin, but discrimination in the larger society compels them to accept underemployment in community groups.

Community work can provide important Canadian work experience for women, the lack of which is a major barrier to employment for immigrants. Working with their own ethnic or racial groups sometimes provides women graduates from Canadian educational institutions with their first job. Community groups may also provide locations where students doing their practicums for educational institutions can test their programs. State agencies sometimes send workers from particular racial or ethnic groups to community groups to gain work experience.

The Filipino Community Centre provides training and upgrading classes in computers, English as a Second Language, and office skills for domestic workers who want to apply for landed immigrant status. The centre also has a volunteer program: 'Starting this year, [our] volunteer training and development program has been expanded to include office apprenticeship. We have a very large volunteer base now. It was helped by the foreign domestic workers' movement. Nannies are required to render volunteer services as part of the evaluation process in becoming immigrants. So we have a large number of people volunteering now ... [but] to accommodate them and to give them good training is a problem' (Interview, 30 Jan. 1992). Some service providers argue that becoming a volunteer in a community group is a useful bridge to paid employment. Volunteer work can be cited by women who have been at home raising children as work experience when they seek paid employment. But it is unpaid labour, and some critics argue that it perpetuates the exploitation and oppression of women (OCASI 1992b).

Race and gender discrimination are barriers to women from Asia, Africa, and the Caribbean who are seeking experience by serving on the board of a mainstream social service agency. The lack of such experience may become an additional obstacle to their career development. Community links are valuable to professional women from Asia, Africa, and the Caribbean working in the larger society – for example, physicians, lawyers, private counsellors, and community outreach workers with various school boards. As a member of the board of a community group, professional middle-class women serve both their own needs and those of women from their own community. Some women from Asia, Africa, and the Caribbean have used their experience in community work to build a political base for themselves. Activist Winnie Ng has been nominated as a candidate for election by the federal New Democratic Party, for example (Interview, 12 May 1992).

Social services for women are provided by a variety of different agencies and groups. Through a system of referrals, mainstream agencies frequently call upon community groups to help with interpreting or to mediate between an immigrant woman and her family, the courts, police, or hospitals. Community groups may provide emergency help to a woman and direct her to other social service agencies – for example, to professional counselling for health problems. A woman who is a victim of violence may be referred to a shelter and the shelter in turn may seek the community group's help in translating or in understanding the woman's cultural norms.

But despite the closely linked services, there is stratification by race and ethnicity among the service providers. Women from Asia, Africa, and the Caribbean predominate in community work, and white women dominate in mainstream agencies. Work within community groups has all the characteristics of 'women's work': it is part-time, temporary, non-unionized, low-paid, and offers few benefits. Work with mainstream agencies is better paid, full-time, and stable, and it permits advancement through the ranks.

The stratification within social services is partially explained by the race and gender biases of the larger society, which limit women's opportunities for employment. Professional associations may not give accreditation to educational qualifications received in Third World countries. Work experience may be devalued or judged irrelevant to the Canadian work environment (Urban Alliance on Race Relations and Ontario Women's Directorate, n.d., 1).

A twenty-five-member coalition of community-based women's group's and antiracist organizations questioned the hiring practices of the Ontario Women's Directorate in a letter to the assistant deputy minister in charge of women's issues: 'It is of great concern to us that the majority of senior and middle management positions as well as permanent full-time positions at all levels of the Ontario Women's Directorate are held by white, middle-class, able-bodied women ... [These conditions] ghettoize women of colour, Aboriginal women, and women with disabilities in unstable, temporary contracts that are dismissed at will by white, middle-class management.' Gender-related responsibilities of domestic work and child care limit women's opportunities in professions and encourage them to compromise by accepting temporary, part-time jobs with community groups. As new immigrants, women frequently need to find a job immediately to ensure the survival of their families. Men, on the other hand, can wait to find a job in their area of expertise.

Women from Asia, Africa, and the Caribbean do not want to be labelled as 'ethnic workers,' and they fear that work with community groups may limit their opportunities for career advancement. Similarly, when they are hired by mainstream agencies for 'multicultural services,' they fear being ghettoized. A South Asian social worker, who has been in Canada a long time, expressed her resentment towards an employer by observing that, despite all the qualifications she had gained from Canadian universities, she was told that she had been hired because of her ethnic identity: 'They could have hired anyone else,' she said. 'It's demeaning to be told that you were hired because you are an ethnic' (Interview, 9 Apr. 1992).

Some of my respondents complained that white counsellors and social workers in such organizations were unwilling to familiarize themselves with issues confronting different cultural groups and to try to make their practices more antiracist (Interview, 28 July 1992). A South Asian woman said that at her agency she was constantly assigned black and South Asian clients: 'That also bothers me, because I feel that people who are working here or in any other agency should be able to deal with any nationality, as long as they do not have a language barrier. If they have an issue that they don't know how to deal with on a cultural level, or [a problem with a] value system, consult me and I'll help them. But I think it is time [that white counsellors] realized and understood and learned how to do cross-cultural counselling. They try to avoid that. It's very annoying. I do not see a strong motivation to learn [or to] incorporate my expertise' (Interview, 9 Apr. 1992).

Service providers within community groups have sometimes come together to identify their common concerns about the inaccessibility of services to members of ethnic and racial groups through mainstream social service agencies. Their report describes a shortage of workers in mainstream social service agencies who have the language needed to serve members of different ethnic groups. The authors of the report complained that 'all services are designed and delivered as if everyone speaks English fluently, subscribes to the same cultural values, and knows where to find the family services they need' (Medeiros 1991, 1).

Multicultural services are now being introduced, and they are a valuable addition to social services offered through mainstream social service agencies. However, they may not form part of the core programs offered by mainstream social service agencies, which therefore may only hire women from Asia, Africa, and the Caribbean on short-term contracts for new programs providing culturally sensitive services to immigrant women. Social service agencies are being pulled in different directions: they need to provide services where possible in the language of the women who come to them, but only women from the same ethnic group are likely to be familiar with the language. The executive director of Family Support Services, a mainstream social service agency, describes some of the problems that are involved in providing culturally sensitive services and integrating women from Asia, Africa, and the Caribbean into the workforce:

I think there is an enormous risk in channelling women to serve women from their own ethnic group ... I think the issue is, from a policy and planning perspective: Does [hiring women from Asia, Africa, and the Caribbean] enshrine a token effort or is it an overall organizational goal? Are they paid less, and is [this] because of rational reasons, or is it related to the kind of clientele they are seeing? Are they treated any differently? Do they have an office? What is the expectation of the other staff who are not from that particular culture – are they also expected to see other [immigrant women] clients? (Interview, 10 May 1992)

Community-based groups criticize the lack of women from Asia, Africa, and the Caribbean in mainstream social service agencies and on that basis demand more resources from state agencies.

Women who work with community organizations have created a special role for themselves as mediators between working-class women and the larger society. Their work has been crucial in raising the consciousness of the larger society about the integrated nature of the oppression of women from their own communities. They have formed coalitions among themselves or with white feminist groups to challenge the sexist and racist biases of legislation. These struggles are analysed in the next chapter.

Feminist research methodology provides some opportunity for suppressed and subordinate voices of women to be heard. But women from Asia, Africa, and the Caribbean question whether academic feminist research will transform the unequal structures of race and class that oppress them. Black women, who have experienced the most oppression, have reason to be sceptical about 'more research.' Legislation on human rights and multiculturalism, despite its progressive and liberal intent and its potential for creating equal opportunity, has brought only marginal gains to women from Asia, Africa, and the Caribbean.

The women's movement has enabled women from Asia, Africa, and the Caribbean to question the biases of society and to struggle against them. Through community groups, women from Asia, Africa, and the Caribbean are attempting to mobilize women to struggle against the race, class, and gender biases of society. The different degrees of power and privilege enjoyed by women, however, challenge them to find ways to reconcile feminist ideals with practical work in community organizations.

8

Immigrant Women and the State

Through its sponsorship of community groups, the state attempts to meet the challenge of securing social equality for members of diverse cultural and racial groups. In allocating resources to community organizations, the state is responding to the dissatisfaction of oppressed groups with institutions controlled by dominant groups – by white, middle-class males of British descent, for example. The state thereby contains and manages the discontent, but it does not attack the underlying causes. Dominant groups continue to exert their power even through the state. Evelyn Kallen, a sociologist, observes: 'Funding bodies are *controlling* agencies. The dominant fund-giving agency sets the terms under which funds are allotted, selects the recipients, and regulates distribution and expenditure. Hence, government funding allows subtle dominant *intervention* in minority affairs. Thus, the ethnic minority is kept in a dependent position and minority ethnic protest is diffused' (1982, 189).

Community groups of women from Asia, Africa, and the Caribbean, like other women's groups, cannot refuse government funding, which enables organizations to provide services to women from their own communities and to mobilize support on behalf of women addressing particular issues. Funds allocated by state agencies help community organizations to gather necessary resources (e.g., research studies), form alliances with other organizations on issues of common concern, and launch legal challenges against discrimination by the government.

Problems of race, class, and gender discrimination are seldom amenable to simple solutions. Women can sometimes overcome differences of class and race among themselves when they work on common issues (e.g., the devaluation of housework or the denial of language training). Local alliances among women's organizations on particular issues (e.g., housework) can overcome the barriers of race and class. Common experiences of class bias generate natural alliances among women's organizations and overcome differences of race among them.

THE STATE AND COMMUNITY-BASED ORGANIZATIONS

Community groups might survive by raising funds privately, but usually they turn to the state for resources to do their work.[1] One survey conducted in 1990 found that 88 per cent of them received some federal funds, 87 per cent received provincial grants, and approximately 65 per cent had some municipal funding. The United Way gave funds to 45 per cent of community groups. But 70 per cent also raised income from other sources (OCASI 1991, 2). These figures are higher than those noted in a 1980 survey of agencies in Toronto serving immigrant women (Women Working with Immigrant Women 1980, 11–15).

Tania Das Gupta observes that the funding criteria of state agencies directly control program development and the delivery of services: 'Community groups are told whom they should or should not serve. Issues such as whether to serve immigrants who have been here for more than three years, whether to serve "refugee claimants" or not, or who is to be defined as "disadvantaged" have all been points of struggle for immigrant women' (1986, 43). Despite the constraints that such grants impose, community groups have opted for obtaining these grants because the programs and services they fund are desperately needed by the women from their groups (Interview, 24 Mar. 1992). A long-term activist in the immigrant community observed: 'We can't function without money ... so [to] get funding you just do what needs to be done for them [funding agencies], keep them out of your hair and carry on the work. But usually the kind of partnership they demand means control over what we can and cannot do. [O]n the other hand is the reality of survival. Our work needs to be recognized and paid for. It is in the interest of the state to have us do their work at a cheap cost' (Interview, 28 Mar. 1992).

State agencies – such as the federal Department of Multiculturalism and Citizenship and the Department of Employment and Immigration and Ontario's Ministry of Community and Social Services and the Ministry of Citizenship – have the mandate to facilitate the settlement and integration of new immigrants. They have a number of programs through which they seek to provide 'equal and equitable' access to all social services for immigrants, and they support programs relating to language training, employment, health, and the family. The Acting Director of the Field Services Branch of the Ontario Ministry of Citizenship noted at the OCASI conference in June 1992 that programs have broadly defined goals and objectives, such as community development, increasing 'understanding of cultural differences,' and 'promoting understanding of new immigrants.' At the same conference an officer of the Department of Multiculturalism and Citizenship remarked that the mandate of state agencies includes promoting race relations through 'education and cross-cultural exchange' and support of ethno-specific organizations. Their programs also support advocacy by ethno-specific organizations, which helps 'mainstream agencies to adapt to change.'

The relations between community-based organizations and state agencies, such as the Department of Multiculturalism and Citizenship and the Department of Employment and Immigration, can be compared to relations between contractors and subcontractors. Generally, contractors impose a set of standards and conditions on subcontractors, who provide services at a cost lower than is available to the contractors themselves. Unlike the contractors, subcontractors have employees who are non-unionized, flexible, and on short-term contracts. The subcontractor's services are contingent on the needs of the contractors. There is a relationship of dependency, but the contractors make no long-term commitment to the subcontractors.

State agencies do not simply allocate funds to community-based groups but 'purchase services' from them. As the primary contractors, state agencies set out the rules and standards that community-based organizations must meet as subcontractors for the delivery of specific services. During the Funders Forum at the 1992 OCASI conference, an officer of the Department of Multiculturalism and Citizenship observed that state agencies are constrained by their own mandates and that the programs available through them must have well-defined objectives. To obtain grants, community-based groups must find some common ground between the needs of women from their group and the goals of the programs offered through a state agency. The needs of the women must be specific, and the community groups must have well-thought-out plans for achieving their goals.

Through the provision of grants, state agencies structure the agendas of community-based organizations. State agencies set the rules that community groups must follow to obtain funding or resources for their activities. Community-based organizations identify a need and volunteer to provide a service. If a need has already been acknowledged by state agencies (e.g., services for women who are victims of violence), a proposal to meet that need has the potential for attracting resources. Knowing that funds are available for specific issues, community groups structure their activities to fit the goals of state agencies. Thus the priorities of the state are adopted by community groups.

The state agency determines whether a proposal falls within its jurisdiction and meets its objectives and goals. State agencies usually fund a proposal for a year, but they like to see a well-developed proposal which sets out long-term objectives for the group. A proposal that outlines plans for only one year generally receives a negative evaluation. But community groups find it difficult to formulate long-range plans, and they are always apprehensive that their funds will be reduced or discontinued (Women Working with Immigrant Women 1986, 5). The chair of the board of the Riverdale Immigrant Women's Centre observes: 'The need is evident. All they have to [do] is to look at the numbers of people who want access to our services. But we have to repeatedly keep pleading and pleading for every dollar. It gets very exhausting ... It's very frustrating' (Interview, 8 May 1992).

A well-developed project may include services that fall under the jurisdiction of several state agencies and may receive funding from each of them. This situation imposes heavy administrative burdens on community groups:

Eighty per cent of the agencies receive grants from four or more funders; more than one-fourth go to ten or more granting agencies for the agency's funds. [T]hese figures ... do not reflect grant applications prepared and submitted but refused, or the rigorous reporting requirements (at least twice per year) accompanying each successful grant application. This waste of essential human energies is compounded by the pressures of conflicting and continually shifting priorities of the different funding bodies. The holistic vision of integrated service provision promoted by community-based agencies is greatly compromised by the necessity to chop and parcel the agency's activities into packages acceptable to the various grants providers. (OCASI 1991, 11)

During the Funders Forum at the 1992 OCASI conference, it was pointed out that one of the most difficult problems for community groups is short-term, annual grants with no promise of long-term funding from state agencies. Delays in the processing and delivery of funds lead to interruptions of services, unpaid staff, and emergency loans from banks. A frustrated community worker complained in the Women

Working with Immigrant Women newsletter: 'After years of effort and hard work, the immigrant and racial-minority community-service groups are still scraping to find enough money to deliver the services ... Family violence, racial discrimination and [racist] attacks do not coincide with the release of government funds [or] the time that we are financially in the position to deal with these issues and provide the necessary services.' In one survey, 50 per cent of community groups complained of inadequate funds (OCASI 1990; 1991). Their limited resources forced them to concentrate on day-to-day work, which left no time to recruit additional members or plan for the future (Interviews, 24 Mar. 1992; 4 Feb. 1992).

A new community group, with no track record, typically receives project funding for a year. At the end of the first year, a new proposal has to be submitted and is re-evaluated. Community groups find this an arduous process, and those who are unable to meet these requirements are judged to be unsuccessful or they carry the stigma of a bad record (Women Working with Immigrant Women 1986, 5).

It was pointed out at the Funders Forum during the 1992 OCASI conference that, after several years of receiving project funding, a community group may be given program funding 'if it develops, changes, builds, and shows promise of being stable ... It must serve multiple needs.' Program funding also requires annual reports, proposals, and evaluations. Since funds are first allocated to programs and then, if resources permit, to projects, community groups lobby to have their proposals categorized as programs.

Only a few groups receive what is termed 'core funding' (also referred to as an annualized budget) from state agencies such as the Department of Health and Welfare or from private organizations such as United Way. In one survey, 50 per cent of community groups complained of lack of core funding (OCASI 1991, 7). Core funding ensures the continuation of primary programs over a period of years, but it brings additional responsibilities. One South Asian woman observed: 'once you get into the funding game, you have now got rules, [and] you spend your entire time writing applications for money and responding to bureaucrats' (Interview, 22 May 1992).

The allocation of core funding is a controversial issue. A Peel Multicultural Council newsletter (vol. 3, no. 5) asked why little core funding was given for 'advocacy, public education, and other initiatives that foster better relations within the community': 'Why, for example, is the Ontario Race Relations Directorate not given the mandate to grant "core funding" to anti-racist organizations? Why should the Ontario Race Relations Directorate be limited to only giving Project Funding? How can an organization function properly if the funds that it could access are only Project Funds?'

Community groups have asked state agencies to recognize their anti-racism struggles by granting them core funds. In 1991 Ontario Minister of Citizenship Elaine Ziemba announced some changes in the government's funding criteria: 'We will – for the first time – provide core funding to community-based groups so they can plan and operate antiracism programs. A stable financial base will enable these local organizations to concentrate on advocating for people who have been excluded from existing programs and services ... Our aim is to provide a voice for those who have been forgotten' (1991, 6). However, in a later address to the Korean-Canadian Women's Association, she said that the recession had eroded the ability of the government to provide such funding, and community groups would have to continue to make do with project funding for a bit longer. The government hoped to strike a balance between its support of antiracism advocacy and its assistance to groups with 'crucial projects' (Korean-Canadian Women's Association 1991, 36–7).

Community groups want to understand how the system works, how to submit proposals and design budgets, and how to identify goals and objectives that coincide with the programs of state agencies. They express frustration at always being 'on the firing line' but accept the need to learn 'how to play the game.' During the OCASI conference in 1992, a facilitator at a workshop on designing and evaluating community programs for women noted: 'We are not trying to change the world, but only provide women with some opportunities, some way to express themselves'; but these goals have to be 'realistic and measurable.'

Community groups describe their services and advocacy in terms of providing equal opportunity and equal access rather than in terms of fighting race and gender discrimination, which might be taken to be critical of state policy. At the OCASI conference in 1992, 280 representatives attended a funders forum where officers from state agencies explained procedures for obtaining funds. A number of representatives complained about the difficulty of providing annual reports and of familiarizing themselves with the maze of programs of different state agencies and about the lack of program funding, which led to interruptions of their programs. But no one in the audience raised questions of gender and race bias or challenged the existing policies of the agencies.

The pragmatic, uncritical approach adopted by community groups is motivated by their desire to keep their funding. While they are reluctant to espouse radical or militant politics, they are vigilant about protecting existing programs, and they lobby state agencies to adopt new goals. Community groups seek representation on the boards of state committees and present their views at public hearings on issues that relate to immigrant women. For example, representatives of women's community groups made joint and individual presentations to the Ontario Training and Adjustment Board, which held public hearings in 1992 for the restructuring of the province's training programs. Representatives of immigrant women's groups noted the advantages of providing training through their community organizations and the desirability of maintaining language-training and employment-readiness programs in immigrant women's organizations. Women testified that services obtained through women's organizations had helped them learn English and acquire marketable skills for successful employment. Immigrant women's groups feared that the special needs of their constituents might not receive sufficient attention in the proposed restructuring of training programs, and they wished to preserve the programs offered through their own organizations.

ADVOCACY BY COMMUNITY GROUPS

'Language Rights Are Human Rights'

The necessity of language training for alleviating oppression and discrimination against immigrant women was identified as early as 1970 by the Royal Commission on the Status of Women report (361–2). Immigrant women's organizations, conferences on immigrant women, reports, royal commissions, and research studies have repeatedly argued that language training is the first step in securing equal access to the resources and opportunities of Canadian society.

Almost all community groups offer English-language training, and extending their programs to accommodate more women has been one of their most consistent demands in recent years. Community groups have been critical of state delivery of language instruction to immigrant women, and they have championed immigrant women's right to language instruction. Community organizations representing women from Asia, southern European countries, and Latin America (such as the Coalition of Visible Minority Women, the National Organization of Immigrant and Visible Minority Women, the Centre for Spanish-Speaking

People, and COSTI-Italian Immigrant Aid Service) have come together to challenge legislation that discriminates against women in language training. The advocacy of community organizations has made language instruction more widely available, increased the number of courses at all levels, and ensured that their content is closely related to women's everyday lives and experiences.

By 1970, 50 per cent of the immigrants to Canada were females and 90 per cent of them were between the ages of fifteen and sixty-four (Boyd 1989; 1990). The changes in immigration policy in 1962 and 1967 resulted in more immigrants being drawn from Third World countries. By 1987, 70 per cent of the immigrants were from Africa, Asia, Caribbean, and South America (Boyd 1990, 275). Consequently, the number of immi- grants residing in Canada who do not speak English or French has been increasing steadily. The 1981 census indicates that females are twice as likely as men not to know either of the official languages. Women from Asia (India, Vietnam, Hong Kong) and southern European countries (Greece, Italy, Portugal) have the most difficulty with language particularly when they first arrive in Canada. Monica Boyd notes: 'These sex differences in language ability most likely reflect sex differences in the opportunities to learn language in area of origin; the existence of institutionally complete communities in Canada for numerically large and geographically concentrated birthplace groups, which reduces the need to gain extensive familiarity with the language of the receiving society; and the difficulties experienced by immigrant women in accessing language-training programs' (1990, 280).

Not knowing the English language limits the ability of women to join the labour market and ghettoizes those who do work on the lower rungs of the labour force. Inability to converse in the English language is associated with 'lower labour-force participation rates (for women), higher unemployment, occupational and industrial concentration and lower weekly wages' (Boyd 1990, 289). In 'Sex Discrimination in the Immigration Act and Its Regulations,' Women Working with Immigrant Women noted that women who do not read or speak English may be unaware of their rights as workers – consequently, they suffer greater exploitation – and they are often unable to gain access to information about community and social services. Without knowledge of English, women are more vulnerable within the household and in society at large (Giles 1987a). They are socially and psychologically isolated, lose self-esteem, and feel that even the traditional status assigned to them as housewives and mothers has been undermined by their inability to speak English.

The struggle by community groups and other women's organizations in the 1980s to ensure immigrant women's equal access to language training exposed the sexist assumptions in the legislation. However, the removal of obvious sexist biases from the legislation did not result in equality of access. Laws that do not specifically take into account the different circumstances of women's lives may simply perpetuate inequality under the guise of neutrality.

The dependent status assigned to women during the immigration process limits their access to language training. The application for immigration formerly required that one person be designated as principal applicant or 'head of household,' and officers automatically assigned this status to the male. Women who accompanied the principal applicant were categorized as 'family class' or sponsored immigrants and became his legal dependants. This situation has now changed, and the family can choose to assign either a male or a female as the principal applicant. However, since males frequently have better educational qualifications and higher marketable skills, families often choose the male as the principal applicant to maximize their chances of being accepted for immigration. Although the explicit bias has been removed, not much has changed from previous years. Between 1981 and 1986, 50 per cent of female immigrants entered Canada in the 'family class,' compared to 40 per cent of male immigrants (Boyd 1989, 18). In 1981, 29,078 men and 31,862 married women were admitted as landed immigrants; of these, 79 men entered as spouses, compared to 18,938 women (Boyd 1986, 46).

'Canada does not have a comprehensive, integrated and universally accessible language-training policy for immigrants' (Boyd 1990, 289). However, there is a wide range of language-training programs offered to immigrants by state agencies at different levels of government. Language training is available to women through the federal Department of Employment and Immigration, the Secretary of State, and provincial agencies such as the Ministry of Citizenship, the Ministry of Education, the Ministry of College and Universities, and the Ministry of Skills Development.[2] The programs available through Employment and Immigration have a labour-market orientation and mostly exclude immigrant women. Other programs are available to women who are at home, but they are offered for shorter durations and do not have any financial allowances (entitlements) attached to them (Giles 1987b; Go 1987).

The most extensive language-training programs are offered through the Department of Employment and Immigration. However, clients must not be sponsored immigrants, and they must be 'destined for the labour market.' A department manual, issued in 1986, states that language training is directed to

1. skilled workers who cannot secure employment in their trade or profession or in a suitable related occupation because of a lack of fluency in a second language, and
2. unskilled workers who cannot be placed in suitable employment because of a lack of fluency in a second language. (Quoted in Giles 1987a, 8)

These eligibility requirements exclude most immigrant women. Immigrant women are denied participation in these programs because they are at home and it is assumed that they do not need language training, or they work in job ghettos with women who speak the same language, or they are classified as not 'destined for the labour market.'

Community groups have criticized programs of the Department of Employment and Immigration because they exclude female immigrants who have the status of 'sponsored or 'family class' immigrants. The reality for many immigrant women, regardless of what is stated in the immigration documents, is that they join the labour force once they enter Canada. Even if women are not immediately destined for the labour market, there is no guarantee that they will not have to go to work eventually. Mary Eberts, a noted authority on human rights, notes: 'The idea of labour-destined skilled workers being eligible for subsidies and in fact being preferred, is ... just the latest version of immigration policies' preference for men. It used to be the head of the family that would get access to these programs. Today this has changed, because it was disreputable and could expose them to a Charter challenge, so it changed to labour-destined workers. The labour-destined worker is almost always a man. It is the old problem with a new coat' (1987, 24).

Being denied language training disadvantages women and ghettoizes them in low-paid occupations where extensive verbal interactions are not required. Once women join these occupations, they lose eligibility for language training because they cannot argue that they need the language to find suitable employment (Giles 1987a, 1987b; Go 1987; Adamson 1991). Community groups have argued that the administration of the program relies on the existence of women's job ghettoes to keep them out of language training. Such exclusions deny equality to immigrant women and relegate them to 'jobs cleaning high-rise office build-

ings where the whole staff is made up of one language group or another'
(Eberts 1987, 24–5).

Sexist biases among employment counsellors are additional obstacles
for women. Employment officers have 'too little training, too many clients, and too little time to do an adequate job of selecting immigrant
women for the program' (Seydegart and Spears, in Adamson 1991, 38).
Amy Go observes: 'Access to training is denied many immigrants
because the counsellors do not believe that they require language facility
for their jobs. It is a common practice of the Canada Employment Centres to refer only one family member to training, usually the male. Immigrant women are particularly victimized by these discriminatory
practices.' In 1986–7, only about 2,000 of 5,100 trainees were females
(1987, 10). Yet twice as many women as men lack the ability to converse
in the English language.

Another site of struggle for community organizations has been the
unequal benefits associated with language training for women. There
are five types of income support available for participants in the Department of Employment and Immigration programs: living allowances
(also referred to as basic training allowances) and allowances for dependent care, commuting, living away from home, and (long-distance)
transportation. 'Family class' and 'assisted relative class' immigrant
women are not eligible for training allowances because their sponsors
are supposed to be responsible for them (Giles 1987, 9). They do have
access to the other training allowances, but these are reduced, sometimes by as much as 50 per cent, based on the earnings of their spouses
(Adamson 1991, 37). Commenting on the unequal benefits available to
immigrant women, Mary Eberts observes: 'Again, this is a clear example
that the government is not acknowledging that the woman is a person in
her own right and that her income is necessary for the family just as
much as the male income. It demeans her as an independent person'
(1987, 25).

Without training allowances, the cost of attending language-training
programs is prohibitive for immigrant families, particularly when there
is only a single wage earner (Paredes 1987, 24). Adamson explains that
the low rate of training allowances 'tends to discourage immigrant
women from attempting to educate themselves and instead tacitly
encourages them to find employment that will pay more than the training allowance' (Adamson 1991, 37). Sometimes women are forced to
take part-time jobs and this adversely affects the learning process. One
woman explains: 'The government gave me $100 a week for allowance.

To buy food, and everything in my apartment, it's nothing. So I had to get a part-time job. I worked for three months. But I stopped because I wasn't learning anything. I didn't have time to study and it was too tiring for me to go to school, work, and take care of my kids and husband' (Paredes 1987, 24).

The Department of Employment and Immigration was lobbied by the National Coalition of Visible-Minority and Immigrant Women to respond to the needs of immigrant women (Go 1987, 15). The new Settlement Language-Training Program was initiated in 1986–7 and was expanded further in 1988 (Boyd 1990, 289). Its primary target group was immigrant women who were not 'immediately destined for the labour force,' and it excluded women who were employed or were Canadian citizens. It provided participants with the cost of public transportation and with free child-care services. According to a department pamphlet issued in 1987, community groups could apply for funds to coordinate and run language-training classes for immigrant women, but the teachers were to be allocated and paid by the local boards of education.

Community groups have asserted that the cultural similarity between themselves and their students makes their language programs more successful. This view is borne out by a study conducted by the Teachers of English as a Second Language Association, which noted that the Settlement Language-Training Program was a success because bilingual teachers were more effective in reaching 'isolated, non-confident immigrant women.' The study found that community-based programs were viewed by immigrant women as less threatening than those offered through colleges and universities. Support services, such as baby-sitting and transportation allowances, were considered to be critical to the program's success (Adamson 1991, 41; Go 1987, 16–17; also Ontario Women's Directorate 1987, 9).

Community groups contend that gender makes a difference in the delivery of language training. In general, immigrant women have lower educational and literacy levels than immigrant men, so the level of instruction and curricula must be appropriate to their specific needs. In addition, account must be taken of the different experiences of women, whether they are at home or in gender-segregated work. The Coalition of Visible Minority Women, for example, offers language instruction that enables immigrant women who were nurses in their countries of origin to prepare for the Test of English as a Foreign Language exam (TOEFL) and the Test of Spoken English (TSE), that must be passed before taking the licensing exam for nursing. The language instruction offered by the organization specifically familiarizes them with the vocabulary of the nursing profession.

Community groups distinguish between the 'grammar-based' curricula offered by various boards of education and community colleges and their own gender-specific and culturally sensitive curricula. They note that their instruction equips women with 'life skills.' Their approach is 'holistic': language instruction familiarizes students with the vocabulary that they require in their everyday lives. Community groups offer different levels of instruction and can reach the most disadvantaged women. They may offer training in job searches and writing résumés as part of their language instruction or a basic course for housewives and women with low levels of literacy and education.

In July 1992, I attended a language-instruction class offered through the Settlement Language-Training Program. The class was divided into two sections. The subject of the first was how to order a meal in a restaurant. Students in the second, more advanced section learned how to ask for directions while using the public transportation system. The women were being taught to use words such as 'north,' 'south,' and 'intersection.'[3] The classes also included reading-comprehension exercises and conversation. One of the classes was taught by a Chinese woman and the other by a South Asian woman. There were about thirty students from working-class families, and all but one were married. Some were young women, accompanied by small children, while others were elderly women. The atmosphere of the class, held in the basement of a church, was more like that of a social gathering than of a formal classroom. The students seemed to feel comfortable with one another and with the teachers.

In 1987, led by the Centre for Spanish-Speaking People and in conjunction with the Legal Education and Action Fund (LEAF), a predominantly white, middle-class organization, community groups began to prepare a challenge to the federal language-training policies. It was the consensus among the participants of the symposium 'Equality in Language and Literacy Training' that the exclusion of immigrant women from language-training programs was discriminatory, that it denied equality and could be contested under the Canadian Charter of Rights and Freedoms.

Rita Cadieux, the deputy chief commissioner of the Canadian Human Rights Commission, supported the participants of the symposium by arguing that there were sufficient grounds for initiating a challenge of discrimination. The Canadian Human Rights Act states: 'Every individual has the right to make for himself or herself the life that he or she is able or wishes to have, consistent with his or her duties and obligations as a member of society, without being hindered in or prevented from doing so by discriminatory practices' (Cadieux 1987, 20). Cadieux noted that discrimination may exist 'when a policy or practice related to employment or services affects differentially a group of persons on the basis of a prohibited ground of discrimination, for example, sex.' The exclusion of immigrant women from language training violated the Canadian Human Rights Act because 'the present policy of teaching English or French as a second language to immigrants seems to have an adverse effect on a group of persons – immigrant women – on the basis of a prohibited ground of discrimination' (Cadieux 1987, 20).

Mary Eberts advised the symposium participants that section 15 of the Charter of Rights and Freedoms could be invoked on behalf of immigrant women:

Section 15 of the Charter guarantees equality before and under the law, and the equal protection and equal benefit of the law. Focusing on this phrase, you would argue that there is a law, or a statute with regulations under it, setting up this program (subsidized language training) and that the benefit is not equally available. It is preferentially available to some and not to others. Focus would also be directed on the fact that sex and national and ethnic origin are all enumerated categories, therefore any plaintiff complaining of denial of access to language training on the basis of her sex would be able to invoke the clear recognition in Section 15 that women and members of minorities are intended to benefit from that section. (1987, 23)

A challenge was launched by the Legal Education and Action Fund on behalf of two immigrant women under section 15 of the Charter. While the case was pending, in 1992 the federal government responded by introducing a new policy, Language Instruction for Newcomers (LINC), which eliminated many of the sexist biases of earlier programs. It changed the focus of language-training programs from training for labour-market entry to 'training driven by immigrant integration objectives.' LINC gives preference to newcomers but specifically excludes Canadian citizens. While some language training is available to all, advanced language training would be provided to those immigrants 'whose occupational objectives can be tied directly to local market needs.' No one is eligible for any training allowances. The role of community organizations in the delivery of language programs is preserved, but the organizations are excluded from participating in the assessment of immigrants to determine eligibility or the extent of language instruction required (Settlement Directorate 1992, 1–7).

Community groups have protested the government's failure to consult with 'language-training stakeholders' in formulating the 'principles or program components' of LINC (OCASI 1992b, 1). They have criticized the elimination of training allowances. Those women who, for financial or family reasons, have been unable to gain access to language training but have acquired Canadian citizenship will no longer be eligible for language training. More significantly, cultural biases may enter into the evaluation and testing of language proficiency. Community groups want to mediate between immigrants and state agencies. They argue: 'Placements based solely on language needs, without regard for psychological, social and cultural needs, will not be effective. Immigrants experiencing social isolation or the aftermath of torture cannot be placed appropriately and will be unable to successfully learn an official language without having their other needs assessed and addressed. This holistic approach to language-training assessment and placement has been successfully implemented by community trainers' (OCASI 1992c, 6).

Community organizations have raised the consciousness of the larger society about how gender discrimination embedded in state policies affects women from their own communities. Community organizations have promoted opportunities for women from Asia, Africa, and the Caribbean by expanding their rights to language training. During interviews, my respondents frequently emphasized the interconnected nature of the many programs offered by their organizations. As one noted, a non-English-speaking woman who is a victim of violence may need social services and legal advice in addition to ongoing help in learning the English language, acquiring job-related skills, and finding employment. The cultural similarity between the women and the community organizations makes their interactions more comfortable and less threatening. Similar situations and experiences enable women to relate to women outside their own specific communities.

Intercede's Advocacy on Behalf of Domestic Workers

Intercede was formed by the Committee to Advance the Status of Housework (CASH) in 1979. According to its brochure, CASH aimed to 'provide an organized point of reference for individuals and groups seeking to upgrade the economic, social, and legal status of housework.'

Intercede, the International Coalition to End Domestic Exploitation, was a specific project of this group, and was co-sponsored by the Immigrant Women's Job Placement Centre. In 1986 it was incorporated as Intercede, the Toronto Organization for Domestic Workers' Rights (Intercede 1987, 4). The change in name marked a shift in the group's perspective: domestic workers are not merely victims (of capitalism, colonialism, imperialism, racism, or sexism) but agents of change who are struggling to overcome their exploitation.

Intercede has simultaneously worked on behalf of domestics and mobilized public opinion in support of changes in legislation. It has improved the regulations under which domestic workers enter Canada by challenging legislation that discriminates against them and by increasing their chances of becoming landed immigrants (permanent residents). It has challenged the exclusion of domestic workers from the Employment Standards Act, the Labour Relations Act, and the Human Rights Code. By representing its case as an example of how society devalues women's domestic work (as shown by the administration of Canadian immigration policies), Intercede has provided a common cause for women from different classes and ethnic and racial groups.

The exploitation of domestic workers is a prime example of race, class, and gender oppression, and domestic workers have become the *cause célèbre* of feminist discourses, rallies, and political organizations. The women's movement has raised awareness of how gender-related responsibilities (child care and housework) have denied women equality in the workplace and have had a detrimental impact on their careers. Hiring domestic workers allows middle-class Canadian women to work outside the home; but in thus liberating themselves, they exploit women from Third World countries. Employing domestic workers presents a problem for 'women's liberation as a collective ideal.' Sedef Arat-Koc observes: 'Domestic work ... rather than solving the problem of gender inequality, adds class and racial dimensions to it. Instead of housework and childcare being the responsibility of *all* women it becomes the responsibility of *some*, with subordinate class, racial and citizenship status, who are employed and supervised by those whom they liberate from the direct physical burdens. Reinforcing the divisions of mental and manual labour, it may perpetuate the low status and pay for domestic service' (1990, 98). Feminists have condemned the oppression and exploitation of domestic workers and have supported Intercede in its struggles to improve their situation in Canada.

Domestic work also raises difficult issues for Canadian policy makers who must decide whether housework is equivalent to other skilled occupations; what the educational requirements are for the job; and what constitutes valid work experience. Government officials and task force personnel have sometimes discussed the paid domestic work of Third World women in Canadian homes as a moral and humanitarian concern. One task force report published in April 1981 argued that, since domestic workers may have had their temporary authorization permits renewed over several years, the government was obliged on humanitarian grounds to 'accept the responsibility' to grant them permanent resident status. The report argued that to abolish the program (to protect the government from allegations of racial and gender biases) would deny Third World women job opportunities available in Canada.

Critics say that the attempts by the immigration department to portray domestic work as a way of helping Third World women are 'misguided' (Bakan and Stasiulis 1992, 36). And the argument of humanitarianism disregards the exploitation of domestic workers who provide a service to middle-class Canadian women at below market rates. Patricia Daenzer maintains that the primary functions of the domestic-workers programs are to support class interests, to maintain gender-specific characteristics in this occupational area, and to reinforce 'the subjugation of cultural and racial minorities entering the predominantly white Canadian labour force' (1991, 268).

Intercede has pushed for equity for domestic workers by seeking changes to Canada's immigration policy. The conditions of entry determine women's subsequent treatment by their employers and may exclude them from labour legislation and the Human Rights Code. Intercede has highlighted the women's situation in the media, developed important links with other women's organizations, and kept its membership informed through its monthly newsletter, *Domestic Cross-Cultural News* (Intercede 1987; 1991). Intercede has struggled to gain citizenship rights for women who have come to Canada with employment authorizations, including their right to stay in Canada permanently. It has challenged the gender and race biases of immigration policies that devalue domestic work or give greater preference to women from developed countries (e.g., the Live-in Caregiver Program of 1992). These struggles of Intercede have brought better wages for domestic workers and more protection from unscrupulous employers.

Throughout this century, immigration policy has attempted to meet the demand for domestic workers in Canadian households by allowing them entry into Canada as a special class of employees.[4] At one level, the situation is simple. The increasing number of Canadian women joining the workforce has created a constant demand for domestic workers. (Arat-Koc 1990; Bakan and Stasiulis 1992, 6–14) There is a virtually inexhaustible supply of domestic workers from Third World countries. The government of the Philippines and the governments in the Caribbean have actively supported the emigration of women as domestic workers as a solution to their own unemployment problems (Calliste 1989, 146–51; Daenzer 1991; Interview, 8 May 1992). But the supply-and-demand equation is complicated by the low status of domestic work and poor working conditions, a situation that encourages workers, once they are in Canada, to move out of this occupation. Canadian immigration policy has devised a number of restrictive measures to keep domestic workers tied to their jobs, but these measures have been challenged for their race, class, and gender biases.

In 1955 the Canadian government established a small quota for domestic workers from the Caribbean to meet the 'unlimited demand' for these workers. The women who immigrated under this program were formally tied to one year of domestic work. If they quit before that time without the sanction of the state, they faced deportation (Satzewich 1991, 125). The number of women who immigrated exceeded the quota. Canadian officials in the Caribbean and at the Department of Citizenship and Immigration expressed doubts about the program. They perceived the immigration of these women as a 'temporary' and 'short-term' solution to a 'permanent problem' and were fearful that the immigration of these women would 'create future problems.' Officials feared that the women, who were presumed to belong to 'lower classes,' would sponsor 'unskilled workers' to join them in Canada. The women were alleged to be immoral and promiscuous (Satzewich 1991, 141–5).

Since 1967 women from Third World countries have been able to apply to enter Canada under the point system either as independent immigrants or as sponsored or nominated relatives. Points are allocated for education and training, occupational demand, occupational skills, arranged employment or designated occupation, in addition to other criteria such as age, ability to speak English or French, having relatives in Canada, and personal assessment by the immigration officer (Parai 1975). Domestic workers might have gained entry under this system, but immigration officers showed gender biases in evaluating domestic work. Domestic workers gained no points for occupational demand (despite a shortage of domestic workers) nor were they adequately credited with occupational knowledge and training (Daenzer

1991, 225–6). Consequently, throughout the 1970s many female domestic workers failed to qualify as landed immigrants. However, women who apply as domestic workers are placed in a special category, and a different set of rules applies to them. These rules are being challenged by Intercede.

Domestic workers have come to Canada primarily from the Philippines, the Caribbean, and Europe, including Britain (Boyd 1989, 4). In the immediate postwar period, a limited number of displaced and refugee women from Europe entered Canada as domestic workers, but by the 1960s a large percentage of domestic workers in Canada came from the Caribbean. At the present time more women come from the Philippines. This change is due to the conditions in the Philippines, the preference of Canadian employers for Filipino domestic workers, the compliance of employment agencies with the racial preferences of the employers, and the biases of immigration officers against women from the Caribbean (Bakan and Stasiulis 1992, 24–5).

It is difficult to estimate the number of domestic workers at any time in Canada because they fit many different categories of work and statistics indicate only how many have come under specific programs, such as the Foreign Domestic Movement Program (Seward and McDade 1988, 40–3). As landed immigrants, domestic workers may not be specifically identified in any statistics. In 1990, over 58 per cent of the 11,000 domestic workers who entered under the Foreign Domestic Movement Program were from the Philippines, compared to just under 25 per cent in 1982 (Bakan and Stasiulis 1992, 18). The paid membership of Intercede in 1991 was 1,794; of these, 94 per cent were from the Philippines, and 6 per cent included women from the Caribbean, south and southeast Asia, and Europe (Villasin 1991).

Domestic workers in Canada have been represented in Toronto's media as vulnerable women who are oppressed by the gender, race, and class biases of the larger society, who work in degrading conditions and are economically and sexually exploited by their employers (Silvera 1983). In a story published in *The Globe and Mail* (19 March 1987), Ann Rahula described the conditions for one woman:

Melita Carbungco used to have a job taking care of two children and doing housework for a professional couple. She did not quit when her work day stretched from 7 in the morning until 8 at night with no extra pay.

She did not quit when she found she was on call to fetch or wipe or baby-sit on her days off.

She did not quit even when her boss asked her to work Saturdays and settle for half of a weekday off instead.

She said no. And she was fired.

And in *The Toronto Star* (5 February 1990), Leslie Papp portrayed the working conditions of another woman:

Her boss has shaken her, yelled at her and humiliated her. But Emma isn't planning to leave.

As a domestic worker, her rights are limited. And Emma, a native of the Philippines, is afraid that the woman employing her to cook, clean, and take care of her children will have her deported.

The situation of domestic workers is reminiscent of the conditions of American slaves. An article in *The Toronto Star* was titled 'Today's "Slaves" – Immigrant Women Working as Maids' (11 Jan. 1979). The reports of Intercede use the evocative terminology of slavery and of bonded and indentured labour to describe the situation of domestic workers who live in the homes of their employers. Intercede has noted that 'the bonding of domestic workers to their employers has been a consistent aspect of Immigration policy regarding domestic workers' (1991, 4). One woman described the situation in *Domestic Cross-Cultural News* (Mar. 1992): 'We are exposed to abuses and threats from our employers. We work like indentured servants, endure loneliness, long working hours, low wages, culture shock because we want to be part of this country. We know we are here because we are needed.' Intercede argues that immigration authorities are afraid that, if these women are accepted as immigrants, they will not remain domestic workers – much less meet the demand for live-in domestic help – which 'is a shameful excuse for allowing any form of slavery to exist in Canada.'

Similar sentiments have been expressed by Doris Anderson, a prominent white feminist: 'since before Confederation, we've had a form of indentured slavery in Canada sponsored and approved by the government' (*Toronto Star*, 24 Jan. 1987). Several employers vehemently condemned such terminology when it was used by Michele Landsberg, but she insisted that it accurately described the condition of domestic workers (*Toronto Star*, 23 Feb. 1991).[5] At a February 1992 rally in Toronto, which was organized by Intercede to protest entry-requirement changes to the Foreign Domestic Movement Program, banners declared 'Temporary Status Equals Slavery' and proclaimed that women 'Good Enough to Work' were 'Good Enough to Stay!' (*Rebel Girls Rag* 1992, 2).

In lobbying the government for changes in immigration policy, Intercede asserted that the government was complicit in the exploitation of Third World women and suggested that one 'underlying reason for the lack of protective legislation is the sexual and national composition of the domestic labour force, which is almost 100 per cent female, and estimated to be 80 per cent non-Canadian-born' (Intercede 1980, 11). Patricia Daenzer argues that the restrictions on citizenship rights and occupational mobility were instituted only when the demographics changed to a predominance of women from the Caribbean and the Philippines (1991).

Between 1973 and 1980, domestic workers were allowed to enter Canada on one-year work permits which tied them to particular employers and to domestic work. They could renew their work permits but could not obtain permanent resident status. In 1981, subsequent to a review of legislation governing the entry of domestic workers, immigration officers were asked by the Department of Employment and Immigration to facilitate the entry of domestic workers as landed immigrants. They were required to grant ten out of a maximum of fifteen assessment points to those with formal training or on-the-job experience in domestic work. A memorandum to the department minister, Lloyd Axworthy, stated that the training was to last 'for a period of time sufficient to have provided the applicants with a developmental opportunity which [would] enable them to earn sufficient income to adequately maintain themselves' (quoted in Daenzer 1991, 232). This language allowed for subjective assessment of what counted as 'sufficient' time or as 'a developmental opportunity' and led to no significant changes in the entry of domestic workers as landed immigrants. Between 1980 and 1985, 8,779 domestic workers were admitted as landed immigrants, compared to 75,689 domestic workers who came with employment authorizations, that is, as temporary workers (Daenzer 1991, 233).

In 1981 when the new Foreign Domestic Movement Program was introduced, domestic workers were able to apply for permanent resident status after two years of domestic service. An immigration officer would assess the candidates' 'potential for self-sufficiency,' and if they were not 'sufficiently established' they would be given an opportunity to upgrade their skills. In its new policy the Department of Employment and Immigration noted that in future 'entrants coming to Canada as domestic workers will be selected on the basis of their personal suitability and demonstrated ability to undertake training or upgrading here which will help them become self-sufficient.' In practice, this meant that for domestic workers to gain landed-immigrant status they had to upgrade their skills (interpreted widely to mean work outside the home), participate in volunteer work (with a community organization, for example), and be able to show evidence of 'financial stability' (Intercede 1990a, 1991).

The new rules were greeted with 'guarded optimism,' but problems remained. The women were required to work as domestic workers for two years. This period of 'indenture' was not applied to any other occupational category by immigration policies. The opportunity to attend classes to upgrade skills was dependent on the good will of the employers to make time available for them. Enrolling in courses was prohibitively expensive because domestic workers were required to pay foreign student fees.[6] Intercede argued that by insisting on upgrading skills the policy implicitly attributed low value to women's work:

The requirement for upgrading leaves the impression among domestic workers that they need to prepare to work in other occupations rather than stay in domestic work in order to qualify for [landed immigrant status] in Canada. In effect, therefore, the specific criteria applied to domestic workers serve to discourage those who are interested in pursuing long-term careers in domestic work and child care from doing so! In the last few years ... those who have been rejected are domestic workers who wanted to stay as housekeepers or caretakers and failed to upgrade themselves in another area. (1990a, 14)

The requirement to do volunteer work was considered an undue hardship for women who already had to endure long hours of work. The regulations left much to the discretion of the immigration officers, who had traditionally shown little sympathy for these women (Intercede 1990a, 12–14). Women could change employers if they could convince the immigration officers that they had a 'valid' reason for leaving, but those who changed more than two or three times were negatively evaluated when they were assessed for immigration status (Intercede 1991, 5). Consequently, some women remained in abusive and sexually exploitative situations rather than jeopardize their chances of becoming permanent residents.

Through its newsletter, Intercede keeps its members informed about how to upgrade their skills and how to prove their self-sufficiency to immigration officers. A legal aid clinic at Intercede provides advice to its

members on immigration regulations and employment-related problems. Through its research and need assessment studies, Intercede has
kept the situation of domestic workers on the government's agenda
(Intercede 1990b). It has won several important victories for domestic
workers, such as minimum wage and over-time work protection, a
forty-four hour work week, and paid public holidays. Intercede continues to struggle to enable domestic workers to form a bargaining unit to
negotiate conditions of work with their employers.

The racial identities of the domestic workers and their employers raise
some problematic issues for Intercede. There are no statistics on the
racial identity of the employers, although some estimates have been
made of household income.[7] A wealthy Chinese family or a black female
physician may hire a nanny from Great Britain, the Philippines, or the
Caribbean. Non-white women may exploit white women of a different
class.

Despite the racial tension inherent in the situation of many domestic
workers and their white female employers, Intercede has been successful in gaining the support of mainstream women's organizations (Intercede 1987, 1991). Judith Ramirez, a white feminist and one of Intercede's
founding members and its executive director for many years, worked
tirelessly on behalf of domestic workers. White women who support
domestic workers demonstrate gender solidarity, although it may have
a negative impact on them. For example, white women who support the
demands of domestic workers for minimum wages or their right to be
paid time-and-a-half for work beyond forty-four hours a week are
increasing their own child-care costs. And in supporting Intercede's
arguments that requiring a woman to put in two years of live-in domestic work before she can apply for landed immigrant status is unjust and
inequitable, they may further diminish the supply of domestic workers
and increase the cost for themselves.

Although domestic work has traditionally been shunned by Canadian
women, live-in domestic work is even less attractive. Domestic workers
complain that employers force them to work during their free time and
attempt to curtail their freedom (for example, by demanding that they
not stay out late at night).[8] There is evidence to indicate that if domestic
workers were not compelled by legislation to live with their employers
they would not, unless working conditions improved substantially. But
'if the nanny is free to walk out the door, the whole structure of the
career woman's life is a teetering house of cards' (Landsberg 1991).

There are some voices of dissent from among employers and from the

Canadian Coalition for In-home Child and Domestic Care, an organization that represents approximately thirty employment agencies.[9] It has argued that the 'pendulum has swung too far in favour of domestic workers and against the employers.' Intercede promotes the cause of domestic workers but may also be endangering their jobs and 'pricing them out of the market.' Hannah Havileck, a spokeswoman for the Domestic Care Coalition, said in a radio interview (1 Oct. 1987): 'Judy [Ramirez], you are concerned about Third World women, and you're not concerned about the Canadian working woman. Have you ever thought of th[em]? ... I have women telephoning me saying that if they have to pay overtime because they simply need the nanny for fifty hours a week ... they are not going to be able to afford a nanny.'

Intercede has attempted to create solidarity along gender lines by identifying structural problems. It has criticized the gender biases of society that place the responsibility of child care on women and assume that the best child care is given in the home by the mother.[10] It has argued that the real problem lies in the state's failure to provide an adequate number of day-care spaces for children.[11] Although day-care costs are subsidized for some women, they are not for middle-class women. The cost of day care for a woman with two or more children is prohibitively expensive, and she is therefore driven to employ a domestic worker who can provide child care at much cheaper cost (Intercede 1981, 3–9).

Intercede's strategy to overcome the differences of power and privilege between women has been to focus on gender solidarity and raise questions about the low value attached to housework by society. A 1980 brief by Intercede to the government of Ontario noted:

Housework has been seen by society in general and governments in particular as having no economic value. The lack of recognition of the value of housework done by women for their own families is extended in the government's eyes to the housework done by a domestic worker in somebody else's home. The fact that a domestic worker does work which is considered of low value, requiring little skill, and which, in fact, could be done by the family members for no pay, means that such workers are often considered not to be 'real workers.' (10)

Intercede has argued that housework is 'productive work' and should be treated on par with other kinds of labour performed in the marketplace. The household is the workplace for domestic workers and should be regulated and monitored like other workplaces (Intercede 1991, 2–3).

The government's reluctance to do so is sometimes interpreted as a sign of its gender and racial biases and its complicity in the exploitation of this group of women.

A 1990 court decision that said a potential domestic worker must be judged simply on her ability to do the work and not on her potential to settle in Canada led to a suspension of the Foreign Domestic Workers Program (Watson 1991). A thorough review of the program was initiated by the Department of Employment and Immigration. A government official analysed the Foreign Domestic Movement program by explicitly identifying the underlying racial tension. He wrote: 'My premise is that the foreign domestic program is really two programs. One is the true temporary worker program involving British nannies and the like. This one should be left alone. The second program involving the Caribbean and the Philippines is, however, a sham ... Very few people from this latter group come with the intention of remaining in domestic work ... And the upgrading courses that we make them take are more show than substance ... It leaves us with a program that pumps people, who have gone through a half-assed selection assessment, into the Canadian labour market' (quoted in Daenzer 1991, 247–8).

The government was sensitive to the high visibility of the domestic workers in the media and the support they enjoyed from large sections of the Canadian women's movement. It had to meet the needs of Canadian employers, appear to treat all applicants equitably, and eliminate explicit gender biases from its policies. In 1992 the new Live-in Caregiver Program replaced the earlier program. According to the new regulations, a domestic worker needs a grade 12 education, six months of full-time training, and the ability to speak, read, and understand English or French (*Globe and Mail* 28 Apr. 1992; *Domestic Cross-Cultural News* June 1992, 1). She has to live with her employers, and at the end of two years of employment, she qualifies for landed immigrant status. There are no additional requirements.

The new guidelines, particularly the education and language requirements, have been denounced by Intercede and Third World women as racist because they discriminate against domestic workers from the Philippines and the Caribbean and favour Europeans (*Globe and Mail* 15 Feb. 1992, 3 June 1992; *Domestic Cross-Cultural News* Jan. 1992, Feb. 1992, June 1992). A spokesperson from the Congress of Black Women argued that the new laws are yet another form of 'systemic and institutional racism and sexism perpetrated against black women and women of colour' (*Domestic Cross-Cultural News* March 1992, 3). And the president of the

Canadian Auto Workers urged the minister to withdraw the new rules and denounced the government's racism in the process:

Is it not ironic that Canada has the most lax rules when it comes to business immigrants, but the toughest when it comes to domestics? What hypocrisy! Is it not outrageous that many employers have had to remove unjustifiable Grade 12 entry requirements under Canadian Human Rights laws and employment equity initiatives, yet your government now suggests that a Grade 12 is necessary to clean the toilet bowls and feed the children of those who can afford to employ domestic labour? What nonsense!

How can you proclaim that Canada is a tolerant society when your own government practises such overt racism? (*Domestic Cross-Cultural News* March 1992, 2–3)

But the Canadian Coalition for In-home Child and Domestic Care supports the new regulations. These new rules enhance the role of employment agencies as 'gatekeepers' for domestic workers, who are 'dependent on private agents to secure an offer of employment as a condition for entry into the country' (Bakan and Stasiulis 1992, 34).

By referring to the workers as caregivers rather than as domestic workers, the new legislation has tried to avoid the debate about the devaluation of housework or women's work in immigration policies. Theoretically, it has raised the status of domestic work by requiring occupational training and educational requirements (Kingston 1992). Unlike in Britain, there are no training programs for domestic workers in the Caribbean or in the Philippines (or in most Third World countries) so the training requirement will probably bar poor women from these countries from entering Canada, 'precisely the women who have been willing to accept the low pay and poor condition of domestic work that has been shunned by Canadian women' (*Globe and Mail* 7 Aug. 1992). Intercede conducted a survey of 213 of its members and came to the conclusion that only 19 per cent of them would qualify under the new Live-in Caregiver Program (*Domestic Cross-Cultural News*, Sept. 1992, 1).

The new program transfers the selection process and the decision making to source countries. Once a domestic worker is selected to come to Canada, she automatically gains the right to become a landed immigrant after two years of employment as a live-in caregiver. But the new program implicitly moves the location of any further protest to the Philippines and the Caribbean (and other Third World countries), which may not be particularly responsive to allegations of class and gender biases in Canadian legislation.

The plight of domestic workers is an issue of class and race as well as of gender. The example of domestic workers shows the valuable role of community organizations in mobilizing women to struggle against gender, race, and class discrimination, and middle-class, white women have shown solidarity with the most disadvantaged women from Third World countries, sometimes in contradiction to their own specific interests. However, integrating feminist ideals into public policy remains problematic.

Funds allocated through a variety of state agencies have enabled middle-class women from Asia, Africa, and the Caribbean to organize women from their own communities. Although the mandate of their community-based organizations is to provide social services, the opportunity to come together with women who are similarly situated increases consciousness of their common experiences of race, class, and gender oppression. Participating in struggles initiated by the groups politicizes middle- and working-class women, and they become more articulate about their own oppressions. It provides women of the same ethnic and racial background with a safe space where they feel more confident in expressing themselves and are not fearful of retaliation by powerful 'others.'

Ethno-specific and immigrant women's organizations provide opportunities for middle-class women to hone their political and organizational skills so they can develop strategies for negotiating coalitions and alliances between different groups and to exercise leadership. These organizations provide an independent political base from which women from Asia, Africa, and the Caribbean can assert their right to speak for themselves and for women from their own communities.

The existence of autonomous immigrant women's or ethno-specific organizations shows the diversity of organizations within the women's movement. The diverse struggles of white, middle-class women and women from Asia, Africa, and the Caribbean and their different circumstances make it necessary to form alliances and coalitions among themselves. But questions of privilege and power arise in ethno-specific and immigrant women's organizations. Middle- and working-class women from Asia, Africa, and the Caribbean have to negotiate among themselves to define their priorities and set up agendas for political struggles. This process creates tension and division and reveals their ideological and political differences.

The emergence and increased popularity of ethno-specific and immigrant women's organizations attest to the difficult conditions of women's lives and give the lie to those who stereotype women from Asia, Africa, and the Caribbean as passive victims. Legal challenges are not easy, but when they occur they give hope to women that some justice is attainable. Such struggles empower them.

9

Immigrant Women and Wife Abuse

Wife abuse is one of the most violent manifestations of patriarchal domination and male power. To help women who need services and support to eliminate the abuse which threatens their lives, community-based groups have lobbied state agencies and politicians to acknowledge the severity of wife abuse and to allocate resources to support abused women. But feminist theory has shown that the state has been complicit in maintaining the patriarchal values that underlie women's oppression. Consequently, the dependence of community-based groups on the state for funds creates a tension between the goals of providing culturally sensitive services to non–English-speaking, working-class women and the patriarchal state and society in which abuse occurs.

State recognition of wife abuse as a serious problem in Canada encouraged community organizations to introduce services for abused women from their ethnic groups. In this chapter I focus on marriage and gender relations because community organizations focus primarily on women who have been abused by their spouses. But the problem of violence also exists between common-law spouses and dating partners and in same-sex relations.

Physical abuse, including sexual abuse, can range from slapping, hitting, or punching to forcing a woman to have sex against her wishes. According to the Ontario Women's Directorate brochure 'Let's Break the Silence,' emotional abuse can include 'insulting a woman; threatening to hurt her; treating her badly in front of others; blaming her for things that are not her fault; controlling where she goes and what she does.' The Ontario Women's Directorate explains that the 'terms "wife abuse" and "wife assault" are used when a man hurts or threatens a woman he is in a relationship with.'

There are distinctions between abuse, assault, and battering. 'Assault' is part of Canadian legal terminology which defines sexual assault as a criminal offence. The term 'battering' suggests physical violence of an extreme kind, but it can cover a variety of situations. Linda MacLeod defines it broadly: '[t]he loss of dignity, control, and safety as well as the feeling of powerlessness and entrapment experienced by women who are the direct victims of *ongoing or repeated* physical, psychological, economic, sexual and/or verbal violence or who are subjected to *persistent* threats or the witnessing of such violence against their children, other relatives, friends, pets and/or cherished possessions, by their boyfriends, husbands, live-in lovers, ex-husbands or ex-lovers, whether male or female' (1987, 16).

'Abuse' is the most general term. An abused woman who seeks services from community organizations may be seeking support or advice but may not wish to lay a formal complaint or press charges against her spouse. And the law does not consider every form of abuse an offence. When a woman goes to a community organization or to a shelter for women to seek help, it is not important to determine whether a woman's complaints fit into a definition of assault, battering, or abuse. That becomes relevant if further legal action is contemplated or if some additional resources are required, such as housing.

At a workshop on wife abuse which included thirty-five service providers, it was argued that a wide interpretation and definition of what constituted wife abuse had to be adopted. Most women who were present agreed that abuse was anything that a woman experienced as control over her and that she believed to be abuse. The service providers asserted that it was not for them to make judgments on what they believed to be abuse; rather, their role was to provide a supportive environment in which a woman could best consider all the options that were available to her.[1] As used by service providers, the term covers any kind of behaviour that is experienced by a woman as abusive.

My account of the role of community organizations in providing services for victims of wife abuse focuses particularly on South Asian women for two reasons. First, my South Asian respondents could assume that I had some familiarity with South Asian norms, and this facilitated free and full discussions. They felt no need to be reserved or defensive in discussing the problem of wife abuse in our community. Second, my knowledge of Indian culture, history, and politics enabled me to analyse the different ways in which wife abuse in Canada and South Asia are manifested and to see how immigration affects wife abuse in South Asian families. In this chapter, black women are less well represented, but some training manuals and booklets include black women in their research samples (see, for example, *Setting the Precedent* by Milagros Paredes [1992]).

COMMUNITY RESPONSES TO WIFE ABUSE

In the mid-1970s the women's movement brought to public attention the abuse that some women were being forced to endure in their homes (Barnsley 1985, 17). Feminist discussions of wife abuse, unlike discussions of family, sexuality, socialization, and images of femininity, recognized that women from Asia, Africa, and the Caribbean might experience wife abuse somewhat differently from white Canadian women (Randall 1989, 4; MacLeod 1987, 26–7). By the 1980s wife abuse had become recognized by public policy, social service agencies, and community groups as a serious problem for women in Canadian society (MacLeod 1987, 3). At the same time, the existence of human rights laws, and their use by oppressed groups to challenge discrimination, encouraged policy makers to respond to wife abuse in ways that would forestall allegations of racial and gender biases. This public ethos favoured the assertion by community groups serving immigrant women that they were best placed to provide social services to women from racial and ethnic groups. They particularly made such a case on behalf of women who did not speak English and were unfamiliar with, or alienated from, white Canadian norms.

Community organizations have documented the prevalence of wife abuse among immigrant women as a group and among immigrant women in specific ethnic and racial groups, and have discussed the violence experienced by immigrant women (OCASI 1992a). For example, the Chinese Family Life Services of Metro Toronto, the South Asian Family Support Services, the Korean-Canadian Women's Association, the Network of Filipino-Canadian Women, and the South East Asian Services (Vietnamese) have documented the occurrence of wife abuse for their communities. Other groups of women have published need-assessment studies to make a case for social services for immigrant and refugee women who are victims of sexual assault (e.g., *Setting the Precedent*). In addition, there are several handbooks (e.g., *Towards Equal Access* by Fauzia Rafiq [1991]) and training manuals (e.g., *Working with Assaulted Immigrant Women* by Monica Riutort and Shirley Small [1985]) which advise service providers about the need to be culturally sensitive, about identifying the kinds of problems immigrant women sometimes encounter, and about explaining how to counsel immigrant women.

The reports produced by community groups on wife abuse make a simple and straightforward argument. Women from ethnic and racial communities confront cultural, social, and racial barriers that obstruct their access to services from mainstream agencies, but the community-based organizations can provide 'culturally sensitive and linguistically appropriate' services to women from their groups. State agencies should allocate resources to community groups to ensure equality of access to social services by all Canadian women. Many of these reports describe the processes that were followed in arriving at these conclusions: group discussions with the users and providers of services, workshops for service providers, or retreats with other service providers. These processes facilitated the emergence of a consensus among community organizations on the need for culturally sensitive services, the inadequacy of funds allocated to them by state agencies, the necessity of extending their programs, and the existence of racial bias in mainstream social service agencies. However, there is no agreement on how to overcome these problems, and no alternative counselling models have yet been proposed. The research and writing of reports provide opportunities for information sharing. But, more significantly, coming together with other women who have similar experiences raises the consciousness of gender, race, and class oppression among the women and politicizes them.

The literature by community groups traces wife abuse to patriarchal domination and gender stratification within the family. The submission of the South Asian Family Support Services to the Canadian Panel on Violence Against Women (1992) states:

We believe that the crucial variable in the explanation of violence against women is patriarchal power and the resulting social inequality between men and women. Capitalism has encouraged the possession of material property and women are also considered property to be possessed and dispensed with. Gender socialization has always emphasized that man is the 'head of the household', 'the bread winner' and 'the lord and master' of all. Women are to be submissive, quiet, and obedient. Assertiveness is equated with selfishness ... [South Asian women] spend most of their lives under strict supervision of the family, in order to acquire appropriate 'gender specific' behaviour.

None of the studies describes abuse as a medical or pathological problem within the family. Rather, they focus on explaining how patriarchal domination in the family's culture constructs gender roles and beliefs and norms that support inequality within the family. The abuse is often precipitated by the spouse's perception of being thwarted in his desire to exercise exclusive authority over the family's resources, including his wife's wages, and over his wife's domestic work (A. Papp 1990; Chan 1989; Paredes 1992).

A South Asian Woman in her late twenties who has survived wife abuse described her situation in this way at a conference on wife abuse organized by the South Asian Family Support Services (26 Apr. 1992).

I waited for over a year for my husband to change to a nice person. I hid from everyone that I was being abused and our newborn son was being assaulted. Not even my brother and sister, with whom we lived in the same apartment, knew of how I was being treated. Every time I would go to the washroom I would come back to the room and find my son lying on the icy cold window. [My husband] would take off all the baby's clothes and put him there all naked. I would come back to find him shivering. When you are upset and you see your own baby treated this badly by his own father, it is just very confusing.

My husband told me that if I always obeyed him, then he would, out of gratitude, be good to me and stop hitting our son. So I figured that since he is going to change, there is no use in letting anyone know about how he is treating me or what he is doing. But things just kept getting worse.

My sister and friends told me that he had told them that he had only married me to come to Canada and he [was] going to leave me after he got his Canadian citizenship. You wouldn't know how hurt I was. So that night when he started fighting with everyone I called the police. The police took him away, and later on he got out of jail on bail. We had a mistrial the last time at court, because all the witnesses were not present and his lawyer declined to proceed with the trial. The judge asked the police to interview some people. The police interviewed my aunt, brother, sister, and brother-in-law. The [police] wanted to find someone who saw my husband hitting the baby or me. And I am saying, how is this possible when he did it in a room that was always locked and we were always in the room, and he had the door always locked? I was too upset to get mad ... The police told me I'd be lucky to send my husband to jail for a while, let alone deport him.

It's very difficult knowing what to do even though you know you have your family support. And now, even though we are separated, I always feel that he is out there waiting for a chance to grab my son and kill him. He didn't show up for the [hearing] of child custody and no one knows of his whereabouts, I feel [scared] even more.

I used to be so scared to go out alone that I always went out with my brother or friend. Just when I thought I had got control of my fear, I had to go to the court to see my coordinator. I made myself go on the bus and I prayed all the way there that I wouldn't see my husband anywhere. But my horror increased when I got to the court. I found out that one of the charges against my husband was dropped. The police had told me that they would be adding more charges from the evidence they had received. I asked my coordinator how this is possible – that a charge can be dropped. She said I will have to wait and talk to the Crown Attorney about it. So I guess I will have to wait and see. But this is very frustrating.

I have been attending a support group, and it has helped me a lot, but it is just not enough. I don't think I will ever be able to get over this experience.

Reports by the Chinese Family Life Services and the Korean-Canadian Women's Association explain that immigration alters traditional gender roles. For example, the wife may have a paid job for the first time in Canada (Korean-Canadian Women's Association 1991, 5–20). These changes create additional stress on the family, resulting in abuse of the wife:

To most immigrants, underemployment and occupational changes are ego-shattering and depress[ing] realities. When traditional men find themselves having to share power and status with their wives, they may resort to further asserting their authority over their wives ... To Chinese-Canadians, the redistribution of power in the family acts as a threat to their concept of manhood and husbandhood. In order to restore familiarity and equilibrium within themselves and in the family, some traditional men resort to violence to regain control and reduce their pain and hurt. Women often find it hard to leave their abusive marriages as they have never expected marital separation, on top of their separation from their country of emigration. (Chan 1989, 2)

Women who do not speak English and who are victims of wife abuse are placed in particularly poignant circumstances. They work in poorly paid jobs that require long, difficult hours, which reinforces their economic dependence on their spouses. Their lack of English isolates them from the larger society, and they may be unaware of legislation regarding wife abuse and the social services available to them (South East Asian Services 1992, 16–24; A. Papp 1990). Perhaps the most serious consequence of their inability to communicate in English is their additional victimization through misinformation. They may not know that, since 1984, sponsored immigrants who are victims of wife abuse have been eligible for welfare and public housing and cannot be deported if it can be formally established that the sponsorship has been severed (Riutort and Small 1985, 10–16; Pope 1991). A women may be told by her spouse that, if she reports the abuse, he will withdraw his immigration sponsorship and she will be forced to return to their country of origin, or that he will withdraw his sponsorship of their family members (A. Papp 1990; South East Asian Services 1992). The woman is intimidated by the spouse with additional threats of having her children taken away by him or removed from her care by a social welfare agency.

A South Asian political activist noted that men frequently keep under their control important documents such as passports, children's birth certificates, their wives' educational certificates, degrees, and diplomas, and even their social insurance numbers (Interview, 8 May 1992). A woman's access to social welfare requires a social insurance number, passport, health card, and bank book (Riutort and Small 1985, 10–14). Without these documents, a woman who is a sponsored immigrant faces a much more complicated process obtaining access to welfare or public housing, finding a job, or relocating her children to new schools. These additional barriers may keep a woman trapped in an abusive home.

Cultural norms and values regarding the family, marriage, and divorce explain why women hide their problems, stay in abusive homes for long periods of time, and refuse to reveal abuse to others within the community or to members of the larger society. The Chinese Family Life Services describes the traditional concepts governing 'proper conduct and attitude' in the family:

The Chinese family concept regards the individual's behaviour as inseparable from that of the family ... An individual's behaviour represents not only the collective qualities of the immediate family but also those of the ancestors. Thus, the faults or virtues of an individual family member's behaviour are shared by the whole family. This concept of 'face' includes the face of the nation and fellow country persons. The preservation of the family/nation's integrity has more importance than the individual's personal interests. An individual is therefore taught to suppress his/her grievances and emotions for the sake of harmony and the name of the family/nation. (Chan 1989, 1)

The cultural behaviour patterns or norms that inhibit women from using social services may not be well understood by white Canadian counsellors and service providers, who may misinterpret the behaviour and attitude of women from ethnic or racial groups by labelling them as 'passive,' 'unresponsive,' 'resistant,' or 'unmotivated' (Interview, 8 Oct. 1992). Women in Third World countries are unfamiliar with social service agencies and are dependent on informal networks for help. They may not understand the code of confidentiality that binds service providers, and they may fear that their personal problems will become widely known in their communities. They therefore opt not to use social services (South East Asian Services 1992; Chan 1989). And a stigma may be associated with being helped by formal service agencies. For example, in India social services are available only to the very poor and desperate, and thus South Asian women are reluctant to seek social services in Canada. Some feminist referral services are available to women in India and Sri Lanka who are victims of abuse, but these may not be widely known (Kurkulasuriya 1991; Forum against Oppression of Women 1990).

Women who do not speak English are dependent on their ethnic or racial community for all their social interactions, and this situation compels them to abide by the norms of the group. In the Filipino community, reporting abuse 'would cause the person, her family, and community embarrassment' (Cervantes 1988, 5). Women from Asia and southern Europe fear that in revealing the abuse they may violate the group's cultural norms and incur ostracization by the community (Pinedo and Santinoli 1991, 67; South East Asian Services 1992, 15). One English-speaking, middle-class South Asian (Sikh) woman told me that she had been abused by her spouse for twenty-one years in Canada. She finally reported the abuse and legally separated from her husband. With no marketable skills, she was forced to accept welfare to support herself and three teenaged children. All her South Asian friends abandoned her because she was a divorced woman on welfare (Interview, 22 July 1992).

The tardiness of agencies in beginning to do outreach among ethnic and racial groups makes it difficult for women in those groups to gain access to social services (Chan 1989, 29; OCASI 1987). Information about social services and shelters may be unavailable to them or available only in English. In the summer of 1992, I called several shelters in Toronto and requested printed information (flyers and brochures) in a language other than English or French. Most shelters apologetically confessed that these were not available as yet because they had no resources to produce translations. This problem is indicative of the priorities of the shelters, because special grants from state agencies are available to finance translations. Information about wife assault is available in several languages from Education Wife Assault, which has produced pamphlets, brochures, flyers, and audio tapes in different languages to reach non–English-speaking women.[2] These are available in some shelters.

Political activists and service providers from Asia, Africa, and the Caribbean complain that media campaigns against wife abuse that encourage women to seek the help of the police are not reassuring for women who come from Third World countries. Women who come from Latin American countries with political dictatorships may have no confidence in the police. Women who come from India, where the police are widely believed to be corrupt, easily bribed, and abusive, would seldom wish to seek police help. Women from the Philippines, particularly during the regime of Marcos, perceived the police as 'intimidating symbols of repression and corruption' (Cervantes 1988, 5; South East Asian Services 1992, 17). It is unlikely that an abused black woman in Ontario would have much confidence in the police force, whose racism has so often been publicly examined and criticized. And many communities would condemn a woman for reporting a man to the police: 'A woman will experience strong feelings of guilt and betrayal if she has to call the police in order to stop the violence. The community [may] ... condemn the woman who called the police or went to court, if the man had been previously jailed or tortured in his country of origin. She, then, will be accused of using a repressive institution to inflict more pain on "the poor man," so to speak' (Pinedo and Santinoli 1991, 67). But such reasoning asks the abused woman to bear the brunt of gender violence so that other members of the group are not exposed to racial oppression.

PROVIDING 'CULTURALLY SENSITIVE' SERVICES

State agencies have responded to the documentation of wife abuse by allocating resources to community organizations to provide services to women in ethnic and racial groups. A whole network of services is now in place to help women who are victims of wife abuse, although service providers note the need to extend existing services and add new ones. Women from Asia, Africa, and the Caribbean can get help from mainstream social service agencies, ethno-specific agencies, immigrant women's centres, and shelters.

Community groups have argued that mainstream social service agencies do not have enough personnel from different ethnic groups to provide effective services. At the same time, they have urged state agencies to compel mainstream social service agencies to institute affirmative action policies in their hiring practices. Community groups assert that hiring procedures and training for boards of directors and staff indicate the extent to which established family services agencies are committed to addressing the needs of diverse ethnocultural and racial communities (Medeiros 1991, 40). The presence of a multicultural workforce would ensure that access to social services was widely available to ethnic and racial groups (OCASI 1988).

A survey of sixteen mainstream agencies in 1989 found that only six had 'formal or informal policies or practices to address the issues of the ethnocultural and racial population of Metropolitan Toronto.' The informal policies included staff training, recruitment of members of racial and ethnic groups to the boards of directors, outreach, and research (Medeiros 1991, 41). Some agencies, such as the Family Services Association of Metropolitan Toronto, have introduced educational programs for identifying wife abuse and have hired women from Asia, Africa, and the Caribbean to direct them (Interview, 20 June 1992). But generally agencies have been slow to 'recognize the dramatic changes in the ethno-cultural and racial composition of Metropolitan Toronto' and to direct resources to serving these populations (Medeiros 1991, 41).

Community-based ethno-specific organizations and immigrant women's organizations play a critical role in reaching abused women. Community workers mediate between the abused woman and the larger society. They inform state agencies of the need for social services for women of their own ethnic communities, and they inform abused women about immigration regulations, legislation regarding wife abuse, and the availability of a variety of social services. Through these organizations, women can 'speak for themselves.' Because their experiences are different from those of their white counterparts, they can 'help to develop the content of their social services by defining the oppressive practices of mainstream societies as well as the oppressive practices within their own culture' (Chaudhry 1992, 12).

News about the existence of a community group helping abused women spreads by word of mouth through the community. Community groups advertise the services they offer in different languages in ethnic and local newspapers and by placing flyers in the neighbourhood. A South Asian woman who had survived wife abuse for twenty-one years finally sought the services of the South Asian Family Support Services after she saw the agency's flyer at the local public library. Frequently, the first contact with an organization is made anonymously over the phone by the abused woman herself, a relative, or a friend. Or a woman may go to an organization under some pretext and only after several meetings reveal the abuse she is experiencing and her need for support and services.

The availability of support and services through community groups can break the isolation of an abused woman and encourage her to come forward to seek help. Community groups provide counselling, sometimes in the woman's mother tongue, and they have introduced support groups for women who are survivors of wife abuse. Community workers (along with the police) may accompany a woman who is a victim of abuse to collect her personal belongings. They escort women to social service agencies, to lawyers' offices, and to the courts. Their support can reassure the woman and enable her to leave an abusive home.

Community workers explain that an abused woman needs a diverse range of services. Her first requirement may be counselling, but counselling is only the beginning of a long process of re-establishing her self-esteem and becoming self-supporting. Settlement services, such as programs for language training, skills development, and employment readiness, are all integral parts of the services that are required by abused women. A South Asian counsellor with the Riverdale Immigrant Women's Centre describes the process:

[Women] come to us in a state of shock, numbed by abuse. They are shattered because their family is broken. A few months later, the same women have wiped away their tears and are beginning to make a life for themselves. Some have joined English as a Second Language classes or job-oriented courses, while others are working. In fact, some of the women are even ready to help others in similar situations. Some of the qualities, i.e., sense of responsibility, patience, and belief in fate, that led them to accept their abusive situation, now help them to come to terms with their new life. (Cloutier 1989, 15)

By arranging and attending workshops and conferences, service providers keep one another informed of issues that are significant for certain ethnic groups. This information enhances their sensitivity to the cultural and social differences between women and facilitates counselling of women from Asia, Africa, and the Caribbean. Community groups may host workshops and conferences to provide service providers with information about legislation and services that are available to women who are victims of abuse. Or they may have professional development days for service providers in a particular ethnic group to share their experiences and suggest or develop solutions to problems they encounter in their delivery of services. For example, the South Asian

Family Support Services held a conference, 'Police and Court Responses to Wife Abuse,' for service providers in April 1992; the Caribbean Association of Peel held a conference, 'A Cultural Perspective on Wife Assault,' in November 1991; and the Korean-Canadian Women's Association held workshops on family law, which referred primarily to violence within the family, in 1988. In September 1992, Education Sexual Assault organized a retreat for women on its advisory committee to discuss the possibility of more research on wife abuse. In addition, in 1992 Education Wife Assault and the Ontario Women's Directorate organized conferences on wife assault and violence against women. These workshops and seminars raise the consciousness of the workers about their own biases (e.g., homophobia) and help them develop strategies for overcoming them.

When an abused woman walks into the offices of a community group, the presence of women like her reduces tension and anxiety. Similar physical appearance is significant since the service provider and user may have different understandings of South Asian cultural and social norms and may have different political commitments. The assumption of commonality facilitates the counselling and the provision of social services. The counsellor and the abused woman can quickly establish 'a relationship of trust so that healing and problem solving can begin' (Riverdale Immigrant Women's Centre 1991, 4). Women who work in community groups note that their familiarity with the cultural and social norms of the abused woman helps to reassure her and provides a supportive environment in which to discuss her problems. They are able to avoid some *faux pas* that might alienate the abused woman and lead her to return to an abusive home.

At a workshop for South Asian service providers organized by Education Wife Assault in June 1992, the group tried to identify the factors that contributed most to their counselling. The thirty-five women who were present named education and a liberal family background, particularly the family support and encouragement they received during their education and in later life. These factors created a basis for inculcating in the women they counselled appropriate attitudes towards other people. The experience of being an immigrant created empathy for abused women. One woman focused on her experience of discrimination: 'I wonder if we are fully accepted, if we have the opportunities to accomplish what we want. The ladies who come to me can't find employment, a place to live, education. The women don't fit in – they believe they are discriminated [against] because of their colour.' Some women argued that the race and gender discrimination that they themselves had experienced created a basis for understanding the women they helped. A lesbian South Asian woman explained that understanding the links between her oppression and the oppression of the abused women she counsels gives her an insight into 'helping the women to help themselves.' Women's experiences of marriage across cultures, religions, and race were regarded as important in helping them to understand the alienation experienced by abused women and their feelings of 'not belonging.' A woman from Sri Lanka who had come to Canada after having lived for periods of time in India and Australia described her dilemma in this way: 'I don't know where I belong. Hindus don't accept me. And when I go to a Christian family, they don't accept me. I try to fit in with South Asians but their ideas don't always please me.' Another woman, who grew up in Britain, observed: 'The women I see are from the old culture – I can relate to them in their need to be accepted for themselves rather than try to become like others. There is the practical and the psychological problem ... we have to accept ourselves first rather than wait for other people to accept us. This idea runs strongly in my counselling.'

Some of the community workers considered their work as just a job, but others were politically committed to feminism and to antiracism. These politically conscious women strongly opposed the use of counselling models that were derived from social work, clinical psychology, or anthropology.

The available literature on cross-cultural counselling is not thought to be particularly useful for cases of wife abuse. Asian women argue that the counselling models derived from the experience of white societies are irrelevant to their needs. The executive director of the Riverdale Immigrant Women's Centre noted that the counsellors had been trained in these clinical and social work models and had to consciously attempt to overcome their own professional socialization (Interview, 16 Sept. 1992; Riverdale Immigrant Women's Centre 1991, 4). Another South Asian woman added:

There has been some work done on culturally-specific counselling but there is no definite paradigm or theoretical framework which has been tried and is known to have worked. Many frontline workers tell us that although they have the required language skills and are also culturally sensitive, their interventions are usually based on the Western model of counselling. For example, most of the theoretical frameworks for counselling assaulted immigrant women get their underpinnings from Western feminist ideology: women are empowered by emphasizing individual rights and freedoms. This type of intervention leads to confusion in the minds of many South Asian women, who usually come from traditional families (Chaudhry 1992, 12).

Umbrella organizations, such as the Multicultural Alliance for Access to Family Services, have been working to develop alternative models and strategies that would be more applicable to the experiences of ethnic and racial groups (Rajan-Eastcott 1992).

When I urged one of my South Asian respondents during an interview (8 May 1992) to explain what she meant by 'culturally sensitive counselling,' she said the difference was the contrast between the Western value of individualism and the family orientation of the South Asians:

In the Western world, empowerment means that you are here for your individual self. You are only responsible for your own self, so you take care of yourself. But that's not the way South Asian women see it. They have to think of everybody else – their father, mother, brothers, sisters – family's prestige. Their behaviour has implications for the entire family. So their language and their philosophy are very different. All they want is the beating to stop, which is very different from empowerment.

Another South Asian woman explained it in this way:

Western therapy often focuses on the individual and her needs ... In many non-white groups, the welfare of the family comes before the welfare of an individual, especially if the individual in question is a woman. Individual counselling is even perceived as being destructive of society as it promotes personal well-being of an individual at the expense of the community ... For [South Asians] the family and its obligations take precedence. Therefore, individualistic desires are not emphasized ... [I]f independence of the client is encouraged, it may be met with strong parental disapproval at home. In fact, some helping professionals or agencies may even be perceived as being 'home breakers' if, for example, they encourage a woman to be independent of an abusive spouse. (Gill 1992, 67)

Community workers understand the social and cultural inhibitions of the women from their groups and can suggest strategies for dealing with abuse in ways that are culturally acceptable. For example, a South Asian woman may want, not to end her relationship with her abusive spouse, but only to find someone to mediate on her behalf and stop the violence in her family. Mediation sometimes stops the abuse; a counsellor or social worker may persuade the abusive spouse to change his behaviour by informing him of the penalties. In other cases, a woman's seeking help may lead to more abuse. And a South Asian woman may be reluctant to obtain separation or divorce, despite the abuse, because she fears that it will have a negative impact on her unmarried siblings or her own unmarried daughters (Valiante 1991). To alleviate the abused woman's guilt and anxiety, community workers from the ethnic group can assure her that, regardless of the choice she makes, their services will continue to be available to her.

The report by the Chinese Family Life Services recommends that service providers use language in ways that make a woman feel comfortable and that facilitate counselling. For example, the report suggests avoiding the use of such words as 'crime,' 'abuse,' and 'problems' and substituting 'against the law,' 'violence,' and 'issues.' This agency's service providers also try to reassure the woman that her choices are within the cultural boundaries of the group; for example, leaving her home or opting for divorce can be seen as protecting the children or saving her husband from further confrontations with the law. The report observed: 'We have found the use of metaphors and Chinese idioms successful in helping clients to increasingly realize the values governing their sense of self and interactional patterns. Challenges to destructive values/destructive interpretation of traditional values were conducted in an educational/discussion/exploratory manner rather than in a direct, empowering or confrontational style' (Chan 1989, 24).

Other community groups recommended avoiding question-and-answer formats, leading up to the problem gradually rather than confronting it immediately, and being sensitive to status (e.g., never asking children to interpret for Vietnamese women). Some groups argued that women from their communities have difficulty adjusting to the formalities of making appointments and having a fixed time for their counselling sessions. Community groups may dispense with these protocols if a woman is undergoing a crisis, or has phoned and wants to come to their offices immediately, or has arranged time off from work and can only see the counsellor at a specified time (George 1992, 9).

The work of community groups is feminist in practice, although feminist theory may not be consciously articulated by them. Feminism in this context means that counsellors support the right of women to live a life free from abuse. At some workshops, elderly and 'traditional' South Asian women spoke vehemently against wife abuse. Community and shelter workers are sensitive to the cultural sanction imposed by their group on divorced women and to the right of the woman to make her own choice, even to return to the abusive spouse, despite their belief that the abuse will only be repeated. In an interview (10 May 1992), one social worker explained: 'We are very clear that it is the woman's choice. We need to protect her and ensure that there is a very clear safety plan and she's aware of it. There are times when we have to be directive around that, when her life is at stake, or we see that her life is at stake and she's not recognizing it. The safety of the women and children is paramount.'

Community workers attempt to inform a woman seeking help about legislation against wife abuse and to explore all the options and choices available to her, including the possibility of retraining and becoming self-supporting. The South East Asian Services advises that 'field workers may have to respect the choice of abused Vietnamese women to stay [with the abusive spouse].' They should 'appreciate the strength and courage that these women show, which, in some cases, has meant enduring the abuses all the way from Vietnam, through refugee camps, to Canada.' But they may point out to her that there are people in her community 'who would interpret such endurance and silence as a sign of the woman's own belief that she has caused the anger and brutality of her husband' (South East Asian Services 1992, 25).

Community groups and service providers are cultural interpreters for women who do not speak English and are unfamiliar with white Canadian norms. Their interpretations of culture represent idealized norms rather than practised values that determine everyday interactions. I examine these problems by analysing the notion of community and culture with specific reference to South Asians.

COMMUNITY AND CULTURE

The term 'South Asian community' covers a wide diversity of regional, social, and cultural differences. As noted in chapter 2, South Asians come from many different parts of the world: India, Pakistan, Bangladesh, Sri Lanka, East Africa, Britain, and the Caribbean. They are divided from each other by caste, class, language, religion, and degrees of urbanization and Westernization. If a community is defined in terms of daily, face-to-face contact, organization, and 'groupness' – *Gemeinschaft* – it is doubtful that we can describe the diverse South Asian population in Toronto as comprising a community. There is not one South Asian community but many South Asian communities. How they are identified depends on who identifies them: *'someone* perceives "togetherness" in a social network, or group of networks or even a social category, and thus labels the individuals in that network or category as a community' (Di Leonardo 1984, 133).

I encounter one community of South Asians in the homes of my sisters. These South Asians come to Canada from different places, they differ in religion, and they belong to different castes. The males have all received post-graduate or graduate degrees from universities in the West, and they are now practising physicians, scientists, engineers, corporate executives, or private businessmen. Their wives are full-time housewives or have 'women's jobs.' They are much more concerned with social mobility for themselves and their children than with maintaining South Asian values and norms. But they resent racial stereotypes and racism, which impede their careers or their children's educational progress. They interact with white Canadians socially in their private lives, and they permit cross-cultural dating for their sons and daughters.

The second community of South Asians with which I am familiar includes South Asian women who are professional colleagues. These are middle-class women who have come to Canada from all over the world; they belong to different religions and castes. I meet the few South Asian women who hold academic positions in Canadian universities at conferences or at my place of work. We are brought together by our common experience of marginality in Canadian universities and exclusion from some academic environments (Naidoo 1990; Brown 1991; Dhruvarajan 1991). The political consciousness of these women is shared by other professional women, such as social workers, teachers, and community workers. Together these women assert their right and that of all members of their ethnic groups to represent and speak for themselves on issues of gender and racial biases in the larger society. They have varying degrees of commitment to maintaining South Asian culture. Some may wear South Asian dress as a symbol of their political beliefs, which range from liberal to radical feminism. They are almost all committed to multiculturalism and to antiracist politics.

A third South Asian community includes the working-class women whom I meet at temples, gurdwaras, mosques, South Asian restaurants and grocery stores, or community centres and offices. These women usually dress in South Asian clothes and speak English hesitantly or not at all. Those who work outside the home are employed in factories or other low-skilled occupations with other South Asian women. Their spouses are factory workers. Their social interactions are exclusively with other South Asians, which reinforces their ties to their South Asian culture. But this reinforcement of their cultural values is counterbalanced by the pull exerted by their children to adopt some white Canadian norms as well.

Community groups advocate only on behalf of working-class South Asian women. They are the primary users of the services available through community organizations and shelters. Middle-class South Asians usually have access to the services of mainstream agencies or of private counsellors. Community groups seldom discuss the socioeconomic background of their users, but they note the cultural and regional diversity of their clients and suggest this complexity makes it hard for white Canadians to understand them. They nevertheless tend to ascribe to South Asians a common set of values and norms.

Immigration may also create cultural and social distance from the prevalent norms and values of communities in South Asia. For example, a South Asian lesbian who came to Canada from Malaysia as a teenager asked a group of thirty-five South Asian service providers at the Education Wife Assault workshop in June 1992 to do an exercise from an American book on homophobia that asked them to identify public images and portrayals of lesbianism from their countries of origin. She seemed to be entirely unaware that South Asian women generally do not feel comfortable discussing sexual relations publicly. Portrayals of heterosexual relations in popular culture are very conservative in South Asian countries, and there is no public discussion of homosexuality. The speaker was more familiar with Western than with South Asian norms, and she seemed insensitive to the culture of the women at the workshop.

Community groups often describe the culture of South Asians in ahistorical terms. (A similar tendency can be observed for Chinese and Vietnamese culture.) They present gender roles prescribed by the culture as an unchanging reality rather than as something transformed by politics and economics (Rafiq 1991; Kohli 1991a). One South Asian social worker attempted to explain the norms of South Asians by observing that 'South Asian generally come to Canada with a number of common family experiences and shared values.' They share 'a lifelong commitment to one marriage and to the maintenance of the family unit.' They recognize the 'male as head of family,' 'respect and honour elderly members of the family,' and accept the 'subordination of the individual to the family.' 'Interdependence and not independence' guides family relationships (Valiante 1991, 96; see also Cloutier 1991; Chawla 1990). But such descriptions do not reflect the realities of the women's lives in Canada or in their countries of origin. They do not show how these values have been transformed by education, urbanization, technological change, women's employment, immigration, or the women's movement in the countries of origin or in Canada. The Imam (priest) of a mosque in Toronto described the results of some of these changes:

The South Asian man [was] expected to be the absolute ruler of his home and his [dependants] were expected to be quiet and submissive ... This has led to tension, division, and violence in the home. In Canada the South Asian Muslim woman, for example, could not bear all the responsibilities of the household for economic pressures forced her out of her home and into the work force. Contact with feminists also affected her outlook on the role of the husband and father. Fatigue, depression, and misunderstanding have combined with cultural isolation and resulted in a very high percentage of family feuds and broken homes. Consequently, children growing up with this tension have inherited a disillusioned outlook on their family, culture, and religion. (Quick 1990, 121–2)

The diversity of communities of South Asians in Canada and of the cultures within these communities means that community-based organizations dealing with wife abuse may adopt an idea of the 'community' they serve that is not representative of all South Asians in the country. But the assumption of shared values and norms increases their legitimacy in the eyes of granting agencies and facilitates their counselling work with abused women.

Immigrant women are separated from the traditional support of their families, and they often feel 'isolated and without any help in Canada. Most of them do not have access to support from friends or family' (A. Papp 1990, 100). But their isolation is also symptomatic of their abusive situation, which they share with women across cultures. Non–English-speaking women may be isolated from white Canadian society, but they can relate to the diverse South Asian communities in Toronto. There are several places of worship (temples, mosques, gurdwaras, Jamat khanas, churches) where South Asians congregate on Sunday. There are thriving business and entertainment districts in the west and east ends of the city. In addition to community groups, there are voluntary organizations which provide social and recreational opportunities with other South Asians. But some women are isolated by the abusive spouses who do not allow any communication with other South Asians.

The significance of an immigrant's loss of family and friends may be somewhat exaggerated. Research on violence against women in India,

England, Scotland, and the United States indicates that friends and neighbours in these countries are reluctant to get involved when they are forced to acknowledge abuse in a friend's or relative's family. They regard it as a 'family matter' and a private affair. Patriarchal values make them reluctant to interfere or support a woman who is experiencing abuse (Dobash and Dobash 1980, 1992; Schechter 1982; I. Taylor 1991). In India or Pakistan, the family can mediate, or some senior and respected member of the family can be brought in to condemn, and thus end, the behaviour of the abusive spouse (A. Papp 1990, 39–40; Interviews 20 July 1989; 10 April 1992).

Sometimes my respondents claimed that the constant informal visiting among families in South Asia acts as a natural deterrent to abusive spouses. The close quarters in which South Asians live, they said, would not provide enough privacy for abuse to be frequent or routine.

Research on violence against women in India does not support the assertion that family and friends can effectively mediate on behalf of the abused woman. In their *In Search of Answers* (1991), Madhu Kishwar and Ruth Vanita report that in-laws, particularly mothers-in-law, are often involved in the abuse of a woman in a South Asian family. Emotional and physical harassment may begin when the spouse and mother-in-law demand additional dowry from the wife's parents and may end in the wife's death. The increasing number of these 'dowry deaths' and 'kitchen deaths' are reported regularly in the newspapers.[3] The lobbying of the women's movement has led to new legislation, so that now when a woman dies within the first few years of marriage the burden falls on the spouse and his family to prove that they are not guilty (Balasubrahmanyan 1985, 154–89).

Wife abuse in South Asian families results from the unequal gender relations. South Asian women share with women across different cultures and races some common dilemmas. Their socialization places the burden of the maintenance of the family unit upon them, and they have the primary responsibility for the physical and emotional well-being of their children. While white Canadian women can get the support of formal social service agencies, racial biases exclude women from Asia, Africa, and the Caribbean from access to, and use of, these services, although community groups give them some measure of support in their difficult circumstances.

Immigration makes available a number of services (however inadequate or insufficient) and provides women with choices and opportunities that are not available to them in their countries of origin. A South

Asian survivor of wife abuse, a woman in her late twenties, told me that she had obtained a divorce from her husband because of his abusive behaviour.[4] She was appreciative of the help given to her by the South Asian Family Support Services, and she was quite proud of having made the choice to live independently (despite having parents in Toronto) with her small child in an apartment in a public housing complex. The opportunity to retrain, live in a separate household, and become self-supporting is available only to upper-middle-class women in South Asia. Most other women cope with abuse until it becomes life-threatening because life in South Asia for a single woman can be enormously difficult emotionally and materially.

The literature on wife abuse prepared by community groups reveals that, although patriarchy is a common underlying cause of wife abuse in all communities, it manifests itself, and is experienced in, culturally specific ways. Immigration aggravates some situations of wife abuse and creates additional sources of dependence and vulnerability for some women.

Community groups have come forward to help victims of wife abuse in their own communities and have struggled to make mainstream social service agencies respond in a culturally sensitive manner to women from different ethnic and racial groups. Community groups cater primarily to working-class and non–English-speaking women. There are differences of class and ideology among service providers and users of services within community groups, but the assumption of shared cultural values and norms facilitates the provision of services. Most significantly, community groups provide opportunities for middle-class and working-class women to come together and share their experiences of gender and racial domination. Such coming together raises their consciousness about their situation and lays the groundwork for solidarity among them.

SHELTERS FOR WOMEN

Shelters are a necessary part of the services offered to immigrant women through community organizations. The primary objective of the shelter is to serve any woman whose life or safety is threatened and who needs emergency housing. Shelters are geared to respond to crisis situations, defined broadly as situations where an individual's coping mechanisms have failed. A crisis could involve immediate physical threat to an individual, an emotional state such as being

extremely depressed or suicidal, or simply not having money for gro-
ceries (Kohli 1991b). With the exception of Shirley Samaroo House,
shelters are not designated by ethnic or racial groups but are used by
women in the neighbourhood or community in which they are located.
During the time that a woman is at a shelter, she is assisted in making
other long-term housing arrangements and is given help getting access
to social services.

Shelters for women are a response to the lobbying of the women's
movement in Canada. Interval House, the first shelter for battered
women and their children in Canada, opened in Toronto in 1973. Some
shelters explicitly state their feminist philosophy, the collective methods
of their work, and their non-hierarchical organization. For example, the
1990 annual report of the Emily Stowe Shelter for Women states:

The Emily Stowe Shelter for Women is a feminist organization that provides
emergency housing and support services to assaulted women and their children.

The shelter is administered on a collective basis; that is, all collective members
equally participate in decision making and share the tasks necessary to keep the
shelter operational ... The Emily Stowe encourages the empowerment of women
who work at and live in the shelter so that these women may challenge the structures that continue to oppress all women.

The philosophy of Shirley Samaroo House focuses more explicitly on
race and class. This shelter was started in 1987 specifically to serve the
needs of immigrant women. A coalition of women from different
groups, including Spanish-speaking women, South Asians, Cambodi-
ans, and blacks, lobbied state agencies, asserting that the needs of
women from their communities were not being met (Interviews, 22 May
1992; 1 May 1992). As stated in its 1988 annual report, the shelter explicitly recognizes the different oppressions encountered by women from
Asia, Africa, and the Caribbean:

The Shirley Samaroo House of the City of York is a feminist organization providing emergency shelter for assaulted women and their children. We recognize the
oppression of women based on gender, race, and class. We are struggling for
economic, political, social, and legal rights that will ensure real alternatives and
choices for all women.

We recognize that woman assault is a crime which results from the patriarchal
and economic structures of society. We also recognize the special needs of immigrant women because of the difficulties in confronting the barriers imposed by

race, class position, language and the pressure to assimilate into mainstream society.

A woman may apply to enter a shelter by simply calling on the telephone. A shelter worker determines whether there is an immediate threat to the life and safety of the woman or her children; if so, the worker gives her the address of the shelter. (To ensure the safety of the workers and residents, the address of the shelter is not advertised.) The shelter worker inquires whether the woman has funds available for a taxi; if not, the shelter offers to pay for her transportation. This route for getting access to the services of a shelter would obviously be difficult for a non–English-speaking woman.

A woman can also be directed to a shelter by a hospital, the police, community groups, or mainstream social service agencies. When women who do not speak English are referred to shelters, the service providers may know the languages that are spoken by the current staff at a particular shelter, or the ethnic identity of the staff, and may therefore seek to match the abused woman with a shelter. However, there are no formal mechanisms for this matching process, and the first priority is to find housing for the woman. Some community groups may continue to counsel or support a woman by telephone; otherwise, the shelter workers take over at that point (Chan 1989, 27).

There are strict rules regarding the maximum age of male children – varying from twelve to sixteen – who can be residents at the shelters. This restriction sometimes poses a problem for abused women who cannot find alternative safe housing for their older sons. My South Asian respondents noted that it imposed a difficult choice for the women, who felt they were being asked to choose between their own safety and the well-being of their male children. But concerns about the safety of the other residents, who have all recently been traumatized by the violence of some male, make such a rule necessary.

Either immediately or when the abused woman is able, the workers attempt to complete a form with her personal information. When a non–English-speaking woman has come to a shelter with a service provider from a community group, that individual may act as an interpreter. Otherwise, the shelter may request a group or individual in the neighbourhood to interpret for the woman. The Barbara Schlifer Clinic provides interpreting services in nine languages,[5] and shelters may use these services.

Each shelter is designed to work as a large family where women live together with their children. This situation was described in 1974 in the pioneering work of Erin Pizzy, *Scream Quietly or the Neighbours Will Hear*. Subsequent studies by Lee Ann Hoff and Donileen Loseke suggest that difficulties can arise when a diverse group of women have to share accommodation. There can be big differences between 'idealized expectations and practical experience' (Loseke 1992, 117–18; Hoff 1990). The difficulties of running a household with women from diverse backgrounds and the bias of state agencies in favour of hierarchical structures have compelled shelters, despite their commitment to collective modes of operation, to introduce greater structure into their organizations. However, the degree of structure and hierarchy varies from one shelter to another.

Theoretically, in the shelter there is no hierarchy of the staff and residents, and everyone shares in the chores of maintaining the household. A woman is assigned a room which she shares with her children or with other women. There are rules that residents are expected to follow, although they vary from shelter to shelter. A woman who refuses to abide by these rules is warned and, if necessary, removed from the premises after repeated violations (Interview, 12 June 1992). The residents are responsible for maintaining their own rooms and caring for their children. The job of food preparation is rotated among the residents, and all residents are also responsible for maintaining the common areas. If a woman has special dietary needs, she is given money to buy food.[6] All residents are given some money for personal expenses and for transportation.

The women who come to the shelters are primarily working-class women with limited resources, and they all suffer degrees of stress. They belong to different ethnic and racial groups and are single or married. Their beliefs about marriage, divorce, and feminism can vary. Conflicts and tensions can sometimes develop among the women, and these tensions are exacerbated by racial biases. My respondents were outraged and embittered by the racism within shelters and in the delivery of social services. A long-term shelter worker, herself a survivor of wife abuse, complained in dramatic terms of suffering from burn-out:

There was no place for me to address the wounding that I experienced on a daily basis [at the shelter]. We have to work with our [women of colour] and white women, as well as fight with the collective and board and demand changes right then at the shelter. It is a very heavy toll. Expectations come when you are working for a violence-free society. I felt totally battered [at the shelters]. I left the system even though my livelihood was at stake. (Interview, 28 Mar. 1992)

Conflicts emerge at the shelters because of interpersonal and structural racism. Overt racist behaviour is monitored and sanctioned by the staff, but more subtle forms of racism result in alienating residents and workers. Some women feel that their child-rearing practices are being disparaged, or that their children's cultural values are being undermined by the other residents, or that they are being excluded from conversations among residents. Negative comments about the food that a woman has prepared for the residents create tension. The South East Asian Family Services argues that Vietnamese and Chinese women have to choose 'between being abused by women of other races/ethnic groups' and 'being abused by their husbands.' Many Vietnamese and Chinese women would rather return to their own homes because they have some hopes of reconciling with their spouses (South East Asian Services 1992, 27). South Asians face similar situations (Rafiq 1991, 11).

At the Shirley Samaroo House, workers faced the dilemma of having to ask a woman to leave the shelter becase of her racist behaviour when she had nowhere else to go. Women from Asia, Africa, and the Caribbean had the right to use the shelter without being verbally abused. The issue was resolved by treating the racist behaviour as an occasion for conflict resolution and by counselling to help the woman overcome her attitudes (Interview, 7 Oct. 1992). The Homeward Family Shelter gives a resident a warning for using a racial epithet and, after a second or third violation, asks the woman to leave the shelter (Interview, 12 June 1992).

The feminist principles that guide the shelters encourage them to emphasize peer support and group discussions, which can also serve as consciousness-raising mechanisms. But group discussions can be problematic:

The shelter's philosophy of empowering the women invited their participation in decision-making. But avoiding traditional institutional controlling tactics is apparently not enough, since the women's participation was less than ideal. Many of these women are very traditional and therefore are not immediately comfortable with this radical feminist value. Thus, exposing battered women to feminist values must be done carefully. Such exposure cannot impose these values, despite the staff's political commitment to changing traditional values they believe are related to women's vulnerability to violence. These complex dynamics and values regarding violence and women's empowerment complicate the problem of including battered women in the everyday concerns of the shelter (Hoff 1990, 150).

Group discussions may be better suited to white, middle-class experience. Working-class women and women from Asia, Africa, and the Caribbean are often impatient with the long process entailed in group discussions (Hoff 1990, 163).

Feminist research has revealed how group dynamics that are set up or led by males alienate and silence women. Similar observations have been made about middle-class versus working-class groups. It is difficult to draw women from different cultures and races into discussions. Individuals in a cross-cultural setting are reluctant to discuss the unseemly aspects of their culture with others or to be critical of their own culture or nationalities. Women from different cultures, and particularly women who belong to stigmatized groups, have difficulty revealing details about their families, culture, or society to others.

Group discussions obviously exclude women who do not speak English. They also exclude women whose limited facility with English prevents them from expressing their personal feelings other than in their mother tongue. In addition, the cultural context in which abuse occurs may also create distance, rather than a sense of shared feelings or a common political consciousness, among the women in group discussions. For example, immigrant women may have concerns about their own or a relative's pending immigration status, which may not have much significance for other women. Immigrant women may also experience anxieties over establishing the breakdown of sponsorship that would make them eligible for welfare and housing, and this concern may also isolate them from others.

Cultural differences can also create issues. For example, abuse in South Asian families sometimes includes recriminations about the wife's parents and relatives. In-laws may be party to the emotional abuse, and the home may include relatives of the spouse. The contribution of these experiences to the woman's sense of being abused is not always appreciated by those who are not familiar with the culture. Group discussions would not reduce such a woman's sense of isolation. And discussions about subjects such as homophobia or lesbianism may be perceived, not as educational, but as extremely threatening to women committed to traditional and conventional norms and beliefs. Such discussions may compel a woman to return to the abusive home.

Shelters also offer opportunities for abused women to discuss their problems privately with shelter workers. Shelter workers reject the professional model of social work that positions the social worker as the 'expert' and an abused woman as her 'client' or 'case.' Friendship is their preferred model for the relationship between shelter workers and residents. Shelter workers seek to validate the woman's experiences. They believe in 'the authority of experience' and give importance to the everyday reality of women's lives. According to an Interval House brochure, 'Feminism at Interval House means that we listen to and believe women, that a woman's personal life experience matters. These personal experiences of abuse are connected to the larger social, economic, and political systems that keep women in a less powerful and dangerous position all over the world. Our feminist perspective values all women and is committed to helping to change a society and a world that does not treat women with respect.'

Interactions between shelter workers and residents may be influenced by racial biases. One South Asian service provider complained that some white shelter workers, with stereotypical understandings of South Asian women, assumed that a resident would return to her spouse (Interview, 28 April 1992). Some white Canadian residents may not wish to discuss their problems with South Asian workers because of racial biases (Interview, 21 Apr. 1992). However, one Filipina woman argued that the women who come to the shelter have low self-esteem and are not in a position to look down on any of the other residents or the workers (Interview, 12 June 1992).

Racism in the hiring of shelter workers is of great concern to women from Asia, Africa, and the Caribbean. As shown in earlier chapters, women from Asia, Africa, and the Caribbean complain that either they are not hired in the larger society or they are hired as part-time workers or on short-term contracts. For services to be equally accessible to all Canadian women, the staff at shelters must be multilingual and multi-ethnic. Shelters in neighbourhoods with a strong presence of one ethnic group usually include some workers who speak that group's language. But none has the ideal mix of workers representing different ethnic and racial groups. The difficulty of representing the diverse number of languages and cultures prevalent in Toronto is compounded by the limited resources of the shelters. Shelter workers may verbally support the need to do more outreach among ethnic and racial groups or to have a more racially and ethnically diverse staff, but they are reluctant to give these issues priority or allocate resources to them (Interview, 21 Apr. 1992). Despite the rhetoric of equality and equal access, the status quo of racial and ethnic inequality is maintained in the shelters, as elsewhere.

Following is a Korean-Canadian woman's account of her stay at a shelter:

Due to problems with my family, I was living at a shelter with my three children. During my stay, I faced many incidents which I felt were cases of racial discrimination. I'd like to share some of my experiences.

1. It was May of 1991. One day, my daughter on her way to the shelter from school, had been badly hurt. I found out that the childcare worker who brings kids home from school had pulled my daughter's ponytail. As a result, my daughter's neck was twisted and she fell.

The childcare worker seemed to treat my children differently. She was fine with the other children but not mine. My daughter, in grade 4 at the time, was crying after her fall but the childcare worker thought it was amusing and only laughed.

I was very upset. I tried to get an explanation with the help of the shelter workers, but they only said the childcare worker was trying to save my daughter from a dangerous situation. The childcare worker had absolutely no intention of apologizing.

It wasn't until the KCWA [Korean-Canadian Women's Association] intervened and disclosed the matter that the childcare worker apologized to my daughter. If KCWA had not been involved, this incident would have ended with my daughter being at fault. I had wanted a formal apology. I was not satisfied with this outcome, but seeing my daughter's neck healing, I thought I'd be better to forget the whole thing.

2. Living in a shelter is like communal living. Everyone had to take turns on various duties of cleaning, taking out garbage, etc. Because I was an immigrant in an unfamiliar country, I didn't want to be blamed for anything. I made sure my children were well-behaved and put in extra effort to give a good impression, sometimes by taking on other people's duties.

Despite all my efforts, I clashed with this one woman, a woman who I thought held an attitude of superiority and looked down upon me.

Once, it was my turn to clean up the cafeteria. I finish[ed] all my duties, even took out the garbage, and went to bed. But the next morning the woman yelled at my kids, 'It was your mom's duty but she didn't do it!' My angry children replied that I had finished my duties but that it was the people who came out to use the cafeteria during the night who didn't clean up. At this the woman mimicked them and called them racist names. The upset children burst into tears as they replied, 'We are Korean.'

3. Another woman comes to mind. A woman by the name of Maria. She had a 14-year-old and a very young daughter. I thought about the hardship she must be going through and wanted to help her. I offered to babysit her children, gave her some clothes, and did her a lot of favours.

However, the woman only discriminated against my children. She would yell at my kids to get up when they were watching TV, made sure my kids wouldn't approach her even to compliment her cooking, and threateningly ask[ed] my daughter if she hid any food in her room. When my children made snacks, her kids would come and steal them. But she ignored all this among many others. There were many other children but she would only pick on my children, making their lives miserable.

Though my children were relatively well-behaved in the shelter, the woman's harsh treatment of them makes me feel victimized and unfairly treated. (Korean-Canadian Women's Association 1992, 12–13)

Shelters provide an example of the additional difficulties confronted by women from Asia, Africa, and the Caribbean in struggling against their oppressions and give the lie to those who argue that their attachment to their culture encourages them to passively accept their traditionally prescribed gender roles. Shelters are needed by all women who are victims of abuse, but women who do not speak English have greater difficulty getting access to them, and women from Asia, Africa, and the Caribbean may experience racism within them. Some feminists at the shelters are sensitive to the interlocking nature of all systems of domination and the need to struggle against them simultaneously. But other shelter workers think of their work as merely doing a job, and residents simply want to obtain the services they need. The gender oppression common to women across race and class lines brings women together in a shelter and provides an opportunity for raising their consciousness and establishing solidarity. But racist behaviour between residents and between staff and residents sometimes wastes this opportunity.

The work of community organizations in providing services to women who are victims of abuse helps women to help themselves. But by emphasizing the needs of individual women and concentrating attention on providing services, community organizations may be ignoring the social origins of the problem. A number of writers have noted the pull between meeting the needs of individual woman and working to bring about social change or transforming the unequal gender relations of society. The risks for the women's movement in moving from social change to social service are described by Emerson Dobash and Russell

Dobash: 'At stake is ... whether they remain activists and advocates contradicting the status quo and competing for adoption of their vision of social change or are transformed into or replaced by hostel managers and therapists supporting the status quo' (1992, 46).

Community groups and shelters need resources to provide services, a situation that encourages them to adopt the priorities of grant-giving agencies. Susan Schechter argues that 'shelters exist within a society that denies resources to women and undercuts their individual and collective power. Without material resources – housing, jobs, and sufficient incomes – empowerment as a universal goal is unreachable.' Focusing on services helps individuals, but 'no challenge is presented to the very ideological framework that men and women incorporate to justify male violence' (1982, 253, 25).

There need not be a polarization between providing services and promoting social change. Women who use the services may change their minds on issues after meeting with other women or listening to alternative views of wife abuse. Their feelings of self-blame may be reduced, and their perspective about the power dynamics of their own personal situation may be altered. Work within community organizations can also raise the consciousness of workers and politicize them. Workers are confronted almost daily with evidence of inequality and its impact on women's lives. They begin to re-examine their own socialization, culture, and gender roles in trying to understand the problems of women who come to them for help. Discussions with other service providers politicizes these women, and their work becomes a way to channel their own outrage at the sexist and racist oppression experienced by women (Interview, 7 Oct. 1992).

Women who work with community organizations on behalf of women from Asia, Africa, and the Caribbean come together in coalitions to struggle against racism in the provision of social services and in shelters for women. These coalitions have sometimes compelled state agencies to recognize the distinctiveness of the experiences of women from Asia, Africa, and the Caribbean. In the process, the women hone their skills in lobbying, organization, and leadership, laying the foundation for further advocacy of antiracist and antisexist social policies.

10

Conclusion

Throughout this century, the experiences of women from Asia, Africa, and the Caribbean in Canada have been marked by race, gender, and class discrimination. But the social and political environment has slowly changed: the explicit racism and sexism of the early part of this century has given way to public disapprobation of any expression of racism, classism, and sexism. Ideals of race, class, and gender equality, however, are not always practised, and blatant and subtle forms of exclusion and discrimination continue to mar the lives of women from Asia, Africa, and the Caribbean. Nevertheless, the expression of such ideals has created an ethos in which subjugated groups can articulate their oppressions and have some hope of being heard.

Race, class, and gender oppression has informed the everyday experiences of women from Asia, Africa, and the Caribbean. Progressive movements had the potential of including the issues of these women in their political agendas, but the integrated nature of their oppressions was not always understood and their issues were not given priority. Women from Asia, Africa, and the Caribbean were marginalized through the greater part of this century in the struggles against racism by members of their own community and in the struggles against sexism by white Canadian women. Deeply entrenched norms of race and gender domination manifested themselves in theoretical writings, in organizations, and in everyday practices of mainstream feminism.

Women from Asia, Africa, and the Caribbean have identified their absence from the discourses of progressive movements and have asserted their right to speak on their own behalf. There is now a growing body of literature by these women which documents the integrated nature of the multiple oppressions experienced by them and its impact on their families, social relations, employment, and activity in feminist and antiracist movements. This literature is a testimony to the struggles of women from Asia, Africa, and the Caribbean and indicates how they have overcome the resistance to including their voice in discourses about women and racialized groups. These accounts are important additions to scholarship and have significant implications for their everyday lives as well. Such writings can inform laws, policies, and educational practices, and they have consequences for the constitution of self, subjectivity, and experience.

In the early part of this century, the lives of Asian and black women were marked by institutional and everyday racism which isolated them from other Canadians and located them in poorly paid jobs. The explicit racism of legislation, popular media, and everyday interactions labelled them as unwelcome foreigners and outsiders. Chinese, Japanese, and South Asian men struggled against racist immigration policies to bring their wives and children to Canada. Racism isolated them from others in Canadian society, and they responded by drawing close to members of their own racial group. This response reinforced the existing cultural ties between men and women in the Chinese, Japanese, South Asian, and black communities. Although they all experienced racial hostility, their struggles did not make a common cause. Despite the many similarities in their everyday lives, there is no documentary evidence to indicate that there was any communication between women from these communities.

The incipient women's movement did not support Asian or black women by addressing the integrated oppressions of race, class, and gender. Rather, racism of the larger society was reproduced within the women's movement and was articulated in a feminist ideology that focused on the gender and class struggles of women. Feminists of this period have been criticized by academics for their explicit enunciation of racism when they referred to racialized groups and for their lack of empathy for the greater oppressions of women from Asia, Africa, and the Caribbean.

The discussion of racism in the first wave of feminist theory and practice has kept the focus on white women, but it does not tell us what significance feminism had for the everyday lives of Chinese, Japanese, South Asian, and black women. The maternal feminism of liberal feminists and the 'militant maternalism' of socialist feminists did not include the concerns of women from Asia, Africa, and the Caribbean. This shortcoming was perhaps inevitable. There were very few women from these communities present in Canada. Many did not speak English, and they frequently worked alongside their spouses to eke out a marginal existence. The politics of socialist parties and the labour movement accommodated the concerns of working-class women and included southern and eastern European women within their ranks, but, with the exception of Co-operative Commonwealth Federation, these groups remained silent on the oppressions of Chinese, Japanese, South Asian, and black women at least until the 1930s. These women, were sexually and economically exploited by men of their own communities and by white Canadians, who kept them at the bottom of the class hierarchy. Only the missionaries supported them, and their work was marred by their adoption of the racist sentiments prevalent at the time.

The women who came to Canada from Asia, Africa, and the Caribbean after the Second World War were very different from those who immigrated in the early years of the century, and the communities they subsequently established in all major metropolitan areas in Canada differed dramatically from those that had been established at an earlier time in British Columbia. Postwar immigration policies encouraged professionals to immigrate, and special immigration programs facilitated the arrival of entrepreneurs and business people. Dependent family members, refugees, and temporary workers added to the diversity of women who came from Asia, Africa, and the Caribbean. Some of these women had professional qualifications, while others had only a high school education; some came alone as domestic workers, while others were accompanied by their families; some spoke English fluently, while others not at all. The women were found in different kinds of occupations, clustered at the upper and lower levels of job hierarchies, and in unionized and non-unionized workplaces. The diverse characteristics of these groups were made invisible by a new, supposedly neutral term – 'immigrant women' – which became part of popular terminology. The term was widely used to refer to only non–English-speaking, working-class women from Third World countries or from southern or eastern Europe.

Middle-class women from Asia, Africa, and the Caribbean challenged the exclusion of themselves and their working-class sisters from feminist theory and politics of the 1970s and 1980s. Dialogue and discussion occurred across national borders. Criticisms made in one country were picked up by racialized women in other countries, who supplemented them with their own experiences. They revealed the inadequacy of gender as an explanatory tool and identified the complexity and specificity of the oppression experienced by women of different races, cultures, and classes.

Throughout the 1970s, white, middle-class feminists had identified gender as the primary source of women's oppression. Women from Asia, Africa, and the Caribbean argued that theories based on gender alone tended to be reductionist and to disregard totally the different ways in which gender oppression is experienced by racialized women. They noted that, although gender is shared by all women, it is more important in shaping the lives of middle-class, white women than it is in the everyday lives of working-class, white women or non-white women. When women from Asia, Africa, and the Caribbean experience oppression or discrimination, it is rare that race, class, or gender alone is the decisive factor. Race, class, and gender biases reinforce each other in subtle and complex ways.

Women from Asia, Africa, and the Caribbean went from being absent to being marginalized in feminist theory and practice – a change that was accompanied by conflict and tension. Middle-class women from Asia, Africa, and the Caribbean accused middle-class, white feminists of dominating the feminist agenda, which led to some soul-searching and crises of conscience. Some white, middle-class feminists attempted to identify and root out their own unconscious exercise of privilege. But the fundamental cause lay in systemic biases of institutions and organizations which distribute power and privilege unequally and in which white, middle-class feminists had limited power to effect change. Within women's organizations, white, middle-class feminists introduced new practices that recognized the systemic discrimination experienced by women from Asia, Africa, and the Caribbean. But their good intentions did not always bring the desired results; feelings of bitterness eroded attempts to change and led to disappointment on all sides. Nevertheless, such initiatives provide some hope that in the near future women might cooperate with each other across lines of race and class in their struggle for equality and social justice.

Women from Asia, Africa, and the Caribbean have asserted their right to speak for themselves in mainstream women's organizations and have come together in 'immigrant women's' organizations and in ethno-specific groups that serve the needs of women from their own communities. These community-based groups are important platforms where they can identify the discriminatory practices of institutions and organizations and demand changes to ensure some measure of equity for women from Asia, Africa, and the Caribbean.

The goals and objectives of the Canadian multicultural policy support the demands for culturally sensitive social services provided, wherever possible, in the language most familiar to the women. The Charter of Rights and Freedoms and human rights legislation further reinforce the arguments of these community-based organizations for additional social services to ensure equal access for non–English-speaking, working-class women. As a result, state agencies have allocated some resources to start community-based groups, to provide social services, and to advocate changes in discriminatory legislation and policies.

A range of community-based groups has come into existence. Some of these groups are ethno-specific and provide services to women from their communities, while others offer social services to a broadly based community of 'immigrant women.' There are also umbrella organizations which attempt to give the demands of community-based groups some political coherence and which advocate on their behalf with state agencies. These organizations act as watchdogs to ensure that the rights and needs of their constituents are considered in new allocations of resources, restructuring of programs, and changes in legislation.

The funding of community-based organizations by state agencies constrains, to some extent, their services and advocacy. Funds from state agencies make them circumspect in their critiques of state policies and fearful of alienating state personnel by militant denunciations of race, class, and gender discrimination. Despite these limitations, their services have empowered non–English-speaking, working-class women to challenge the oppressions of race, class, and gender biases.

Community-based groups provide alternative services that are also available to women from Asia, Africa, and the Caribbean through mainstream agencies. The social services offered by community-based groups take into consideration the cultural norms of the women, their difficulty with the English language, and their feeling of discomfort in environments dominated by white Canadians. Community-based groups also offer services to meet the settlement and adaptation needs of new immigrants (e.g., how to start looking for a job), and they help them get access to social services (e.g., housing, welfare, and legal aid). At other times, community-based groups provide supportive services to help the women overcome their unfamiliarity with, and alienation from, Canadian norms. They escort women to courts or to doctors' offices and organize support groups for them.

Services provided by middle-class women in these organizations are valued by working-class women and by the ethnic and racial communities. Common culture, language, and status as immigrants in Canada create a bond among women from the same ethnic and racial groups. Working-class women feel reassured that their needs will be understood and met by women from their own communities. The comfort and familiarity among women from the same ethnic or racial group lead quickly to identifying problems and finding solutions that are acceptable to the clients. Establishing such confidence would require more work and time across lines of race and class. For example, working-class, non–English-speaking women do not have to persuade sceptical service providers of the racism of society or explain or defend their cultural norms when they are victims of violence. In community-based groups, clients can assume that service providers are familiar with their cultural norms and are sympathetic about the racism, sexism, and classism they experience in the wider society.

Women's resistance to their multifaceted oppressions is, to some extent, determined by the social context. Immigrant women may lack the support of their families in resisting male violence in Canada, but in their countries of origins they were stymied by the lack of social services and by financial insecurity. In Canada some South Asian women, who are stereotypically thought of as 'traditional,' have refused to accept the violence in their own homes. They are supported by community-based service providers who explain their rights, assist them in laying charges, and help them to gain access to welfare, housing, and legal aid. If they decide to start a life away from their abusive spouses, counsellors give them information about how to enrol in language programs and to gain some job-related skills. Support groups for victims of violence help women build the self-esteem they have lost during their years of abuse.

Institutional biases of race, class, and gender have impeded the life chances of women from Asia, Africa, and the Caribbean. Working-class, non–English-speaking women have experienced gender discrimination in gaining access to language-training programs. Domestic workers have confronted deterioration in the conditions that were imposed upon them when they came to Canada. Language training and restricted entry into Canada for domestic workers have cut across lines of race and ethnicity. Community groups, however, have come together to challenge the race, class, and gender discrimination inherent in some legislation. In these cases, advocacy eliminated the discrimination, but it also conveyed an important message to society at large: the women were not passive victims of their circumstances but could overcome their differences to struggle against the racism, sexism, and classism of Canadian society.

Community-based groups empower middle-class and working-class women from Asia, Africa, and the Caribbean. They organize conferences and workshops to give information about women to mainstream agencies. Service providers meet together to share ideas and devise strategies for dealing with common problems. These meetings demonstrate to the women that they are not alone in being oppressed by race, class, and gender discrimination, that their experiences are shared by other women. Meetings between women who share experiences of race, class, and gender discrimination direct their attention away from blaming themselves and focus their energies on identifying and naming their oppressions. Such meetings provide opportunities to women to hone their skills in organization, negotiation, and leadership.

Women from Asia, Africa, and the Caribbean in Canada have encountered white, middle-class domination in the women's movement and in society at large. They have sometimes struggled alongside white, middle-class women to challenge the class, race, and gender biases of society, and they have come together with women from their own ethnic and racial groups to challenge racism and classism. These struggles have empowered and motivated them to further resist and challenge their multifaceted oppressions in the hope that their efforts will eventually be successful in gaining equality and social justice for themselves and for future generations.

Women's Organizations Consulted

Achievers Community Services
Afghan Women's Group
Asian Lesbian Group
Cambodian Women's Association
Caribbean Community of Peel
Coalition of Visible-Minority Women
Council of Agencies Serving South Asians
Cross-Cultural Communication Centre
Driftwood Community Centre
Education Wife Assault
Ejarma Cooperative
Family and Children's Services
Family Services Association of Metropolitan Toronto
Filipina Women's Group
Filipino Community Centre
Homeward Family Shelter
Immigrant Services Organization
Immigrant and Visible-Minority Women against Abuse
Immigrant Women's Job Placement Centre
India Rainbow Community Services of Peel
Intercede
Iranian Women's Association
Korean-Canadian Women's Association
Malton Neighbourhood Centre Multicultural Association
Noah's Reception Centre
Ontario Human Rights Review Task Force
Ontario Women's Directorate

Peel Multicultural Association
Red Door Shelter
Rexdale Immigrant Women's Centre
Riverdale Community Health Centre
Riverdale Immigrant Women's Centre
Somalian Women's Group
South Asian Family Support Services
South Asian Women's Group
Thorncliffe Neighbourhood Office
Toronto Asian Community Centre
United Way, Peel Region
Women Working with Immigrant Women
Women's Health in Women's Hands
Woodgreen Community Centre

Notes

1: INTRODUCTION

1 Women from Asia, Africa, and the Caribbean vociferously articulated their exclusion from feminist theories and practices at the annual conference of the Canadian Research Institute for the Advancement of Women (CRIAW) in 1992. See also paper by Joanne St Lewis (1993), and the conversation recorded in Makeda Silvera's 'Organizing exclusion: Race, class, community and the white women's movement' (1986). For an American example, see the debate between Catharine MacKinnon and women of colour in *Yale Journal of Law and Feminism* (1991).

2 I have not examined the experience of immigrant women from Latin America, North Africa, or southern and eastern Europe (including Russia). The race, class, and gender oppressions experienced by First Nations women have some resonance with those of women from Asia, Africa, and the Caribbean, but their history and politics are very different from those of the immigrant groups that are studied here.

3 Robert Miles defines racialization as 'a dialectical process by which meaning is attributed to particular biological features of human beings, as a result of which individuals may be assigned to a general category of persons which reproduces itself biologically' (1989, 76–7). Skin colour is the most prominent of these features, but individuals may be racialized (e.g., as 'non-white') by others of the same skin colour on the basis of ethnic or religious differences.

4 These remarks were made by Judy Rebick at the Conference of the Canadian Research Institute for the Advancement of Women in Toronto (14 Nov. 1992), during the session on women's organizations and the state.

5 The term 'white women' includes a diverse number of European groups, some of which were stigmatized while others were accorded privileges. For

example, in the early 1900s Irish and Ukrainian women experienced discrimination because of their countries of origin, Jewish women because of their religion, and Finnish women because of their socialist beliefs. Some southern and eastern European groups, such as Ukrainian, Jewish, and Italian people, were also racialized. But historians have analysed the experiences of these women by defining them as ethnic rather than racial groups.

In the early 1900s Ukrainian and Jewish women made common cause with other white women in struggling for women's issues in socialist parties and in the labour movement. Although they remained somewhat separate from other white women in these organizations, their issues were represented (however marginally) within these forums. There is no documentary evidence to suggest that Chinese, Japanese, South Asian or black women made common cause with white feminists or participated in any way in their organizations. Thus my use of the term 'white feminist' in this period refers to women of northern European (primarily British) descent.

2: THE EXPERIENCE OF RACE AND GENDER DISCRIMINATION

1 A critical analysis of the literature on women from Asia, Africa, and the Caribbean appears in chapter 5. There I argue that ethnic histories at first subsumed accounts of women's experiences under those of males. Women's history, at least up to the 1970s, emphasized the contributions of white, middle-class women and used the unitary category of 'women' as if they were describing the experience of all women.

See also Medjuck (1990) for a discussion of how race excluded women from Asia, Africa, and the Caribbean from women's history and how gender excluded them from the literature on ethnicity and race.
2 For examples, see the Women's Book Committee of the Chinese Canadian National Council 1992; Brand 1991; Nipp 1983; Silvera 1983; Yee 1987; and Shibata 1980. Others have edited personal letters written by first-generation immigrants; for example, Oiwa (1991) and Kitagawa (1985). And Rosemary Brown, a woman from the Caribbean, has written an autobiography describing her struggles against race and gender discrimination (1989).
3 In contrast, Protestant churches outside British Columbia supported the right of South Asians to immigrate and to bring their wives and children to Canada (Ward 1978, 85).
4 For example, see Strong-Boag 1976; Cleverdon 1974; Bacchi 1983; Cramer 1992.
5 For a discussion of how beliefs held by white Canadians constructed Chinatown as a 'vice-town,' see Anderson 1991, 92–105.

6 An example of women helping women outside a church context is the work of lay women in the Jost mission in Halifax. Middle-class women helped find employment and provided child-care services for working-class women. Christina Simmons explains that this interaction across lines of class allowed the women who received these services to retain 'a strong sense of dignity and pride.' But she does not note the ethnicity of the middle-class women who provided services or of the recipients (1986, 157).

3: RACE, CLASS, AND FEMINIST THEORY

1 There is extensive literature on this subject. See, for example, Kline 1989a, 1989b; hooks 1984, 1988; Lorde 1984; Thornhill 1989; Spelman 1988; Parmar 1989; Carby 1986.
2 See, for example, Medjuck 1990; Adamson, Briskin, and McPhail 1988; Armstrong and Armstrong 1990; Brand 1984; Collins 1991.
3 See, for example, MacKinnon 1991; Thornhill 1989; Silvera 1986, 1989; Open Letters to Catharine MacKinnon 1991; Persad 1992; Javed 1992; Romany 1991; Rhode 1991.
4 Canadian universities are now required under the Federal Contractor Program of the Ministry of Employment and Immigration to conduct a census of their populations. The publication of such data will indicate, among other things, the racial and gender composition of the university's personnel.
5 Feminist literature of the first wave explores these themes, particularly women's struggle for the suffrage. See, for example, Bacchi 1983; Cleverdon 1974. Anthologies on women also discuss many of these themes; see, for example, Stephenson 1973; Campbell et al. 1972; and Fitzgerald, Guberman, and Wolfe 1982.
6 See, for example, Wilson 1982; Bourne 1985.
7 Elizabeth Spelman (1988) has analysed the writings of Simone de Beauvoir and Nancy Chodorow to expose their racist biases. Similarly, Margaret Simons (1979) exposes the biases of Simone de Beauvoir, Kate Millet, Shulamith Firestone, and Mary Daly. And Marlee Kline (1989a) examines some legal writings for their racial biases.
8 In using this and other examples, I do not mean to suggest that the authors have not incorporated the understanding of the integrated nature of race, class, and gender oppression in some of their later works.
9 In contrast, Pat Armstrong and Hugh Armstrong in *Theorizing Women's Work* (1990) integrate an analysis of race, class, and gender throughout the book.
10 Meg Luxton and Harriet Rosenberg in *Through the Kitchen Window: The Politics of Home and Family* (1986) do not include the topic of women's paid domestic

work. The second edition of the book (1990) includes a chapter on Filipinas and Caribbean women's paid domestic work written by Sedef Arat-Koc.

11 Although the threat of rape may be experienced by all women, racial identity still divides them. Makeda Silvera, a black feminist, describes one incident in this way:

> A couple of nights ago I was waiting for the train and this drunk guy, big redneck, came up and started shouting, 'Bitch! Bitch!' I'm really frightened because this guy is really big and I'm wondering what would happen if he came up and attacked me physically. What was I going to do? This white woman walks up on the platform and he starts up again. We kind of look at each other in solidarity and I feel less scared because at least there is another woman. But then, this drunk started calling out 'Nigger! Nigger!' and looking directly at me. That woman, she just looked right through me and there wasn't that kind of connection, that solidarity anymore. It was really frightening. I didn't know what to do. I was angry, I was filled with rage, I wanted to attack the man, I wanted to cry, and suddenly I felt really embarrassed. I didn't know why. (1989, 9–10).

4: RACE, CLASS, AND FEMINIST PRACTICE

1 For example, see the articles in Albrecht and Brewer 1990 and in Wine and Ristock 1991.

2 For another example of the difficulty of developing a theory and practice that retains the significance of gender while acknowledging the diversity of women's experiences, see Ramazanoglu 1989.

3 Gloria Anzaldúa discusses some of the tensions in forming alliances among women across lines of race: 'Despite changes in awareness since the early eighties, racism in the form of "your commitment has to be to feminism, forget about your race and its struggles, struggle with us not them" is still the biggest deterrent to coalition work between white-women and women-of-color' (1990, 221–2). For a discussion of the power relations involved in the experience of women from Asia, Africa, and the Caribbean in feminist theory and practice, see Spelman 1988.

4 For a discussion of Canadian immigration policies, see chapter 6.

5 For example, see Brand and Bhaggiyadatta 1986; Agnew 1990; Khosla 1983; Ghosh 1981; Women Working with Immigrant Women 1988a.

6 This is discussed in detail in chapter 7.

7 State funding of community groups is discussed extensively in chapter 8.

8 For a Canadian example of the power struggle and tension among white feminists and feminists from Asia, Africa, and the Caribbean, see Dewar 1993, 32–47.

9 I refer here to traditional norms and values. South Asian women who have

lived in the West or are identified as 'Westernized' in South Asia may not feel so inhibited in discussing women's sexuality.

10 In this discussion I focus primarily on the differences that class creates between white women and women from Asia, Africa, and the Caribbean. But there are also class divisions among women from Asia, Africa, and the Caribbean which make it difficult for them to form alliances among themselves. Work with community organizations brings working-class and middle-class women together to struggle against racism and sexism. This is explored in chapters 7, 8, and 9.

11 Language can also be used to set up subtle hierachies and 'to reinscribe the politics of domination.' bell hooks has argued that highly abstract, jargonistic language, although highly valued by academic feminists, is inaccessible to large segments of the population and alienates students in women's studies courses and working-class men and women (1991, 1–12).

12 For example, in 1991 the rally of the NAC to Parliament Hill in Ottawa and attempts to meet with various ministers were broadcast on CBC's national evening news and were the subject of a CBC documentary.

The NAC championed the cause of some refugee women in 1993 and brought it to the attention of national media. Two articles appeared in the *Globe and Mail* on 5 March 1993: '"Siege" of immigration offices threatened' (André Picard) and 'Fourteen face violence if deported, committee says.'

13 Delegates representing women from English Canada, French Canada, women from Asia, Africa, and the Caribbean, and lesbian woman were present at all plenary sessions, meetings with the minister in charge of women's affairs, press conferences, and entertainment.

14 The quotation is from the unedited response to 'Changing the Politics of the Women's Movement,' prepared by Salome Lucas (Women Working with Immigrant Women), Judy Vashti Persad (Cross-Cultural Communication Centre), Gillian Morton (South Asian Women's Group), and Nada El Yassir (Palestinian Women's Association).

5: THE POLITICS OF DISCOURSE

1 Feminist critiques of the embeddedness of power relations in epistemology are extensive. See, for example, Smith 1987, 1990; Harding 1986; Jaggar and Bordo 1990; Diamond and Quinby 1988; Code 1991. For a discussion of the power exercised through Western interpretations of Third World societies and the consequent distortion of their experiences, see Harding 1986, 163–96; Lazreg 1990; Mudimbe 1988; Miller 1990.

2 Doreen Indra did a content analysis of news reported in the Vancouver press

from 1905 to 1976 and concluded that 'women have never figured prominently in it; ethnic individuals in the press are inevitably male' (1981, 64).

3 The debate about the exclusion of 'other' groups was spearheaded by the
Ukrainians. Senator Paul Yusyk put forward the idea of a 'third force' in his
first speech to the Senate (Kallen 1988, 236; Burnet 1988, 224).

4 Immigration policy discriminated against some groups on the basis that they
were not likely to assimilate to Canadian norms. Scholars have frequently
interpreted the assimilation argument as a racist rationalization for the differential treatment accorded to immigrants from 'non-preferred' nations (Roy
1989a, 1989b; Li 1988a, 18–22).

   Franca Iacovetta argues that social workers 'were strongly committed to
the process of guiding the integration of the post-war immigrants into Canadian life' and imposed their own, middle-class view of what constituted an
'ideal family' onto the immigrants (1992, 295).

5 This theme is well discussed in John Marlyn's *Under the Ribs of Death* (1971),
which is set in Winnipeg before the Second World War. A Hungarian boy is
driven by the need to be 'like the English' which he associates with being
middle-class and having higher social status. He rejects his own family, but
the larger society continues to perceive him as an ethnic and an outsider.

6 The racism involved in stigmatizing Chinese and Chinatowns is discussed in
Kay Anderson's *Vancouver's Chinatown: Racial Discourse in Canada, 1875–1980*
(1991). Anderson argues that the discourses of the dominant white society
construct the values and norms which are presumed to signify who is a
'Chinese' and what constitutes a 'Chinatown.'

7 Peter Li has also written extensively on race relations and racism in Canada;
see, for example, Li 1980, 1988a, 1988b, 1990; also Li and Bolaria 1983.

8 See, for example, Anita Beltran Chen 1980, 1983, 1987, 1990.

9 For work on the garment industry see, for example, Johnson 1982; Gannage
1986; Seward 1990. For domestic work, see Calliste 1989; Arat-Koc 1990;
Cohen 1991; Daenzer 1991; Bakan and Stasiulis 1992. For a discussion of
immigrant women in the labour force, see Arnopoulos 1979; Giles and
Preston 1991.

10 For a discussion of this topic, see Das Gupta 1987; Ng 1981. Immigrant
women are particularly described as victims of race, class, and gender in
discussions of their paid work.

11 Chapters 7, 8, and 9 examine the literature produced by community-based
groups of women from Asia, Africa, and the Caribbean.

12 There is little literature on this subject. Community groups that provided
services to women from Somalia in 1991–2 frequently described the special
programs initiated on their behalf as necessary to help them overcome

their sexual victimization. Victim status was further heightened by the recent arrivals of refugees escaping a volatile political situation in Somalia.

13 Chapters 7, 8, and 9 elaborate upon these points.

6: SYSTEMIC RACISM

1 My discussion examines racial biases in immigration policies against Third World populations. But immigration policies have also displayed biases towards other ethnic groups, such as Jewish and Italian people (Troper 1982; Harney 1988). And people who were suspected of being sympathetic to communist regimes were frequently denied entry to Canada on grounds of national security (Whitaker 1987).

2 The goal of family reunification is critiqued by some immigrant groups, who argue that the government's definition of family is Eurocentric. The government's definition recognizes only relationships that exist in a nuclear family and does not take into account extended families, which include aunts, uncles, nephews, and nieces. Under the present law, only spouses, children under the age of twenty-one, fiancées, and parents who are at least sixty years old can be sponsored. Immigrant groups have argued that the denial of opportunity to sponsor other family members is discriminatory (Canada, House of Commons, 1984, 58).

3 An example of how race and gender biases can influence assessment by immigration officers is revealed through my own experience. In 1970, I intended to come to study for a PhD in Canada, having obtained admission to the universities of Toronto and Waterloo. But I chose to immigrate and was sponsored by my physician brother. I travelled from Bombay to Delhi for my interview with immigration officers. I was interviewed in a cursory manner for less than five minutes: questions referred primarily to my parents' socioeconomic situation. At the end, the immigration officer remarked that my 'value' in the 'marriage market' had risen substantially by his granting me immigration.

4 Between 1981 and 1986, 40 per cent of women came in the 'family class' and as accompanying dependants of principal applicants (Boyd 1989, 17–19).

5 The 1978 Immigration Act confirms in domestic law Canada's international obligations to protect refugees under the UN Convention. 'The key provisions of that Convention are reflected in sections 4, and 55 of the Act.' They include:

Convention refugees legally in Canada may not be removed unless they are a threat to national security or public order.

Any decision to remove a Convention refugee must be reached in accordance with the due process of law. Unless they are a danger to Canada's security or have been convicted of a serious crime, Convention refugees cannot be removed to a country where their lives or freedom would be threatened on account of race, religion, nationality, political opinion, or membership in a particular group.

6 This point was made in two recent court decisions. In one case, a woman from Guyana claimed that she was fleeing wife abuse and, since no social services were available to her in Guyana, if she was deported and forced to return, her life would be in danger. She was denied refugee status. In another case, a woman from Saudi Arabia argued that she was escaping gender persecution. The Refugee Board that heard her appeal denied her status, arguing that gender was not an enumerated category. However, subsequent to the intervention of Ed Broadbent (former leader of the federal New Democratic Party and now president of the International Centre for Human Rights and Democratic Development), she was granted a ministerial permit and allowed to stay on humanitarian grounds. The minister's decision 'to intervene was a unique ministerial prerogative that does not by itself indicate a change in policy' (York 1993).

7 The United Nations Economic Commission Report for Africa emphasized the difficulty of acquiring data about women. It observed: 'Being the most marginal of poor rural and displaced people, the women take a low profile in an alien environment and are the least accessible population for purposes of data collection. Such women, when reached, are often unwilling to talk partly because of fear. When persuaded to talk, they misreport the required information mostly as a result of their state of illiteracy.' However, there are data to show that 75 per cent of refugees from Afghanistan in camps in Pakistan are female and 90 per cent of refugees from Somalia are female (quoted in NAC, 1987, 15).

8 The Canadian Employment and Immigration Commission has introduced a small Women at Risk program in recognition of some of the additional difficulties that refugee women may encounter. A few women from Third World countries have come to Canada under this program (Spencer-Nimmons and Wong 1989, 42–4).

9 For more discussion of racism at the workplace, see Henry and Ginzberg 1989; Billingsley 1985; Ng 1988a, 1988b; Women Working with Immigrant Women 1988b.

10 This example was cited in *Equality Now* (1984). On 29 December 1979, an immigrant from Jamaica received a letter signed by an evaluation officer of the Ontario Ministry of Education and the Ministry of Colleges and Universi-

ties. The person concerned had a BA from Harvard University and a PhD from Stanford University. The letter stated:

To Whom It May Concern

Based upon information available to the Ministry of Education and the documents provided, ... this person's educational attainment in the United States may be considered comparable to the completion of at least Grade Thirteen in the current Ontario school system.

8: IMMIGRANT WOMEN AND THE STATE

1 One shelter for battered women in Toronto has an annual budget of $1.2 million. Most of this money comes from the provincial and federal governments and from the municipality of Metro Toronto. Only one-sixth of the money is from private donations (Dewar 1993, 35). In contrast, the South Asian Family Support Services is entirely dependent on funds from various governmental and private agencies.
2 For details of the language classes and programs offered through state agencies, see Giles 1987b.
3 Instruction in the use of words like 'north,' 'south' is an example of cultural sensitivity in language learning. In India one does not give or ask for directions with these compass points but refers to some landmark: a store, market, temple, or restaurant. Many immigrants may at first feel confused by the change and be reluctant to identify the problem for fear of being considered ignorant.
4 In the period preceding the Second World War, British women were brought in to work in Canadian households. For a full discussion of this, see Roberts 1990; Barber 1985. Some Finnish women were also employed as domestic workers; for details of their work experiences, see Lindstrom-Best 1986. In the 1940s and 1950s, a limited program was initiated to bring in women from Europe who were displaced or were refugees. There was not much enthusiasm for this program within Canada, and the German government, after making inquiries about the conditions under which their citizens would work, declined to proceed further with this program. For an excellent account of the policies under which domestic workers have been brought into Canada since the 1940s, see Daenzer 1991.
5 The use of this terminology has been widely adopted in academic accounts of domestic workers as well. See, for example, Bakan and Stasiulis 1992; Arat-Koc 1990; Daenzer 1991.
6 Domestic workers brought in under the Foreign Domestic Movement Pro-

gram are legally entitled to get time off for attending classes. Their employers are also required to contribute a small sum towards the cost of courses. However, it is difficult to enforce these regulations. Few domestic workers complain about their employers for fear of losing their jobs. For more details, see Intercede 1990.

7 The income of a household employing domestic workers has been estimated to be $65,000 annually, which is $20,000 above the national combined average annual family income. See Oziewicz 1992b.

8 For example, employers may expect a domestic worker to play with the children or keep an eye on them during her free time. The employers argue that since the nanny is part of the family such duties are not real work but part of the interaction among family members. Or employers may be critical of a nanny who is out late, or they may not allow her to entertain friends (see Silvera 1983).

9 Some employment agencies have shown hostility towards Intercede, arguing that it is too militant, 'almost a union,' and is 'giving Filipino nannies a bad name.' For more details, see Bakan and Stasiulis 1992, 32–3.

10 For a discussion of the attitudes towards different kinds of child care, see Bakan and Stasiulis 1992, 6–14.

11 In 1989 there were only 240,000 day-care spaces for 630,000 children of working parents. See Flavelle 1990.

9: IMMIGRANT WOMEN AND WIFE ABUSE

1 Conference of the Ontario Council of Agencies Serving Immigrants, workshop on wife abuse, June, 25 1992.

2 Education Wife Assault has information in Hindi, Mandarin, Portugese, Punjabi, Spanish, Vietnamese, and Urdu.

3 It is a custom among South Asian families to provide jewellery, household goods, and other gifts to their daughters when they marry. Though usually given voluntarily, some families may negotiate the extent of the dowry. This practice has become more widespread in the last twenty years, and failure to meet the 'requests' of the spouse's family sometimes leads to the harassment of the wife and may result in her homicide, or 'dowry death.' The term 'kitchen deaths' refers to deaths of young women that occur in suspicious circumstances and in which the husband or his family are the prime suspects. South Asians commonly use a kerosene stove for cooking. An unhappy man or his family, whose requests for additional dowry have been turned down, may pour kerosene on the woman and burn her. Such a death can easily be passed off as an 'accident,' but more stringent regulations in investigating

'kitchen deaths' are now being lobbied for by the women's movement in India.

4 I use 'survivor of wife abuse' to refer to women who have left an abusive relationship. But even women who stay can be called 'survivors,' and this term may come to supplant the more negative term 'victims.' See Dobash and Dobash 1992, 40.

5 In 1994 the Barbara Schlifer Clinic offered interpretation in Amharic, Chinese (Cantonese and Mandarin), Hindi, Italian, Portugese, Punjabi, Spanish, Urdu, Vietnamese.

6 Workers at the Shirley Samaroo House had to negotiate with state agencies for a larger budget for food because they had to provide for the diets of many different ethnic and racial groups. The shelter workers argued that providing food which a woman was accustomed to was necessary in creating a comfortable environment for her and lessening her alienation. At first this argument was not accepted by state agencies; but now most shelters have some additional resources to provide for the specific dietary needs of women from different ethnic and racial groups (Interview, 7 Sept. 1992).

References

Abella, Rosalie Silberman. 1984. *Equality in employment* (royal commission report). Ottawa: Canadian Government Publishing Centre.

Abraham, Ammu. 1991. Case studies from the women's centre, Bombay. In *Women and violence: A country report*, ed. M. Krishnaraj, 59–90. Bombay: Research Centre for Women's Studies.

Acker, Joan, Kate Barry, and Johanna Esseveld. 1991. Objectivity and truth: Problems in doing feminist research. In *Beyond methodology: Feminist scholarship as lived research*, ed. M. Fonow and J. Cook, 133–53. Bloomington: Indiana University Press.

Adachi, Ken. 1976. *The enemy that never was*. Toronto: McClelland and Stewart.

Adamson, Nancy, Linda Briskin, and Margaret McPhail. 1988. *Feminists organizing for change: The contemporary women's movement in Canada*. Toronto: Oxford University Press.

Adamson, Shelagh. 1991. *Working paper on immigrant women: Education, training, employment*. Toronto: COSTI-IIAS.

Adilman, Tamara. 1984. A preliminary sketch of Chinese women and work in British Columbia, 1858–1950. In *Not just pin money: Selected essays on the history of women's work in British Columbia*, ed. B. Latham and R. Pazdro, 53–78. Victoria: Camosun College.

Agnew, Vijay. 1990. Women's work with women. *Polyphony* 12 (2–3): 64–72.

– 1991. South Asian women in Ontario: The experience of race, class, and gender. In *Women changing academe*, ed. S. Kirby, 13–32. Winnipeg: Sororal.

– 1993a. Canadian feminism and women of color. *Women's International Studies Forum* 16 (3): 217–27.

– 1993b. South Asian women and feminism. In *Identity, ethnicity, and migration: The South Asian context*, ed. M. Israel and N. Wagle, 142–64. Toronto: South Asian Centre.

Albrecht, Lisa, and Rose Brewer, eds. 1990. *Bridges of power: Women's multicultural alliances*. Philadelphia: New Society.

Alcoff, Linda. 1988. Cultural feminism versus post-structuralism: The identity crisis in feminist theory. *Signs* 13 (3): 405–36.

Amos, Valerie, and Pratibha Parmar. 1984. Challenging imperial feminism. *Feminist Review* 17, 3–15.

Anderson, Alan, and James Frideres. 1981. *Ethnicity in Canada: Theoretical perspectives*. Toronto: Butterworths.

Anderson, Doris. 1987. Ontario should heed domestics' plight. *Toronto Star* (24 Jan.).

Anderson, Kay. 1991. *Vancouver's Chinatown: Racial discourse in Canada, 1875–1980*. Montreal: McGill-Queen's University Press.

Anzaldúa, Gloria. 1990. Bridge, drawbridge, sandbar or island: Lesbians-of-colour. In *Bridges of power: Women's multicultural alliances*, ed. L. Albrecht and R. Brewer, 216–33. Philadelphia: New Society.

Arat-Koc, Sedef. 1990. Importing housewives. Non-citizen domestic workers and the crisis of the domestic sphere in Canada. In *Through the kitchen window*, ed. M. Luxton, H. Rosenberg, and S. Arat-Koc, 81–103. Toronto: Garamond.

Armstrong, Pat, and Hugh Armstrong. 1977. *The double ghetto: Canadian women and their segregated work*. Toronto: McClelland and Stewart.

– 1990. *Theorizing women's work*. Toronto: Garamond.

Arnopoulos, Sheila. 1979. *Problems of immigrant women in the Canadian labour force*. Ottawa: Canadian Advisory Council on the Status of Women.

Ayukawa, Michiko Midge. 1987. Japanese pioneer women in Canada. Unpublished paper.

– 1991. Meiji mothers, Canadian daughters: Confusion and conflict. Paper presented at the Learned Societies Conference, Kingston.

Bacchi, Carol. 1983. *Liberation deferred? The ideas of the English-Canadian suffragists, 1877–1918*. Toronto: University of Toronto Press.

Backhouse, Constance. 1990. Women faculty at the University of Western Ontario: Reflections on the employment equity award. *Canadian Journal of Women and the Law* 4 (1): 38.

Bakan, Abigail, and Daiva Stasiulis. 1992. Making the match: Domestic placement agencies and the racialization of women's household work. Paper presented at the CRIAW conference, Toronto.

Balasubrahmanyan, Vimal. 1990. *In search of justice: Women, law, landmark judgements and media*. Bombay: Research Centre for Women's Studies.

Bannerji, Himani. 1986. Popular images of South Asian women. *Tiger Lily*: 23–7.

– 1987. Introducing racism: Notes towards an anti-racist feminism. *Resources for Feminist Research* 16 (1): 10–12.

– 1991. But who speaks for us? Experience and agency in conventional feminist paradigms. In *Unsettling relations: The university as a site of feminist struggles*, ed. H. Bannerji et al., 67–108. Toronto: Women's Press.

Barber, Marilyn. 1985. The women Ontario welcomed: Immigrant domestics for Ontario homes, 1870–1930. In *The neglected majority*, ed. A. Prentice and S. Trofimenkoff, 102–21. Toronto: McClelland and Stewart.

Barnsley, Jan. 1985. *Feminist action, institutional reaction: Responses to wife assault*. Vancouver: Women's Research Centre.

Barrett, Michele. 1987. The concept of 'difference.' *Feminist Review* 25: 29–41.

Barrett, Michele, and Mary McIntosh. 1985. Ethnocentricism and socialist feminist theory. *Feminist Review* 20: 23–47.

Basavarajappa, K.G., and Ravi Verma. 1990. Occupational composition of immigrant women. In *Ethnic demography: Canadian immigrant, racial and cultural variations*, ed. S. Halli, F. Trovato and L. Driedger, 297–314. Ottawa: Carleton University Press.

Basran, G.S. 1983. Canadian immigration policy and theories of racism. In *Racial minorities in multicultural Canada*, ed. P. Li and B. Singh Bolaria. Toronto: Garamond.

Baureiss, Gunter. 1987. Chinese immigration, Chinese stereotypes, and Chinese labour. *Canadian Ethnic Studies* 19 (3): 15–34.

Bégin, Monique. 1992. The Royal Commission on the Status of Women in Canada: Twenty years later. In *Challenging times: The women's movement in Canada and the United States*, ed. C. Backhouse and D. Flaherty, 21–38. Montreal: McGill-Queen's University Press.

Berger, Thomas. 1982. *Fragile freedoms: Human rights and dissent in Canada*. Toronto: Clarke Irwin.

Bhavnani, Kum Kum, and Margaret Coulson. 1986. Transforming socialist-feminism: The challenge of racism. *Feminist Review* 23: 81–92.

Billingsley, Brenda. 1985. *No discrimination here? Toronto employers and the multi-racial workforce*. Toronto: Social Planning Council of Metropolitan Toronto.

Bissoondath, Neil. 1992. 'I'm just a writer' – That's the voice that matters. *Globe and Mail* (18 Apr.).

Black, Naomi. 1988. The Canadian women's movement: The second wave. In *Changing patterns: Women in Canada*, ed. S. Burt, L. Code, and L. Dorney, 80–102. Toronto: McClelland and Stewart.

– 1992. Ripples in the second wave: Comparing the contemporary women's movement in Canada and the United States. In *Challenging times: The women's movement in Canada and the United States*, ed. C. Backhouse and D. Flaherty, 94–109. Montreal: McGill-Queen's University Press.

Bolaria, B. Singh, and Peter Li, eds. 1988. *Racial oppression in Canada*. Toronto: Garamond Press.

Bordo, Susan. 1990. Feminism, postmodernism, and gender-scepticism. In *Feminism/postmodernism*, ed. L. Nicholson, 133–56. New York: Routledge.

Bourne, Jenny. 1984. *Towards an anti-racist feminism*. London: Institute of Race Relations.

Bourne, Paula, ed. 1985. *Women's paid and unpaid work: Historical and contemporary perspectives*. Toronto: New Hogtown.

Boyd, Monica. 1986. Immigrant women in Canada. In *International migration: The female experience*, ed. R. Simeon and C. Bretell, 45–61. London: Allenheld.

– 1989. *Migrant women in Canada: Profiles and policies*. Ottawa: Employment and Immigration Canada.

– 1990. Immigrant women: Language, socio-economic inequalities and policy issues. In *Ethnic demography: Canadian immigrant, racial and cultural variations*, ed. S. Halli, F. Trovato, and L. Driedger, 275–93. Ottawa: Carleton University Press.

– 1991. Gender, visible minority and immigrant earnings inequality: Reassessing an Employment Equity premise. Working paper 91–96. Department of Sociology and Anthropology, Carleton University, Ottawa.

Brand, Dionne. 1984. Black women in Toronto: Gender, race, and class. *Fireweed* (Summer/Fall): 26–43.

– 1991. *No burden to carry*. Toronto: Women's Press.

Brand, Dionne, and Krisantha Sri Bhaggiyadatta. 1986. *Rivers have sources, trees have roots: Speaking of racism*. Toronto: Cross-Cultural Communication Centre.

Briskin, Linda. 1991. Feminist practice: A new approach to evaluating feminist strategy. In *Women and social change. Feminist activism in Canada*, ed. J. Wine and J. Ristock, 24–40. Toronto: James Lorimer.

Broadfoot, Barry. 1979. *Years of sorrow, years of shame: The story of the Japanese Canadians in World War II*. Don Mills, Ont.: Paperjacks.

Brouwer, Ruth. 1991. *New women for God*. Toronto: University of Toronto Press.

Brown, Louise. 1979. Today's 'slaves' – immigrant women working as maids. *Toronto Star* (11 Jan.).

Brown, Lyn, and Carol Gilligan. 1992. *Meeting at the crossroads: Women's psychology and girls' development*. Cambridge: Harvard University Press.

Brown, Rosemary. 1989. *Being brown*. Toronto: Random House.

– 1991. Overcoming sexism and racism – How? In *Racism in Canada*, ed. O. McKague, 163–78. Saskatoon: Fifth House.

Buchignani, Norman. 1984. Social science research on Asians in Canada. In *Asian Canadians: Aspects of social change*, ed. V. Ujimoto and J. Naidoo, 1–29. Guelph: University of Guelph.

– 1987. Research on South Asians in Canada: Retrospect and prospect. In *The South Asian diaspora in Canada: Six essays*, ed. M. Israel, 113–26. Toronto: Multicultural History Society of Ontario.

Buchignani, Norman, and Doreen Indra. 1985. *Continuous journey: A social history of South Asians in Canada*. Toronto: McClelland and Stewart.

Bulkin, Elly, Minnie Bruce Pratt, and Barbara Smith. 1985. *Yours in struggle*. New York: Long Haul.

Bunch, Charlotte. 1990. Making common cause: Diversity and coalitions. *In Bridges of power: Women's multicultural alliances*, ed. L. Albrecht and R. Brewer, 49–57. Philadelphia: New Society.

Burnet, Jean. ed. 1986. *Looking into my sister's eyes: An exploration in women's history*. Toronto: Multicultural History Society of Ontario.

– 1988. *'Coming Canadians': An introduction to a history of Canada's peoples*. Toronto: McClelland and Stewart.

Cadieux, Rita. 1987. The language of equal opportunity. In *Report of the colloquium: Equality in language and literacy training*, 17–22.

Calliste, Agnes. 1989. Canada's immigration policy and domestics from the Caribbean: The second domestic scheme. In *Race, class, and gender: Bonds and barriers*, ed. J. Vorst et al., 133–65. Toronto: Between the Lines.

Campbell, Bonnie, et al. *Women unite: An anthology of the Canadian Women's Movement*. Toronto: Canadian Women's Educational Press.

Canada. Secretary of State for Multiculturalism. 1981a. *The immigrant woman in Canada: A right to recognition*, part 2. Ottawa: Minister of Supply and Services.

– Employment and Immigration. 1981b. Domestic workers on employment authorization: A revised policy. Unpublished.

– House of Commons. 1981c. Domestic workers on employment authorization. Ottawa: Minister of Supply and Services.

– House of Commons Special Committee on the Participation of Visible Minorities. 1984. *Equality now: Report of the special committee on visible minorities in Canadian society*. Ottawa: Minister of Supply and Services.

– Employment and Immigration. 1987. Terms and conditions, Settlement language training programs. Pamphlet.

– Employment and Immigration. 1989. *Canada's immigration law*. Ottawa: Minister of Supply and Services.

Canadian Research Institute for Advancement of Women. 1992. Annual conference, Toronto.

Cancian, Francesca. 1992. Feminist science: Methodologies that challenge inequality. *Gender and Society*. 6 (4): 623–42.

Cannon, Margaret. 1989. *China tide: The revealing story of the Hong Kong exodus to
Canada*. Toronto: HarperCollins.

Carby, Hazel. 1986. White women listen! Black feminism and the boundaries of
sisterhood. In *The empire strikes back: Race and racism in 70s Britain*, ed. Centre
for Contemporary Culture Studies, 212–35. London: Hutchinson.

Carty, Linda. 1991. Black women in academia: A statement from the periphery.
In *Unsettling relations: The university as a site of feminist struggles*, ed. H. Bannerji
et al., 13–44. Toronto: Women's Press.

Carty, Linda, and Dionne Brand. 1989. 'Visible minority' women – A creation of
the Canadian state. *Resources for Feminist Research* 17 (3): 39–40.

Cayenne, Carol. 1991. Letter to A. M. Gardner (28 Oct.).

Centre for Women's Health Steering Committee. 1988. *Proposal to establish a
community health centre for women*. Toronto: Women's Health in Women's
Hands.

Cervantes, Nena. 1988. *From fright to flight*. Toronto: Network of Filipino-
Canadian Women.

Chadney, James G. 1984. *The Sikhs of Vancouver*. New York: AMS.

Chan, Anthony B. 1983. *Gold mountain: The Chinese in the new world*. Vancouver:
New Star.

Chan, Sui-Lin. 1989. *Wife assault: The Chinese family life services experience*. Toronto: Chinese Family Support Services of Metro Toronto.

Chandrasekhar, S. 1945. *Indian emigration to America*. Bombay: Oxford University
Press.

Chaudhry, Ushi. 1992. Beyond need assessment and problem identification.
Sanvad: Canadian Punjabi Journal 5 (45): 11–12.

Chawla, Saroj. 1990. The Punjabi Hindu family in Ontario: A study in adaptation. *Polyphony* 12: 72–6.

Chen, Anita Beltran. 1980. Filipinos in Canada: A socio-demographic profile. In
Visible minorities and multiculturalism in Canada, ed. V. Ujimoto and G. Hiaba-
yashi, 301–22. Toronto: Butterworths.

– 1983. Kinship and internal migration: Filipinos in Thunder Bay. In *The
south-east Asian environment*, ed. D. Webster, 191–204. Ottawa: University of
Ottawa Press.

– 1987. Filipino Canadians at the Lakehead. *Polyphony* 9 (2): 99–103.

– 1990. Studies on Filipinos in Canada: State of the art. *Canadian Ethnic Studies*
12 (1): 83–95.

Cheng, Tien-Feng. 1931. *Oriental immigration to Canada*. Shanghai: Commercial
Press.

Childers, Mary, and bell hooks. 1990. A conversation about race and class. In *Conflicts in feminism*, ed. M. Hirsch and E. Fox Keller, 60–81. New York: Routledge.

Chinese Canadian National Council, Women's Book Committee. 1992. *Jin Guo: Voices of Chinese Canadian Women*. Toronto: Women's Press.

Chodorow, Nancy. 1978. *The reproduction of mothering: Psychoanalysis and the sociology of gender*. Berkeley: University of California.

Chow, Rey. 1991. *Woman and Chinese modernity: The politics of reading between west and east*. Minnesota: University of Minnesota Press.

Christian, Barbara. 1987. The race for theory. *Cultural Critique* 6: 51–63.

– 1989. But what do we think we're doing anyway? The state of black feminist criticism(s), or my version of a little bit of history. In *Changing our own words*, ed. C. Wall, 57–74. New Brunswick: Rutgers.

Clark, Lorenne, and Debra Lewis. 1977. *Rape: The price of coercive sexuality*. Toronto: Women's Press.

Cleverdon, Catherine. 1974. *The woman suffrage movement in Canada*. Toronto: University of Toronto Press.

Cloutier, Naini. 1989. Family violence in the South Asian community. *Diva* 1 (4): 13–15.

Coalition of Visible-Minority Women. 1989. *Newsletter* 1 (1): 1–6.

Code, Lorraine. 1988. Feminist theory. In *Changing patterns. Women in Canada*, ed. S. Burt, L. Code, and L. Dorney, 18–50. Toronto: McClelland and Stewart.

– 1991. *What can she know? Feminist theory and the construction of knowledge*. Ithaca: Cornell University Press.

Cohen, Rina. 1991. Women of color in white households: Coping strategies of live-in domestic workers. *Qualitative Sociology* 14 (2): 197–215.

Collins, Patricia. 1989. The social construction of black feminist thought. *Signs* 14 (4): 745–73.

– 1990. *Black feminist thought: Knowledge, consciousness, and the politics of empowerment*. New York: Routledge.

– 1991. Learning from the outsider within: The sociological significance of black feminist thought. In *Beyond methodology: Feminist scholarship as lived research*. ed. M. Fonow and J. Cook, Bloomington: Indiana University Press.

Con, Harry, et al., eds. 1982. *From China to Canada. A history of the Chinese communities in Canada*. Toronto: McClelland and Stewart.

Cook, Ramsay. 1974. Introduction. In *The woman suffrage movement in Canada*, ed. C. Cleverdon. Toronto: University of Toronto Press.

Cook, Ramsay, and Wendy Mitchinson, eds. 1976. *The proper sphere: Woman's place in Canadian society*. Toronto: Oxford University Press.

Courtney, Alice, and Thomas Whipple. 1978. *Canadian perspectives on sex stereo-

typing in advertising. Position paper for the Advisory Council on the Status of
Women.

Cramer, Michael. 1992. Public and political documents of the woman's suffrage
campaign in British Columbia, 1871–1917: The view from Victoria. In *British
Columbia reconsidered: Essays on women*, ed. G. Creese and V. Strong-Boag, 55–
72. Vancouver: Press Gang.

Creese, Gillian. 1988–9. Exclusion or solidarity? Vancouver workers confront the
'Oriental Problem.' *British Columbia Studies* 80: 24–49.

– 1992. The politics of dependence: Women, work, and unemployment in the
Vancouver labour movement before World War II. In *British Columbia reconsid-
ered: Essays on Women*, ed. G. Creese and V. Strong-Boag, 364–90. Vancouver:
Press Gang.

Cumming, Peter. 1993. Workshop on anti-racism. Organized by the Tamil
Senior's Club, Toronto (16 Jan.).

Daenzer, Patricia. 1991. Ideology and the formation of migration policy: The
case of immigrant domestic workers, 1940–90. PhD diss., University of
Toronto.

Daley, Jaqueline. 1991. Letter (1 Nov.).

Das Gupta, Tania. 1986. *Learning from our history: Community development by
immigrant women in Ontario 1958–1986.* Toronto: Cross-Cultural Communication Centre.

– 1987. Involving immigrant women: A case of participatory research. *Canadian
Woman Studies* 8: 14–15.

Davis, Angela Y. 1983. *Women, race, and class.* New York: Vintage.

Delhi, Kari. 1991. Leaving the comfort of home: Working through feminisms. In
Unsettling relations: The university as a site of feminist struggles, ed. H. Bannerji et
al., 45–66. Toronto: Women's Press.

Delmar, Rosalind. 1986. What is feminism? In *What is feminism? A reexamination*,
ed. N. Cott et al., 8–33. New York: Pantheon Books.

Dewar, Elaine. 1993. Wrongful dismissal: Angry anti-racists drove June Callwood from Nellie's, the shelter for women she created, because she couldn't
share her 'white-skinned privilege.' *Toronto Life* (March): 32–47.

Dhruvarajan, Vanaja. 1991. The multiple oppression of women of colour. In
Racism in Canada, ed. O. McKague, 101–4. Saskatoon: Fifth House.

Diamond, Irene, and Lee Quinby. 1988. *Feminism and Foucault.* Boston: Northeastern University Press.

Di Leonardo, Micaela. 1984. *The varieties of ethnic experience: Kinship, class, and
gender among California Italian-Americans.* Ithaca: Cornell University Press.

Dill, Bonnie Thornton. 1988. 'Making your job good yourself': Domestic service
and the construction of personal dignity. In *Women and the politics of empower-*

ment, ed. A. Bookman and S. Morgen, 33–52. Philadelphia: Temple University Press.

Di Stefano, Christine. 1990. Dilemmas of difference: Feminism, modernity, and postmodernism. In *Feminism/postmodernism*, ed. L. Nicholson, 63–82. New York: Routledge.

Dobash, Emerson, and Russell Dobash. 1980. *Violence against wives: A case against the patriarchy*. London: Open Books.

– 1992. *Women, violence, and social change*. London: Routledge.

Driedger, Leo. 1989. *The ethnic factor: Identity in diversity*. Toronto: McGraw-Hill Ryerson.

DuCharme, Michele. 1986. The coverage of Candian immigration policy in the *Globe and Mail* (1980–1985). *Currents*: 6–11.

Eberts, Mary. 1985. The use of litigation under the Canadian Charter of Rights and Freedoms as a strategy for achieving change. In *Minorities and the Canadian state*, ed. N. Nevitte and A. Kornberg, 53–70. Oakville, Ont.: Mosaic Press.

– 1987. Language training policy under the Charter of Rights. In *Report of the colloquium: Equality in language and literacy training*, 23–7.

Education Wife Assault. 1992. Workshop for South Asian service providers on sexual assault (30 June).

Egan, Carolyn, Linda Gardner, and Judy Persad. 1988. The politics of transformation: Struggles with race, class, and sexuality in the March 8th coalition. In *Social movements/social change: The politics and practice of organizing*, ed. F. Cunningham et al., 22–47. Toronto: Between the Lines.

Eichler, Margrit. 1973. Women as personal dependents: A critique of theories of the stratification of the sexes and an alternative approach. In *Women in Canada*, ed. M. Stephenson, 36–55. Toronto: New Press.

Eisenstein, H. 1983. *Contemporary feminist thought*. Boston: G.K. Hall.

Eisenstein, Zillah. 1981. *The radical future of liberal feminism*. Boston: Northeastern University Press.

Elliott, Jean Leonard, and Augie Fleras. 1990. Immigration and the Canadian ethnic mosaic. In *Race and ethnic relations in Canada*, ed. P. Li, 51–76. Toronto: Oxford University Press.

Emily Stowe Shelter for Women. 1990. *Annual report*. Toronto: The Shelter.

Errington, Jane. 1988. Pioneers and suffragists. In *Changing patterns: Women in Canada*, ed. S. Burt, L. Code, and L. Dorney, 51–79. Toronto: McClelland and Stewart.

Essed, Philomena. 1991. *Understanding everyday racism: An interdisciplinary theory*. Newbury Park: Sage.

Estable, Alma. 1986. *Immigrant women in Canada: Current issues*. Ottawa: Canadian Advisory Council on the Status of Women.

Ferguson, Edith. 1970. Immigrant women in Canada: Report prepared for the Royal Commission on the Status of Women. Unpublished (microfilm).

Findlay, Sue. 1987. Facing the state: The politics of the women's movement reconsidered. In *Feminism and political economy: Women's work, women's struggles*, ed. H. Maroney and M. Luxton, 31–50. Toronto: Methuen.

– 1988. Feminist struggles with the Canadian state, 1966–88. *Resources for Feminist Research* 17 (3): 5–9.

Fisher-Manick, Beverley. 1981. Race and class: Beyond personal politics. In *Building feminist theory*, ed. G. Steinem and C. Bunch. New York: Longman.

Fitzgerald, Maureeen, Connie Guberman, and Margie Wolfe. 1982. *Still ain't satisfied: Canadian feminism today*. Toronto: Women's Press.

Flavelle, Dana. 1990. The dilemma over domestic workers. *Toronto Star* (1 Feb.).

Fleras, Augie and Jean Leonard Elliott. 1992. *Multiculturalism in Canada*. Scarborough: Nelson.

Forum Against Oppression of Women. 1990. Report of the National Meeting of Women's Organizations against Rape. Bombay: N.p.

Foster, Cecil. 1991. *Distorted mirror: Canada's racist face*. Toronto: HarperCollins.

Fowler, Marian. 1982. *The embroidered tent: Five gentlewomen in early Canada*. Toronto: Anansi.

Fox, Bonnie. ed. 1980. *Hidden in the household: Women's domestic labour under capitalism*. Toronto: Women's Press.

Frankenberg, Ruth. 1993. *The social construction of whiteness: White women, race matters*. Minneapolis: University of Minnesota Press.

Frye, Marilyn. 1983. *The politics of reality: Essays in feminist theory*. Trumansburg, NY: Crossing.

Gannage, Charlene. 1986. *Double day, double bind*. Toronto: Women's Press.

Geiger, Susan. 1990. What's so feminist about women's oral history? *Journal of Women's History* 2 (1): 169–82.

George, Usha. 1992. Ethnocultural agencies. Unpublished manuscript.

Ghosh, Ratna. 1981. Minority within a minority: On being South Asian and female in Canada. In *Women in the family and economy*, ed. G. Kurian and R. Ghosh, 413–26. Westport: Greenwood.

Giles, Winona. 1987a. Language rights are human rights: A discussion paper. In *Report of the colloquium: Equality in language and literacy training*, 1–23.

– 1987b. Language rights are women's rights: Discrimination against immigrant women in Canadian language training policies. *Resources for Feminist Research* 17 (3): 129–32.

Giles, Winona, and Valerie Preston. 1991. Ethnicity, gender and labour markets in Canada: A case study of immigrant women in Toronto. Paper presented at the annual Canadian Association of Anthropology and Sociology, Kingston, Ontario.

Gill, Bhupinder. 1992. Value differences and therapy. *Diva* 3 (2): 65–70.

Gilligan, Carol. 1982. *In a different voice.* Cambridge: Harvard University Press.

Glenn, Evelyn Nakano. 1986. *Issei, Nisei, war bride: Three generations of Japanese-American women in domestic service.* Philadelphia: Temple University Press.

Go, Amy Teng-Teng. 1987. *Discussion paper on E.S.L. funding for submission to the OCASI Board of Directors.* Toronto: OCASI.

Gorham, Deborah. 1979. Flora MacDonald Denison: Canadian feminist. In *A not unreasonable claim: Women and reform in Canada, 1800s–1920s,* ed. L. Kealey, 47–70. Toronto: Women's Press.

Grant, Bruce. 1979. *The boat people: An 'age' investigation.* Markham, Ont.: Penguin.

Greaves, Lorraine. 1991. Reorganizing the National Action Committee on the Status of Women, 1986–1988. In *Women and social change: Feminist activism in Canada,* ed. J. Dawn Wine and J. Ristock, 101–16. Toronto: James Lorimer.

Green, Alan. 1976. *Immigration and the postwar Canadian economy.* Toronto: Maclean-Hunter.

Gupta, Nila, and Makeda Silvera. 1989. We appear silent to people who are deaf to what we say. In *The issue is 'ism: Women of colour speak out,* ed. M. Silvera and N. Gupta. Toronto: Sister Vision.

Guttel, Charnie. 1974. *Marxism and feminism.* Toronto: Women's Press.

Harding, Sandra. 1986. *The science question in feminism.* Ithaca: Cornell University Press.

– 1990. Feminism, science, and the anti-enlightenment critiques. In *Feminism/postmodernism,* ed. L. Nicholson, 83–106. New York: Routledge.

Harney, Robert. 1981. *Toronto: Canada's new cosmopolite.* Toronto: Multicultural History Society of Ontario.

– 1988. 'So great a heritage as ours': Immigration and the survival of the Canadian polity. *Daedalus* 117: 51–97.

Harris, Kathryn. 1989. New alliances: Socialist-feminism in the eighties. *Feminist Review* 30: 34–41.

Hartsock, Nancy M. 1987. The feminist standpoint: Developing the ground for a specifically feminist historical materialism. In *Feminism and methodology,* ed. S. Harding, 157–80. Bloomington: Indiana University Press.

– 1990. Foucault on power: A theory for women? In *Feminism/postmodernism,* ed. L. Nicholson, 157–75. New York: Routledge.

Hawkesworth, Mary. 1989. Knowers, knowing, known: Feminist theory and claims of truth. *Signs* 14(31), 533–557.

Hawkins, Freda. 1970. Women immigrants in Canada: Report prepared for the Royal Commission on the Status of Women. Unpublished (microfilm).
- 1988. *Canada and immigration: Public policy and public concern* (2nd ed.). Kingston: McGill-Queen's University Press.
Head, Wilson. 1975. *The black presence in the Canadian mosaic: A study of the practice of discrimination against blacks in Metropolitan Toronto.* Toronto: Ontario Human Rights Commission.
Henry, Frances. 1973. *Forgotten Canadians: The blacks of Nova Scotia.* Don Mills, Ont.: Longman.
- 1978. *The dynamics of racism in Toronto: Research report.* Toronto: n.p.
- 1986. *Race relations research in Canada today: A 'state of the art' review.* Ottawa: Canadian Human Rights Commission.
Henry, Frances, and E. Ginzberg. 1984. *Who gets the work? A test of racial discrimination in employment.* Toronto: Social Planning Council and Urban Alliance on Race Relations.
Hernandez, Carmencita. 1988a. Immigrant women. *Globe and Mail* (11 Feb.).
- 1988b. The Coalition of Visible-Minority Women. In *Social movements/social change*, ed. F. Cunningham et al., 157–68. Toronto: Between the Lines.
- 1992. Nanny rule will have racist outcome. *Globe and Mail* (15 Feb.).
Hoff, Lee Ann. 1990. *Battered women as survivors.* London: Routledge.
hooks, bell. 1984. *Feminist theory from margin to center.* Boston: South End Press.
- 1988. *Talking back: Thinking feminist, thinking black.* Toronto: Between the Lines.
- 1991. Theory as liberatory practice. *Yale Journal of Law and Feminism* 4: 1–12.
Hoy, David Couzins, ed. 1986. *Foucault.* Oxford: Basil Blackwell.
Hutcheon, Linda, and Marion Richmond, eds. 1990. *Other solitudes: Canadian multicultural fiction.* Toronto: Oxford University Press.
Iacovetta, Franca. 1992. Making 'New Canadians': Social workers, women, and the reshaping of immigrant families. In *Gender conflicts: New essays in women's history*, ed. F. Iacovetta and M. Valverde, 261–303. Toronto: University of Toronto Press.
Immigrant and Visible-Minority Women. 1985. Brief from Immigrant and Visible-Minority Women to Flora McDonald, Minister of Employment and Immigration. Unpublished.
Indra, Doreen. 1981. The invisible mosaic: Women, ethnicity and the Vancouver press, 1905–1976. *Canadian Ethnic Studies*, 13 (1): 63–74.
Intercede. 1980. The status of domestic workers in Ontario: Recommendations for legislative change. A brief to the government of Ontario. Unpublished.
- 1981. The status of domestic workers in Ontario: An update of the recommen-

dations presented to the government of Ontario in December 1980. Unpublished.

– 1987. *Intercede: Annual report*. Toronto: Intercede.

– 1990a. *Report and recommendations on the foreign domestic movement program*. Toronto: Intercede.

– 1990b. *Report to the 1990 annual general meeting*. Toronto: Intercede.

– 1991. *The bare essentials: A needs assessment of foreign domestic workers in Ontario*. Toronto: Intercede.

International Women's Day Celebrations. 1986. *Newsletter*.

Isaac, Barbara. 1991. Letter to senior policy analyst Jim O'Neill, Community Services Branch, Ontario Ministry of Community and Social Services.

Jaggar, Alison. 1983. *Feminist politics and human nature*. Totowa, NJ: Rowman and Allanheld.

Jaggar, Alison, and Susan Bordo, eds. 1990. *Gender/body/knowledge: Feminist reconstructions of being and knowing*. New Brunswick: Rutgers University Press.

Javed, Nayyar. 1992. Global enemy-divided feminists-racism in the women's movement. *Feminist Action* 3 (June).

Jayaratne, Toby, and Abigail Stewart. 1991. Quantitative and qualitative methods in the social sciences: Current feminist issues and practical strategies. In *Beyond methodology: Feminist scholarship as lived research*, ed. M. Fonow and J. Cook, 85–106. Bloomington: Indiana University Press.

Jensen, Joan M. 1988. *Passage from India: Asian Indian immigrants in North America*. New Haven: Yale University Press.

Johnson, Laura. 1982. *The seam allowance: Industrial home sewing in Canada*. Toronto: Women's Press.

Johnston, Hugh. 1979. *The voyage of the* Komagata Maru: *The Sikh challenge to Canada's color bar*. Delhi: Oxford University Press.

Juteau-Lee, Danielle, and Barbara Roberts. 1981. Ethnicity and femininity. *Canadian Ethnic Studies* 13 (1): 1–15.

Kalbach, Warren. 1990. A demographic view of racial and ethnic groups in Canada. In *Race and ethnic relations in Canada*, ed. P. Li, 18–50. Toronto: Oxford University Press.

Kallen, Evelyn. 1982. *Ethnicity and human rights in Canada*. Toronto: Gage.

– 1988. Multiculturalism as ideology, policy, and reality. In *Social inequality in Canada: Patterns, problems, policies*, ed. J. Curtis et al., 235–46. Scarborough: Prentice-Hall.

Kealey, Linda. 1984. Canadian socialism and the woman question, 1900–1914. *Labour/Le Travail* 13: 77–100.

Khosla, Prabha. 1983. Profiles of working-class East Indian women. *Fireweed* 16: 43–48.

Kingston, Anne. 1992. Coping with new rules in the nanny game. *Financial Times of Canada* (10 Feb.)

Kishwar, Madhu, and Ruth Vanita, eds. 1991. *In search of answers: Indian women's voices from Manushi*. Delhi: Horizon India.

Kitagawa, Muriel. 1985. *This is my own: Letters to Wes and other writings on Japanese Canadians, 1941–1948*. Vancouver: Talon.

Kline, Marlee. 1989a. Race, racism, and feminist legal theory. *Harvard Women's Law Journal* 12: 115–51.

– 1989b. Women's oppression and racism: A critique of the 'feminist standpoint.' In *Race, class, and gender: Bonds and barriers*, ed. J. Vorst et al., 37–64. Toronto: Between the Lines.

Kogawa, Joy. 1981. *Obasan*. Toronto: Lester and Orpen Dennys.

Kohli, Rita. 1991a. Living on edge. *Diva* (March): 16–22.

– 1991b. Understanding the nature of crisis. In *Towards equal access*, ed. F. Rafiq, 81–6. Ottawa: Immigrant and Visible-Minority Women Against Abuse.

Korean-Canadian Women's Association. 1988. *Annual report 1987–8*. Toronto: The Association.

– 1989. *Annual report, 1988–9*. Toronto: The Association.

– 1991. Report: *Anti-racism and systemic racial discrimination workshops*. Toronto: The Association.

– 1992. *Voice of Korean–Canadians on racism*. Toronto: The Association.

Kurkulasuriya, Lasanda. 1991. Wife assault: Sri Lanka. *Diva* (March): 26–34.

Ladner, Joyce. 1987. Introduction to tomorrow's tomorrow: The black woman. In *Feminism and methodology*, ed. S. Harding, 74–83. Bloomington: Indiana University Press.

Lai, Chuen-Yan. 1972. The Chinese Consolidated Benevolent Association in Victoria: Its origins and functions. *British Columbia Studies* 15: 53–67.

Landsberg, Michele. 1991. It's nannies vs. employers in this ploy. *Toronto Star* (23 Feb.).

Lawrence, Errol. 1986. Just plain common sense: The 'roots' of racism. In *The empire strikes back: Race and racism in 70s Britain*, ed. Centre for Contemporary Cultural Studies, 47–94. London: Hutchinson.

Lazreg, Marnia. 1990. Feminism and difference: The perils of writing as a woman on women in Algeria. In *Conflicts in feminism*, ed. M. Hirsch and E. Keller, 326–48. New York: Routledge.

Leila Khalid Collective. 1970. Position paper. Available from Toronto Women's Movement archives.

Li, Peter. 1980. Income achievement and adaptive capacity: An empirical comparison of Chinese and Japanese in Canada. In *Visible minorities and multicul-*

turalism: Asians in Canada, ed. V. Ujimoto and G. Hirabayashi, Toronto: Butterworths.

– 1988a. *The Chinese in Canada*. Toronto: Oxford University Press.

– 1988b. *Ethnic inequality in a class society*. Toronto: Wall and Thompson.

Lindstrom-Best, Varpu. 1986. 'I won't be a slave!' – Finnish domestics in Canada, 1911–1930. In *Looking into my sister's eyes: An exploration in women's history*, ed. J. Burnet, 33–54. Toronto: Multicultural History Society of Ontario.

Lips, Hilary M. 1991. *Women, men, and power*. Palo Alto: Mayfield.

Lorde, Audre. 1984. *Sister outsider: Essays and speeches*. Trumansburg, NJ: Crossing.

Loseke, Donileen. 1992. *The battered woman and shelters: The social construction of wife abuse*. Albany: State University of New York Press.

Luxton, Meg, and Harriet Rosenberg, eds. 1986. *Through the kitchen window: The politics of home and family*. Toronto: Garamond.

McClung, Nellie. 1925. *Painted fires*. Toronto: Thomas Allen.

– 1972 [1915]. *In times like these*. Toronto: University of Toronto Press.

McDaniel, Susan. 1988. The changing Canadian family. In *Changing patterns: Women in Canada*, ed. S. Burt, L. Code, and L. Dorney, 103–28. Toronto: McClelland and Stewart.

Mackie, Marlene. 1983. *Exploring gender relations: A Canadian perspective*. Toronto: Butterworths.

– 1985. Stereotypes, prejudice, and discrimination. In *Ethnicity and ethnic relations in Canada*, ed. R. Bienvenue and J. Goldstein, 219–39. Toronto: Butterworths.

MacKinnon, Catharine. 1991. From practice to theory, or what is a white woman anyway? *Yale Journal of Law and Feminism* 4: 13–22.

MacLeod, Linda. 1987. *Battered but not beaten*. Ottawa: Canadian Advisory Council on the Status of Women.

Malarek, Victor. 1987. *Haven's Gate: Canada's immigration fiasco*. Toronto: Macmillan.

Man, Guida. 1991. Silent partners: The experience of women in recent middle-class Chinese immigrant families from Hong Kong. Paper presented at the Learned Societies Conference, Kingston.

Marlyn, John. 1971. *Under the ribs of death*. Toronto: McClelland and Stewart.

Martin, Biddy. 1988. Feminism, criticism, and Foucault. In *Feminism and Foucault*, ed. I. Diamond and L. Quinby, 3–20. Boston: Northeastern University Press.

Martin, Biddy, and Chandra Mohanty. 1986. Feminist politics: What's home got to do with it? In *Feminist studies/critical studies*, ed. T. de Lauretis, 190–210. Bloomington: Indiana University Press.

Medeiros, John. 1991. *Family services for all: Study of family services for ethnocultural and racial communities in Metropolitan Toronto*. Toronto: Multicultural Coalition for Access to Family Services.

Medjuck, Sheva. 1990. Ethnicity and feminism: Two solitudes. *Atlantis* 15 (2): 1–10.

Mies, Maria. 1986. *Patriarchy and accumulation on a world scale*. London: Zed.

Miles, Robert. 1989. *Racism*. London: Routledge.

Mill, John Stuart. 1970 [1869]. The subjection of women. In *Essays on sex equality*, ed. A. Rossi, 125–242. Chicago: University of Chicago Press.

Miller, Christopher L. 1990. *Theories of Africans*. Chicago: University of Chicago Press.

Millman, Marcia, and Rosabeth Kanter. 1987. Introduction to another voice: Feminist perspectives on social life and social science. In *Feminism and methodology*, ed. S. Harding, 29–36. Bloomington: Indiana University Press.

Minh-ha, Trinh T. 1989. *Women, native, other*. Bloomington: Indiana University Press.

Mistry, Rohinton. 1990. Interview. In *Other solitudes: Canadian multicultural fiction*, ed. L. Hutcheon and M. Richmond, 235–62. Toronto: Oxford University Press.

Mitchell, Alana. 1993. New rules create greater nanny shortage. *Globe and Mail* (23 Jan.).

Mitchell, Juliet, and Ann Oakley. 1986. Introduction. In *What is feminism?* ed. N. Cott et al., 1–8. New York: Pantheon.

Mitchinson, Wendy. 1977. Social reform in the nineteenth century: A step towards independence. *Atlantis* 2 (2): 58–75.

Mohanty, Chandra. 1989. Under western eyes: Feminist scholarship and colonial discourses. *Feminist Review* 31: 61–81.

– 1991. Cartographies of struggle: Third-world women and the politics of feminism. In *Third-world women and the politics of feminism*, ed. C. Mohanty, A. Russo, and L. Torres, 1–50. Bloomington: Indiana University Press.

Morse, Eric. 1936. Some aspects of the *Komagata Maru* affair, 1914. *Report*. Ottawa: Canadian Historical Association.

Mudimbe, V.Y. 1988. *The invention of Africa: Gnosis, philosophy, and the order of knowledge*. Bloomington: Indiana University Press.

Murphy, Emily. 1973 [1922]. *The Black Candle*. Toronto: Thomas Allen.

Naidoo, Josephine. 1980. Women of South Asian and Anglo-Saxon origins in the Canadian context: Self perceptions, socialization, achievement aspirations. In *Sex roles: Origins, influences, and implications for women*, ed. S. Adamec, 50–69. Montreal: Ewen.

– 1990. Immigrant women in Canada: Towards a new decade. Paper presented at the CEIAC symposium on Immigrant Settlement and Integration, Toronto.

Narayan, Uma. 1990. The project of feminist epistemology: Perspectives from a nonwestern feminist. In *Gender/body/knowledge: Feminist reconstruction of being and knowing*, ed. A. M. Jaggar and S. R. Bordo, 256–72. New Brunswick: Rutgers University Press.

National Action Committee on the Status of Women. 1986. Presentation to the standing committee of the Secretary of State.

– 1987. *Refugee women and Bill C-55*. Toronto: NAC.

Newton, Janice. 1992. The alchemy of politicization: Socialist women and the early Canadian left. In *Gender conflicts: New essays in women's history*, ed. F. Iacovetta and M. Valverde, 118–48. Toronto: University of Toronto Press.

Ng, Roxana. 1981. Constituting ethnic phenomenon: An account from the perspective of immigrant women. *Canadian Ethnic Studies* 13 (1): 97–107.

– 1986. Immigrant women in Canada: A socially constructed category. *Resources for Feminist Research* 15 (1): 13–14.

– 1988a. *The politics of community service*. Toronto: Garamond.

– 1988b. Immigrant women and institutionalized racism. In *Changing patterns: Women in Canada*. ed. S. Burt, L. Code, and L. Dorney, 184–203. Toronto: McClelland and Stewart.

Nipp, Dora. 1983. Canada-bound: An exploratory study of pioneer Chinese women in western Canada. Master's thesis. University of Toronto, Toronto.

Nonqaba, Msmiang. n.d. New directions for Canadian women: Profile of and interview with Glenda Simms. *Tiger Lily* 11: 35–42.

Nyman, Judy. 1988. Minority groups 'insulted' by report of women's council. *Toronto Star* (9 Feb.).

Oakley, Ann. 1981. Interviewing women: a contradiction in terms. In *Doing Feminist Research*, ed. B. Roberts, 30–61. London: Routledge.

Oiwa, Keibo. Ed. 1991. *Stone voices: Wartime writings of Japanese Canadian Issei*. Montreal: Vehicule.

Ondaatje, Michael. 1990. Interview. In *Other solitudes: Canadian multicultural fiction*, ed. L. Hutcheon and M. Richmond, 196–202. Toronto: Oxford University Press.

Ontario Council of Agencies Serving Immigrants (OCASI). 1987. Immigrants and social assistance: A brief to the Social Assistance Review Committee.

– 1988. Immigrants and access to community and social services. Brief to John Sweeney, Ontario Minister of Community and Social Services.

– 1990. *Focus on immigrant women: A study of immigrant women's needs and programs in the OCASI network*. Toronto: OCASI.

– 1990. Member agency bulletin. *Research Update* 1 (2): 1–14.

– 1991. Immigrant services database. *Research Bulletin* 2 (1): 1–13.

– 1992a. Communities respond to violence against women. *Newsletter* 47.

– 1992b. Discussion paper: Language instruction for newcomers to Canada (LINC). Unpublished.

- 1992c. LINC: A community response presented to Bernard Valcourt, Minister of Employment and Immigration. Toronto: OCASI.
Ontario Human Rights Code Review Task Force. N.d. *Getting human rights enforced effectively.* Toronto: N.p.
Ontario Women's Directorate. N.d. *Let's break the silence.* Brochure.
- 1983. *Conference report* Toronto: The Directorate.
- 1987. *Report of the 1987 community workshops with visible minority and immigrant women.* Toronto: The Directorate.
Open letters to Catharine MacKinnon. 1991. *Yale Journal of Law and Feminism* 4: 177–90.
Owaisi, Lateef, and Zafar Bangash. 1978. *Visible minorities in mass media advertising.* Ottawa: Minister of Supply and Services.
Oziewicz, Estanislao. 1991. Ottawa ending nanny program. *Globe and Mail* (20 Dec.).
- 1992a. Nanny employers must bare finances. *Globe and Mail* (28 Apr.).
- 1992b. Nanny policy called necessary protection. *Globe and Mail* (29 Apr.).
- 1992c. Immigrant nannies must have grade 12 under new rules. *Globe and Mail* (30 June).
- 1993. Why a change of heart does not change policy. *Globe and Mail* (5 Feb.).
Padolsky, Enoch. 1990. Establishing the two-way street: Literary criticism and ethnic studies. *Canadian Ethnic Studies* 13 (1): 22–37.
Palmer, Hazella. 1991. Health centre staff locked out by board. *Healthsharing* (Fall): 8.
Papp, Aruna. 1990. *Report on abused South Asian women in Scarborough.* Scarborough: South Asian Family Support Services.
Papp, Leslie. 1990. Immigrant domestics seeking protection. *Toronto Star* (5 Feb.).
Parai, Louis. 1975. Canada's immigration policy, 1962–1974. *Canadian Review of Sociology and Anthropology* 12 (1): 449–77.
Paredes, Milagros. 1987. Immigrant women and second-language education: A study of unequal access to linguistic resources. *Resources for Feminist Research* 17 (3): 23–7.
- 1992. *Setting the precedent: Process as change in meeting the needs of immigrant and refugee women surviving abuse and sexual violence.* Toronto: Education Sexual Assault.
Parmar, Pratibha. 1986. Gender, race, and class: Asian women in resistance. In *The empire strikes back: Race and racism in 70s Britain,* ed. Centre for Contemporary Cultural Studies, 236–75. London: Hutchinson.
- 1989. Other kinds of dreams. *Feminist Review* 31: 55–65.
- 1990. Women, native, other: Pratibha Parmar interviews Trinh Minh-ha. *Feminist Review* 36: 165–75.

Pateman, Carole. 1987. Feminist critiques of the public/private dichotomy. In *Feminism and equality*, ed. A. Phillips, 103–26. Oxford: Basil Blackwell.

Peel Multicultural Council. Peel multicultural scene. *Newsletter* 3 (5).

Pennell, Joan. 1992. Qualitative analysis for collaborative action research within the battered-women's movements. Unpublished manuscript.

Persad, Judy. 1992. Good enough to work? Good enough to stay! *Rebel Girls Rag* 6 (2): 2.

Peter, Karl. 1981. The myth of multiculturalism and other political fables. In *Ethnicity power and politics in Canada*, ed. J. Dahlie and T. Fernando, 56–67. Toronto: Methuen.

Pettigrew, Joyce. 1981. Reminiscences of fieldwork among the Sikhs. In *Doing Feminist Research*, ed. H. Roberts. London: Routledge.

Pettigrew, Thomas, et al. 1982. *Prejudice*. Cambridge: Harvard University Press.

Picard, André. 1993. 'Siege' of immigration offices threatened: NAC urges Ottawa to stop deporting women victims of conjugal violence. *Globe and Mail* (5 Mar.)

Pinedo, Rosa Maria, and Ana Maria Santinoli. 1991. Immigrant women and wife assault. In *Towards equal access*, ed. F. Rafiq, 65–80. Ottawa: Immigrant and Visible-Minority Women against Abuse.

Pitman, Walter. 1977. *Now is not too late*. Report submitted to the Council of Metropolitan Toronto by the Task Force on Human Relations.

Pizzy, Erin. 1974. *Scream quietly or the neighbours will hear*. London: If Books.

Platt, H.L. 1908. *Story of the Years: Women's Missionary Society*. N.p.

Pope, Lori. 1991. Immigration law and wife assault. *Diva*: 38–48.

Powell, Cynthia, et al. 1991. Open letters to Catharine MacKinnon. *Yale Journal of Law and Feminism*, 4, 177–90.

Pyke, S. W. 1976. Children's literature: Conception of sex-roles. In *Canada: A sociological profile*, ed. W. Mann and L. Wheatcroft, 158–170. Toronto: Copp Clark.

Quick, Abdullah. 1990. Muslim rituals, practices, and social problems in Ontario. *Polyphony* 12: 120–24.

Rafiq, Fauzia. 1991. Wife assault: Pakistan, An overview. *Diva* (March): 5–15.

Rahula, Ann. 1987. Groups poised to fight for domestics. *Globe and Mail* (19 Mar.).

Raj, Samuel. 1980. Some aspects of East Indian struggle in Canada, 1905–1947. In *Visible minorities and multiculturalism: Asians in Canada*, ed. V. Ujimoto and G. Hirabayashi, 63–80. Toronto: Butterworths.

Rajan-Eastcott, Doris. 1992. Our ways: Anti-racist and culturally appropriate approaches to combatting women assault. Unpublished manuscript.

Ramazanoglu, Caroline. 1986. Ethnocentricism and socialist-feminist theory: A response to Barrett and McIntosh. *Feminist Review* 22: 83–6.
– 1989. *Feminism and the contradictions of oppression.* London: Routledge.
Randall, Melanie. 1988. Feminism and the state: Questions for theory and practice. *Resources for Feminist Research* 17 (3): 10–17.
– 1989. The politics of woman abuse: Understanding the issues. A discussion paper. Toronto: Education Wife Assault.
Rebick, Judy. 1992 . Paper delivered at Canadian Research Institute for Advancement of Women, annual conference, session on women and the state, Toronto.
Reid, Robbie. 1941. The inside story of the 'Komagata Maru.' *British Columbia Quarterly* 5: 1–23.
Reinharz, Shulamit. 1992. *Feminist methodology in social science research.* New York: Oxford University Press.
Rhode, Deborah. 1991. Enough said. *Yale Journal of Law and Feminism* 4: 35–8.
Richmond, Anthony. 1967. *Post-war immigrants in Canada.* Toronto: University of Toronto Press.
Ristock, Janice. 1991. Feminist collectives: The struggles and contradictions in our quest for a 'uniquely feminist structure'. In *Women and social change: Feminist activism in Canada*, ed. J. Dawn Wine and J. Ristock, 41–55. Toronto: James Lorimer.
Riutort, Monica, and Small, Shirley. 1985. *Working with assaulted immigrant women.* Toronto: Education Wife Assault.
Riverdale Immigrant Women's Centre. 1991. *Annual report.* Toronto: The Centre.
Roberts, Barbara. 1990. Ladies, women, and the state: Managing female immigration,1880–1920. In *Community organization and the Canadian state*, ed, R. Ng, G. Walker, and J. Muller, 108–130. Toronto: Garamond.
Roberts, Wayne. 1977. Six new women: A guide to the mental map of women reformers in Toronto. *Atlantis* 3 (1): 145–63.
– 1979. 'Rocking the cradle for the world': The new woman and maternal feminism, Toronto, 1877–1914. In *A not unreasonable claim: Women and reform in Canada 1880s–1920s*, ed. L. Kealey, 15–45. Toronto: Women's Press.
Rollins, Judith. 1985. *Between women: Domestics and their employers.* Philadelphia: Temple University Press.
Romany, Celina. 1991. Ain't I a feminist? *Yale Journal of Law and Feminism* 4: 23–34.
Rose, Barbara. 1992. Trouble at Nellie's. *Globe and Mail* (9 May).
Roszak, Theodore, and Betty Roszak. 1969. Redstocking manifesto. In *Masculine/feminine*, ed. B. Roszak and T. Roszak, 272–4. New York: Harper.

Rothenberg, Paula. 1990. The construction, deconstruction, and reconstruction of difference. *Hypatia* 5 (1): 42–57.

Roy, Patricia E. 1989a. *A white man's province*. Vancouver: University of British Columbia Press.

– 1989b. British Columbia's fear of Asians, 1900–1950. In *A history of British Columbia*, ed. P. Roy, 285–99. Toronto: Copp Clark Pitman.

Royal Commission on the Status of Women. 1970. *Report*. Ottawa: Information Canada.

Russo, Ann. 1991. We cannot live without our lives: White women, antiracism, and feminism. In *Third-world women and the politics of feminism*, ed. C. Mohanty, A. Russo, and L. Torres, 297–313. Bloomington: Indiana University Press.

Saheli. 1985. *Saheli: The first four years*. New Delhi: n.p.

Said, Edward W. 1979. *Orientalism*. New York: Vintage.

St Lewis, Joanne. 1993. Paper presented at the Ontario Council of University Faculty Associations Conference.

Samuel, John. 1990. Third-world immigrants and multiculturalism. In *Ethnic demography: Canadian immigrant, racial and cultural variations*, ed. S. Halli, F. Trovato, and L. Driedger, 383–98. Ottawa: Carleton University Press.

Sangster, Joan. 1989. *Dreams of equality: Women on the Canadian left, 1920–1950*. Toronto: McClelland and Stewart.

Sarick, Lila. 1991. Mediator called in at women's clinic. *Globe and Mail* (2 Nov.).

Satzewich, Vic. 1991. *Racism and the incorporation of foreign labor*. London: Routledge.

Sawicki, Jana. 1986. Foucault and feminism: Toward a politics of difference. *Hypatia* 1 (2): 23–36.

Schechter, Susan. 1982. *Women and male violence: The visions and struggles of the battered-women's movement*. Boston: South End Press.

Segal, Lynne. 1987. *Is the future female?: Troubled thoughts on contemporary feminism*. London: Virago.

Settlement Directorate (Ontario Region). 1992. Background paper on language instruction for newcomers to Canada (LINC).

Seward, Shirley. 1990. Immigrant women in the clothing industry. In *Ethnic demography. Canadian immigrant, racial and cultural variations*, ed. S. Halli, F. Trovato, and L. Driedger. Ottawa: Carleton University Press.

Seward, Shirley, and Kathryn McDade. 1988. *Immigrant women in Canada: A policy perspective*. Ottawa: Canadian Advisory Council on the Status of Women.

Seydegart, K., and G. Spears. 1985. *Beyond dialogue: Immigrant women in Canada, 1985–1990*. Unpublished manuscript.

Sheth, Anita, and Amita Handa. 1991. The jewel in the frown: Striking accord between Indian feminists. *Resources for Feminist Research* 20 (3–4): 65–79.

Shibata, Yuko. 1980. Coping with values in conflict: Japanese women in Canada. In *Visible minorities and multiculturalism: Asians in Canada*, ed. V. Ujimoto and G. Hirabayashi, 257–76. Toronto: Butterworths.

Shirley Samaroo House. 1988. *Annual report.* Toronto: Shirley Samaroo House.

Silvera, Makeda. 1983. *Silenced.* Toronto: Williams-Wallace.

– 1986. Organizing exclusion: Race, class, community and the white women's movement. In *Fireworks: The best of Fireweed*, ed. M. Silvera, 176–85. Toronto: Women's Press.

Simmons, Alan. 1990. 'New wave' immigrants: Origins and characteristics. In *Ethnic demography: Canadian immigrant, racial and cultural variations*, ed. S. Halli, F. Trovato, and L. Driedger, 141–60. Ottawa: Carleton University Press.

Simmons, Alan, and Kieran Keohane. 1992. Canadian immigration policy: State strategies and the quest for legitimacy. *Canadian Review of Sociology and Anthropology* 29 (4): 421–52.

Simmons, Christina. 1986. Helping the poorer sisters: The women of the Jost mission, Halifax, 1905–1945. In *Rethinking Canada: The promise of women's history*, ed. V. Strong-Boag and A. Fellman, 157–77. Toronto: Copp Clark Pitman.

Simms, Glenda P. N.d. Rapunzel, can you hear me? The women's liberation movement and its relationship to minority women. N.p.

Simons, Margaret. 1979. Racism and feminism: A schism in the sisterhood. *Feminist Studies* 5 (2): 384–401.

Singh, Khushwant. 1977. *A history of the Sikhs, 1839–1974.* Delhi: Oxford University Press.

Siu, Bobby. 1979. The great leap inward: A critique of Canadian studies of women's movements. Paper presented at the Canadian Sociology and Anthropology Association, University of Saskatchewan, Saskatoon.

Smith, Dorothy. 1985. *Women, class, family and the state.* Toronto: Garamond.

– 1987. *The everyday world as problematic: A feminist sociology.* Toronto: University of Toronto Press.

– 1990. *The conceptual practices of power: A feminist sociology of knowledge.* Toronto: University of Toronto Press.

Smith, Valerie. 1989. Black feminist theory and the representation of the 'other'. In *Changing our own words: Essays on criticism, theory, and writing by black women*, ed. C. Wall, 38–57. New Brunswick: Rutgers University Press.

Solomos, John, et al. 1986. The organic crisis of British capitalism and race: The experience of the seventies. In *The empire strikes back: Race and racism in the 70s Britain*, ed. Centre for Contemporary Cultural Studies, 9–46. London: Hutchinson

South East Asian Services. 1992. *Working with abused wives from Vietnam: A manual for front line workers.* Toronto: South East Asian Services.

Spelman, Elizabeth V. 1988. *Inessential woman: Problems of exclusion in feminist thought*. Boston: Beacon.

Spencer-Nimmons, Noreen, and Chow-Ying Wong. 1989. Refugee women: Canadian considerations of an international burden-sharing need. Paper presented at the international symposium, The refugee crisis: British and Canadian responses, Oxford.

Staff. 1988. The Canadian Advisory Council on the Status of Women's report – Immigrant women in Canada: A policy perspective. *Cross-Cultural Communication Centre* 17 (3): 2.

Stasiulis, Daiva. 1990. Theorizing connections: Gender, race, ethnicity and class. In *Race and Ethnic Relations in Canada*, ed. P. Li, 269–305. Toronto: Oxford University Press.

Stephenson, Marylee, ed. 1973. *Women in Canada*. Toronto: New Press.

Strong-Boag, Veronica. 1976. *The parliament of women: The National Council of Women of Canada, 1893–1929*. Ottawa: National Museum of Man.

– 1986. 'Ever a crusader': Nellie McClung, first-wave feminist. In *Rethinking Canada: The promise of women's history*, ed. V. Strong-Boag and A. Fellman, 178–90. Toronto: Copp Clark Pitman.

Sunahara, Ann. 1981. *The politics of racism*. Toronto: James Lorimer.

Taylor, Imogen. 1991. For better or worse: Caring and the abused wife. In *Women's caring: Feminist perspectives on social welfare*, ed. C. Baines, P. Evans, and S. Neysmith, 204–33. Toronto: McClelland and Stewart.

Taylor, K.W., ed. 1991. Racism in Canadian immigration policy. *Canadian Ethnic Studies* 33 (1): 1–20.

Terrelonge, Pauline. 1984. Feminist consciousness and black women. In *Women: A feminist perspective*, ed. J. Freeman, 555–67. Palo Alto: Mayfield.

Thornhill, Esmeralda. 1989. Focus on black women. In *Race, class, and gender: Bonds and barriers*, ed. J. Vorst et al., 26–36. Toronto: Between the Lines.

Troper, Harold. 1982. *None is too many: Canada and the Jews of Europe*. Toronto: Lester & Orpen Dennys.

Ubale, Bhausaheb. 1977. *Equal opportunity and public policy*. A report of the South Asian Canadian Community on their place in the Canadian mosaic, submitted to the Attorney General of Ontario.

Ujimoto, K. Victor. 1988. Racism, discrimination and internment: Japanese in Canada. In *Racial oppression in Canada*, ed. B. Singh Bolaria and P. Li, 127–60. Toronto: Garamond Press.

– 1990. Studies of ethnic identity and race relations. In *Race and ethnic relations in Canada*, ed. P. Li, 209–30. Toronto: Oxford University Press.

Urban Alliance on Race Relations and Ontario Women's Directorate. N.d. *Employment equity for visible-minority women*. N.p.

Valiante, Waheeda. 1991. Social work practice with South Asian Women: Issues, concerns and problems. In *A reader in South Asian studies*, ed. S. Chandraseker, 95–119. Toronto: South Asian Studies Graduate Students Union, University of Toronto.

Valpy, Michael. 1993. The women persecuted for being women. *Globe and Mail* (11 Mar.).

Valverde, Mariana. 1991a. *The age of light, soap, and water*. Toronto: McClelland and Stewart.

– 1991b. As if subjects existed: Analyzing social discourses. *Canadian Review of Sociology and Anthropology* 28 (2): 173–87.

– 1992. 'When the mother of the race is free': Race, reproduction, and sexuality in first-wave feminism. In *Gender Conflicts*, ed. F. Iacovetta and M. Valverde, 3–26. Toronto: University of Toronto Press.

Van Dieren, Karen. 1984. The response of the WMS to the immigration of Asian women, 1888–1942. In *Not just pin money*, ed. B. Latham and R. Pazdro, 79–97. Victoria: Camosun College.

Van Kirk, Sylvia. 1980. *Many tender ties*. Winnipeg: Watson.

Vickers, Jill. 1988. Politics as if women mattered: The institutionalization of the Canadian women's movement and its impact on federal politics, 1965–1988. Paper presented at ACSANZ, Canberra.

– 1991. Bending the iron law of oligarchy: Debates on the feminization of organization and the political process in the english Canadian women's movement. In *Women and social change: Feminist activism in Canada*, ed. J. Wine and J. Ristock, 75–95. Toronto: James Lorimer.

– 1992. The intellectual origins of the contemporary women's movement in Canada and the United States. In *Challenging Times*, ed. C. Backhouse and D. Flaherty, 39–60. Montreal: McGill-Queen's University Press.

Villasin, Feli. 1991. *Report of the annual general meeting*. Toronto: Intercede.

Wagle, Iqbal. 1990. Bibliographical and archival data on the South Asian diaspora in Canada: The formative period of 1905–1920. Paper presented at Conference on Ethnicity, Migration and Identity, University of Toronto.

Walker, Gillian. 1990. *Family violence and the women's movement: The conceptual politics of struggle*. Toronto: University of Toronto Press.

Ward, W. Peter. 1978. *White Canada forever: Popular attitudes and public policy toward Orientals in British Columbia*. Montreal: McGill-Queen's University Press.

– 1989. Class and race in the social structure of British Columbia 1870–1939. In *A history of British Columbia*, ed. P. Roy, 259–77. Toronto: Copp Clark Pitman.

Watson, Paul. 1991. Domestic plan won't be killed. *Toronto Star* (21 Dec.).

Whitaker, Reg. 1987. *Double standard: The secret history of Canadian immigration.* Toronto: Lester and Orpen Dennys.

Whyte, William, David Greenwood, and Peter Lazes. 1991. Participatory action research: Through practice to science in social research. In *Participatory action research*, ed. W. Whyte, 19–55. London: Sage Publications.

Williams, Patricia J. 1991. *The alchemy of race and rights.* Cambridge: Harvard University Press.

Wilson, S.J. 1982. *Women, the family, and the economy.* Toronto: McGraw-Hill Ryerson.

Wine, Jeri Dawn, and Janice L. Ristock, eds. 1991. *Women and social change: Feminist activism in Canada.* Toronto: James Lorimer.

Winks, Robin W. 1971. *The blacks in Canada: A history.* Montreal: McGill-Queen's University Press.

Wollstonecraft, Mary. 1986 [1792]. *Vindication of the rights of woman.* Harmondsworth: Penguin.

Women Working with Immigrant Women. N.d. Sex discrimination in the immigration act and its regulations. Unpublished.

– 1980. Community analysis. Toronto: Women Working with Immigrant Women.

– 1985–86. Annual report. N.p.

– 1986. Sponsorship concerns, funding concerns. Toronto: Women Working with Immigrant Women.

– 1988a. *Racial minority women and race relations.* Toronto: Women Working with Immigrant Women.

– 1988b. *The effect of Canadian immigration policies on racial minorities in general and racial minority women in particular.* Toronto: Women Working with Immigrant Women.

Women's Health in Women's Hands. 1992. Thanks for support. *Healthsharing* (Winter/Spring): 4.

Women's Missionary Society. N.d. *Our Jubilee Story, 1864–1924.* N.p.

Wong, Nellie. 1991. Socialist feminism: Our bridge to freedom. In *Third-world women and the politics of feminism*, ed. C. Mohanty, A. Russo and L. Torres. Bloomington: Indiana University Press.

Woodsworth, J.S. 1972 [1909]. *Strangers within our gates; or, coming Canadians.* Toronto: University of Toronto Press.

Wright, Carolann. 1991. Sworn statement (28 Oct.).

Yee, May. 1987. Chinese Canadian women: Our common struggle. *Canadian Ethnic Studies* 19 (3): 181.

Yee, Paul. 1988. *Saltwater city: An illustrated history of the Chinese in Vancouver.* Vancouver: Douglas & McIntyre.

York, Geoffrey. 1993. Policy shift too late for women. *Globe and Mail* (3 Feb.)

Young, Iris. 1990. *Justice and the politics of difference*. Princeton: Princeton University Press.

Ziemba, Elaine. 1991. Notes for address to Parliament.

Index